if we have no
peace

Anto Ljoljic

Anto Ljoljic
info@AntoLjoljic.com

Editor: Cynthia Cavalcanti
Cover Art: Jamileh Rose
Photography: Adam Brioza

Ordering Information:
Quantity sales. Special discounts are available on quantity purchases by corporations, associations, media and others. For details, contact the publisher at the email address above.

ISBN 978-0-9989419-0-5 (paperback)
ISBN 978-0-9989419-1-2 (hardback)
ISBN 978-0-9989419-2-9 (Ebook - EPUB)
ISBN 978-0-9989419-3-6 (Ebook - PDF)
ISBN 978-0-9989419-4-3 (Ebook - Kindle)
ISBN 978-0-9989419-5-0 (Ebook - Mobipocket)

Printed in the United States of America

Note to Readers:

This work is a memoir. It reflects the author's present recollections of his experiences over a period of many foggy years. Certain names, locations, and identifying details have been changed and some stories depicted are concatenated from multiple events. Dialogue and events have been recreated from memory.

if we have no
peace

introduction

Let us now discuss, with unrestrained honesty, the evolution of my corrupted mind. The number of times I've been brought to desperation, to a curled-up ball of tears begging for it to be over, leaves me no other choice but to consider the possibility of my being insane. I understand life brings difficulties, and many have been brought to their knees before me, but the sheer volume, and cyclic nature, of my calamities forces even the casual observer to suspect something deeper at play here.

I'm not sure exactly what it is that I'm looking for, but I know what it is not. I am not looking for a fix that will merely mask the pain. I want to be free from the madness whirling around in my head, and I want to help spark the revolution that saves the world. I suppose what I'm really searching for is truth. I'm trying to understand truth with a sense of awe—the way I sometimes feel when staring up at the sun and thinking about how long humans have turned to the sky and stood in amazement.

My stories are about redemption and hope through the fog of modern neurosis. This is my grand confession to how I made myself sick and how the misery in my head lead to the greatest liberation of my life. All I have to offer is testimony of a phenomenon. Something is making the people ill, and I believe we need to do something other than quantifying and solving at breakneck speed. Many of us are sick in a way that betrays a fundamental paradox in our way of living. More and more, we are seeing that people who

1

live in the most economically comfortable parts of the world are afflicted with illnesses that are not caused by traditional pathogens but seem to be symptoms of lifestyle. I don't just mean exercise and food-choice lifestyle; I'm talking about ancient wisdom and reverence of Earth lifestyle, or the lack thereof.

I didn't know what to do anymore, so I'm going to talk about it— all of it, every last deviant thought, with no escape hatch left for me to use and claim ignorance or slander. At this point, I see no sense in continuing the pretense. Lies, versions, angles, and manipulations were the cornerstones around which I had built my entire life, and they proved to be poor building blocks. Where did I go wrong?

I started asking that question a few years ago, and it lead to some fascinating conversations. Many are willing to offer advice, but few are comfortable discussing the darkness of the mind. Everyone seems to have an opinion on how I can fix my life, but people who offer advice usually have something obvious missing from their presence. I'm looking for that undefined IT, the essence of the kernel of the source, serenity, the great calm, equanimity, compassion and understanding. Anyone who spends too much time telling others which path to take is trying too hard for my taste. I'm looking for someone who, or something that, radiates with truth, and I'll know it when I feel it in my heart.

The frenzy of self-help books infecting literature today is atrocious. Rehearsed smiles plastered on shiny book jackets make for a grim tableau of manufactured hope. It's not that I'm against people trying to help others; after all, that is the basic premise of this whole project. But most of the stories out there seem incomplete at best. Only a few have ventured deep enough into the darkness to satisfy my affliction. Most seem to follow the same banal pretext: I wasn't happy, I felt stuck, and something needed to change. Then come seven magical steps for happiness, and poof!—Just like that, you, too, can be cured of your misery.

I'll give them credit for not using my old principles of survival, which involved changing the way I felt by distraction, ego games, or chemical means, but still I am bothered by two points. One, everyone's message has to break down into an easily digestible, cookie-cutter approach so it can be manufactured at scale and pumped to the masses, which then betrays an inorganic source instead of the generous detachment I am looking for. Nature doesn't draw in straight lines, and wisdom doesn't present itself in bullet points. My second point of contention is that no one has purged his or her soul in public before offering their message. I need to know who you are before I trust you.

My theory is simple: One must drop all masks before offering anything in the form of advice. Even then, if they stand before their people naked, their advice is better served in the form of personal experience, which can only be absorbed as analogy or allegory. Otherwise, we focus too much on the achievement of others and how we think that will make us feel if we mimic them, instead of allowing our own path to reveal itself. We have a surfeit of instructions but a lack of guidance.

To be frank, no one has been raw enough, or shown enough vulnerability, for me to be convinced of his or her authenticity. There have been a few authors who came close, but those usually have had the momentum of success already at their backs, thus allowing them to venture into the abyss with greater security than most. What about the commoner? What about the story before the shift? What happened in those years of darkness, before you saw the light, before a hand reached out, before there was hope?

It may be sadistic of me to demand truth in such vile detail, but such was the only method of reprieve I found satisfactory when I was contemplating suicide. I needed to know I was not the only one. I needed to belong to a group and be accepted regardless of my defects. In my search for a cure, I became infatuated by the maelstrom of dark minds; and every time I was deprived of the fine grit, of the filthy details of depravity, I was thrown back into the lonely tumble of depression. Was no one else as maladjusted as me?

I volunteer to disclose fully, to stand naked with no story to hide behind and tell you I have no idea what I'm doing. What I can say is I think I found something among my many follies that appears to be a pattern of clues, and those clues all seem to be pointing toward the same ethereal concept. But the first step must be a purge, so please excuse my indecency.

Once we have a baseline, once we have agreed just how far past deranged I had wandered, then we may begin discussing a path forward, or perhaps even a better way of living. But let us establish one axiom to begin with: The modern design for living my life is shit. I'm not looking for a functioning system that will allow me to get through the day and check the boxes that need to be checked. The whole system is fucked, and I will not accept justification to be part of it.

On the other side of my brash statement lies the sad truth that, relatively speaking, I have nothing to complain about. I was born a white male, in an upper-middle-class home, in thriving Silicon Valley—first-world USA. Who am I to gripe about pain? Perhaps I am spoiled and simply need to grow up and take responsibility for my actions. Perhaps the stories I keep telling myself are old and tired. I will leave that for you to determine.

It seems the more I try to forget my stories, the louder they rattle in my mind when the darkness falls upon me again. I have tried nearly every method of healing and purification shy of exorcism, but I don't think there is a cure because what I have, well, I hesitate to call it a disease. I was fucked up in the head, and the majority of it I did to myself, but I kept enough of it hidden by playing a role every day since I was a child. But I did suffer, and that pain led me to search for some kind of relief.

Dejection, loneliness, and melancholy have crippled me over my lifetime and robbed me of even the most basic ability to function in the world. I had been avoiding it for years, trying to tough it out or self-medicating with a hofbrau of drugs, sex, and vice ad nauseam. Over time, the monster grew beyond my control, and when it ravaged me, I was left in bed for weeks, crying and begging for mercy. The good news is, it has gotten better, and I can feel something shifting inside of me. The only thing I have found that helps is so unbelievably simple that I still struggle with the mere concept. Truth is my medicine, and pain is the required precursor.

I don't have a solution, and I am not a leader. I am merely the voice of a desperate soul—a soul that seems to be connected to everyone around me, to everything on this planet, to the planet itself, and to something else deep in the distance that I do not understand, but I have felt from time to time. There are times today when I feel more terrified than ever, so I want to make clear that this is not meant to be a safe guide or a roadmap for those who deal with similar troubles. You must find your own way. But maybe this can help inspire something you already know. One day, I woke up and realized I had been living in a prison my entire life. These stories are the beginning of my awakening.

the eyes tell the whole story

I took off after him at a full sprint. It was difficult to run grace-fully with a backpack full of fourth-grade curriculum hanging from my shoulders; it acted as a perfect counterweight to each step and smacked my lower back right in the sensitive part next to the spine. When I realized I wasn't going to catch him with my initial charge, I slipped the straps off and let the bag fall as I committed to the chase.

It was a warm spring day, fragrant with orange blossom sweetness, and I was walking home after school. My walk consisted of a short three minutes from school to front door, but along the path, the kids were all funneled into a narrow alley.

"Well at least I'm not a fat-ass like you," said one kid walking near me. I knew him but never hung out with him. He lived just down the street from me and was one year my senior, but he was frail, part of the nerdy science kids who never played sports with us during recess, and he spoke with a saliva-laden lisp. I was twice Robbie's size and nearly the largest kid in elementary school, even though there were two grades above me. I'm sure I had said some-thing to provoke his nasty comment, but I do not remember. What I do remember is the fire that rose in my belly and the recklessness with which I abandoned myself to as soon as I heard one of the nearby girls giggling.

I lunged toward him, grabbing at his t-shirt with my left hand, and

7

delivering a sloppy overhand right that landed on his collarbone. The other kids started clucking and hollering as the commotion began, and Robbie pushed my hand away and took off down the alley while looking back intermittently. I ran after him.

My view was only that of tunnel vision as the periphery became blurs and streaks of color. Robbie turned a sharp left at the end of the alley and tried to pick up steam again, but his angle was too acute, and he did not possess the natural athletic ability to stop and start on a dime. I reached for his backpack, spun him around, and punched him on the cheek. He threw a backhand left as he kept spinning—a flailing, open-hand attempt. The blow landed on my shoulder. He peered at me through his squinted eyes, anticipating retaliation. I squared up, put my hands up in a boxer's pose, and took a couple short steps toward him, waiting for him to commit to the fight.

Robbie was certainly not a fighter, and the truth is, neither was I, but that day I stumbled on a concept that would serve me for years to come: I did something mainly because I could, not because I needed to. Robbie dropped his backpack and stood his ground. His stance was awkward and his countenance more symbolic than authentically aggressive, but there he was about to fight me—a kid twice his size. We fought as kids do, with our heads back, eyes nearly closed, and wild punches flailing about, but it did not matter. Although in a competitive event the judges would have likely awarded me the victory, the fact was I did not win the fight in impressive fashion. Robbie's face was red and puffy in a few spots, but no blood was leaking, and no knockdowns were scored. We expended all our energy then walked off our separate ways, exhausted.

The next day, around the same time, in the same alley, I saw Robbie walking ahead of me. He was walking with a friend, unaware and unconcerned, and I was walking alone when someone nearby began to jeer.

8

"Hey, Anto. Doesn't look like Robbie lost any fights recently."

Indeed the boy had a valid point. Robbie's face did not look any worse than the day before, and he seemed to be walking with a gingerly step. There is pretext and there is truth. The precursor to pretext is fear, and most of us are taught to avoid the arduous path, so pretext tends to win out.

"Hey, Robbie! How's your face?" I shouted so all the kids could hear.

Robbie turned his head back toward me at a downward angle. He displayed only the left side of his face, but that was all I needed to gauge his response. His mouth was closed and his eyebrow raised and his eyes as peaceful and passive as a fawn. His eyes convicted me of my crime before it ever happened. He turned his head back around and continued on.

"Hey! Robbie! I'm talking to you!" I shouted.

Robbie barely turned his head, not even enough to get one eye on me, and returned my insult perfectly.

"Fuck you, Anto."

I took off after him at full speed.

His head start afforded him a temporary advantage, but his gallop was clumsy, all bones, and he hadn't shed his backpack in anticipation of full effort on my part. As we rounded out of the alley, he darted past my house, which was the nearest to the fence line, then ran across the road and cut back in a looping fashion. I cut off his angle and caught him on the sidewalk against my neighbor's fence. I began throwing blows immediately, not allowing for any repositioning, and he covered up his face and turned his body sideways, cornered by the fence.

9

Robbie ducked down and slipped my barrage of punches, then squirted out through an opening and took a couple of leaps away from me. I lurched toward him with both hands and pushed him from the side, knocking him off balance and sending him crashing into an unkempt Myrtle bush. A cloud of yellow powder billowed from the bush, seasons of pine dust absorbed and settled, only to be awoken as a witness to this melee. Robbie closed his eyes and tried to roll off, but his grimace betrayed his pain; something was stabbing at his back. I swung, I punched, I missed, and I hit. All the while, Robbie was trapped by the irregular gravity of the over-grown Myrtle. He kicked at me with savage ferocity, managed to clear some room, and gesticulated his way out of the bush and back to his already running feet. I gave chase, right on his heels.

From behind I could see his shirt was ripped, and his back was scratched and bleeding. Nobody seemed to notice the two kids running wild in the street. No cars stopped, no neighbors came out of their houses, so I was free to continue. Nothing is wasted in this universe, energy only transfers, however unobservable to the human eye.

I caught up to him on the other side of the street, and he surrendered the few lead steps he had in a way that can only be described as broken. He was tired and scared, and his will to fight was gone. He turned around and looked at me, inviting the crescendo so he might finally escape the persecution. Still running in stride, I put my head down and tackled him, taking him off his feet and landing on my next-door neighbor's lawn. A scrum ensued, and I quickly ended up in full mount, raining down blows onto the defenseless boy beneath me.

When I was little, I once watched my grandmother cut the throat of a lamb she planned to cook for a family gathering. She held it close, one arm around the neck and shoulders, and the other firm-ly under the jaw, as she pulled outward so as to stretch the neck to allow the cut maximum efficacy and bleed the beast out as quickly as possible. The look on her face was that of calm and reverence as she did what she did in the dance of life. But the lamb was not so graceful. The lamb kicked its back legs initially and tried to slip out of the chokehold with vigor while instinctively emptying its lungs to the sound of hollow bleats that escaped through the throat, not through the mouth, thus producing more of a gurgling cough than anything else. The eyes of the lamb looked straight up, strange for an animal with eyes squarely on the side of its head, as it gazed in astonishment at the perpetrator of this great betrayal.

Disbelief and sorrow and the eyes of a broken heart; that was all I saw when I finally stopped beating on Robbie. He wouldn't stop staring at me—staring with deep contempt, his nose dripping with blood—even as he walked off down the sidewalk.

Later that night, while my mom was cooking dinner and I was watching television, the doorbell rang. The house smelled of sautéing onions and peppers, and my mom answered the door with a kitchen towel draped over her shoulder. I continued watching whatever I was hypnotized by on the tube.

"Anto, come over here," she called out from the hallway.

I sprang up and began walking toward the door. Moving forward, I caught a glimpse of Robbie standing there with his older brother, who looked to be late high school or early college age. My heart began racing wildly as a sense of heavy compunction fell over me. I looked at Robbie. The eyes of contempt had turned into the glare of anger, and he beamed an invisible spear through my heart.

"Anto, did you have a fight with Robbie today?" my mother asked. She was looking down at me with a stern gaze, and Robbie's brother held the same arresting position. All eyes on me, and I didn't think or hesitate—I just reacted.

"No. I didn't fight with Robbie today," I replied surreptitiously.

Robbie scoffed and chuckled, and his brother placed his hand on

11

the younger boy's shoulder.

"Do you know how Robbie got these marks on his face?" the brother asked.

"I don't know," I offered, eyes pointing straight at my feet.

"Anto. Don't lie. Tell mama the truth," my mom admonished with a thick Croatian accent.

"I am telling the truth."

We all stood there for a moment, first all of them looking at me, then the brother and my mom looking at each other in silence, and then to my amazement, my mother pivoted. Speaking to the brother, she stated:

"Well, I'm sorry, but my son says he didn't do it. So maybe something else happened that we don't know about."

Robbie's jaw dropped as his seething anger instantly turned to shock. The brother, stunned that my mother would believe such an obvious lie, was speechless for a moment then fumbled for a retort. He tried in vain, and my mother dispelled the last of his case, then apologized for not being able to help them. As she began to close the door, I was left staring directly into Robbie's eyes. Finally, the door closed, forcing the scene to come to an end.

followtheline

A voice came blaring through the intercom of my eighth-grade science class: "Ms. Carino, please send Anto Lajolick to the office with his backpack and belongings."

"Oooooohhhhhh," the class erupted in unison.

I stood petrified because I knew what had come back to haunt me. Ms. Carino raised her eyebrows and offered a conciliatory profile as I put my books in my backpack, then she quieted the class down and continued her lesson. Katie was the girl who sat next to me, and she happened to be my all-consuming junior high crush. I hadn't had the courage to profess my heart to her, but we were good friends nonetheless, and she sensed what was approaching. She looked at me with deep concern. I played the tough-guy card, but inside I was saying goodbye to my love in a Shakespearean soliloquy.

The walk from classroom to office was no more than 50 yards, but it afforded me plenty of time to panic. In this section of the school, the courtyard was open—one big square of concrete with a few dry patches of lawn clinging to life by a blade. Around the perimeter were two rows of lockers, once a rich Dodger blue but presently more of a faded denim, and oversized brown wooden benches straddled the borders.

I thought back to a day a year earlier in that courtyard when I let my friend take a whiff of the fresh bag of weed I had so proudly brought to school. That gesture landed me in juvenile hall, which had devastating effects on my family. Things had not been comfortable since.

Following my arrest, I did what any industrious teenager would do: I doubled down on my resolve and pushed even harder to stay with my hooligan tribe. Since my arrest for possession of marijuana, I had been subject to court-ordered drug testing by the likes of my probation officer, but that didn't stop me from getting intoxicated in all kinds of different ways. This was a time before Google, so I called the Santa Clara County Poison Control center and pretended to be a concerned father who suspected his son of using drugs. My plan was to catch my son via a surprise drug test but, in order to catch him at the right time, I wondered if they might share with me the duration of time each of the major drugs stayed detectable in the system. I was given a lengthy dissertation.

It turned out marijuana was the only real issue, with a possible 30-day detection window, but other narcotics only stayed three to five days. More interestingly, alcohol was out in 24 hours and LSD wasn't even detectable in a standard urine test, certainly not the kind of test a budget-strapped public bureaucracy was willing to spend money on, so I gave up smoking pot in favor of being a garbage can for nearly every other illicit substance available.

Cupertino, California is famous for being the birthplace of Apple computer, but there is a second landmark there, a place that fostered the last gasps of a flightless revolution and an epicenter for the ethos I came to live by.

Coffee Society was located just across the street from De Anza College in suburban Cupertino. I never could figure out why it became such a hive, but that place was to my early drug career what Minton's Playhouse was to jazz. At any time of the day, you could find at least a handful of people hanging out in front of Coffee Society, on steps or benches, reading, talking, smoking, or nursing a hangover. On some nights, you would think the place was overspill from a nightclub because the density of loiterers was so thick that civilian patrons of the shopping center wouldn't dare walk through the bedlam.

It was a mix of stoners and comic-book nerds, small time crooks, ex-cons, junkies and artists, poets, high school and college students, high school and college dropouts, shift workers, thugs and runaways, taggers, skaters, punk rockers and dealers, couples, crews, lovers, loners, and me. Everyone knew everyone there, and it became my home away from home. I could usually score any drug I wanted there. If that didn't work out, the option was always available to ask one of the older guys to buy me booze from the local liquor store; all I had to do was throw in a standard six-pack for his troubles.

Those who wanted to drink, smoke weed, snort a line, or engage in illegal transactions would politely excuse themselves to the park 50 yards northeast of the shopping center. I have never seen a higher concentration of nefarious activity than Memorial Park circa 1994. True, it didn't compare to Grateful Dead parking lots, or inner-city housing projects, but for an upper-middle-class suburb, that park certainly held its own. People got high and drunk in that place at all hours; arrests were made, punches were thrown, and blowjobs were given, all within the sanctity of our fair neighborhood park. Cops were constantly cruising the parking lots or trying to sneak up on us from a blind spot, which meant sometimes, if you walked through the park before noon, you might be lucky and find a bag someone ditched in a bush as they were fleeing the previous night.

Life at home was ever more volatile with my constant barrage of lies and parries. My mother still attempted to rein me in with some semblance of parental control, so I was not free to vagabond the streets recklessly like some of my friends seemed to be. Some were kids from truly broken homes who had no rules to live by, and I yearned so deeply to be like them, to be defined, to know my place, to be liberated from playing dual roles and plunge into

15

street virtue with abandon. Regardless of my assessment of the stability and morality of my own household, I still had parents who cared about me, and that meant curfews and check-ins. On the one hand, I think the rules my mother tried to instill very well may have saved me from the unforgiving outcomes other people from that time were doomed to face. Obviously, I wasn't a model citizen at that point, but many of my friends ended up in darker places far more tragic than mine. On the other hand, I see this period as the time I learned to bend the rules, avoid consequences, and lie in the interest of self-gratification. I knew where the limits were, I had constant practice at pushing them, and it was my mother I used as target practice the most.

I walked into the principal's office to accept my fate. As soon as I stepped through the door, I saw a police officer standing next to my principal, and both had the same look on their faces. It seemed more and more adults in my vicinity all had a similar scowl of disappointment and a folded pair of arms across their chests.

"Are you Anto?" the officer asked.

"Yes."

"Is this your ID?" he asked, while holding up a clear plastic Ziploc bag with my junior high identification card inside.

"Yes."

My principal stayed quiet but attentive while the officer began his monologue, and I stood quietly and let my eyes wander.

"You're under arrest for theft of alcohol."

The officer was portly with a mustache so thick it nearly reached the tip of his nose. His uniform was green and tan, Boy Scout colors, and the short sleeves had a sharp crease from shoulder seam to cuff. The shirt became quite snug around his rotund waistline, and the shiny utility belt added even more cause for attention.

When he reached for his handcuffs, the movement was difficult for him, as everything seemed to be working against his angle of approach. I was also taller than he, so the whole thing felt silly. He turned me around and cinched the bracelets on my wrists, colder and heavier than I remembered, then turned me back around to face him in restraints. He reached into his front shirt pocket, pulled out a laminated yellow note card, and began reading me the Miranda Rights while pausing excessively like a child reading aloud to a class for the first time. As he read, I watched his mustache undulate laboriously to the choppy rhythm of his words.

All heads turned as I exited the principal's office and passed the front desk. The secretaries had already seen me paraded in such fashion, so they just shook their heads softly and scolded in silence like good Christians. A few students who were walking by outside stopped in their tracks and stared with their mouths open. The officer led me out the back door to his waiting cruiser while clutching my right bicep from half a pace behind.

The back of a police car was uncomfortable to begin with, but trying to sit with my hands tied behind my back while the metal divider sliced into my knees was quite the test of patience. My hands were void of circulation, and I was sitting sideways so I could steal a little more legroom. I stared at the impressive shotgun secured in the front seat and listened to the officer as he notified dispatch of his status and location.

The drive from Kennedy Junior High in Cupertino to the main jail in downtown San Jose took about twenty minutes. Every driver and passenger along the route couldn't help but double-take in my direction when they saw me sequestered in the back seat. People love to stare at evidence of their own righteousness.

Much to my surprise, after stealing a bottle of peppermint Schnapps from the same grocery store, during the same shift, every day for two weeks, I was caught by the astute store manager who managed to spoil my fun. Instead of heisting one bottle that day, I decided we needed two, and it was greed that brought down my racket like all the great crime bosses of old. Lifting one bottle was manageable. I would wait at the end of the liquor aisle and pretend to be shopping for whatever item was in the abutted section, usually something refrigerated like milk or butter, while I scanned the traffic for a clearing. When I thought I had a moment, I went for it, never waiting for the perfect moment because perfect moments never come. Then I would walk down the displays of shiny bottles while looking straight ahead, hoping no one entered from the opposite end. I would grab a bottle, quickly tuck it into my belt line, then continue walking as if that was never the aisle I intended to peruse in the first place. Lifting two bottles meant I had to make two nocuous strolls down the same aisle and, as I found out abrasively, I had to stuff a second bottle into a belt line where the real estate was already sparse.

"Hey! What do you think you're doing?" the manager shouted as he rounded the corner. His stare seemed to disable my motor skills, leaving me completely frozen, and I stood there and did absolutely nothing.

"Uhhhh. I'm buying Schnapps. I just forgot to get a cart," I said.

He was standing face-to-face with me at that moment, and I think my answer caught him off guard because he fumbled just a second before finding an appropriate response.

"Let me see your ID. You don't look 21."

Well played, good sir. I admitted to indeed being under the legal age required to purchase alcohol and started handing him back one of the bottles. Still insistent on what he deemed to be a valid question, he asked for my identification again. The Velcro from my wallet screamed in horror as I opened myself to what would be my fatal mistake. I handed over the only ID one possesses when he is fourteen years old; a cheap laminate with a heading of Kennedy Junior High across the front. He examined the card with thorough aptitude, exuding a slight whiff of authority, which was just enough to sound the alarm in my head. Modern-day grocery stores are bright and disorienting, taking their queue from the conniving architects of Las Vegas. Even though I wore a baseball hat low over my brow for camouflage, I felt the glare from the fluorescents as the light from above reflected from the white linoleum below. I decided then and there to flee.

I was already crashing out of the front exit by the time I heard him shouting behind me. The automatic doors were slow to open, so I forced my way out when the second bottle of Schnapps fell from my waistline, right out through the bottom of my shorts, and danced on the concrete, pinging in high falsetto tenor. My friend was playing the role of lookout, sitting on his BMX bike, leaning against the soda machine, and smoking a cigarette. When he saw me come barreling out, his eyes grew wide. He flicked his cigarette, propped up my BMX bike, and got it slowly rolling, giving me a slightly moving vehicle to jump onto and make my getaway. We pedaled with fervor, and when we were far enough away from the store, we found a place to hide and catch our breaths. I didn't tell him about the ID. I just hoped everything would go away.

The police car pulled into the main gate, but the intercom stopped us, and we were told to park off to the side. Apparently, a violent criminal was due to arrive shortly, and we had to wait until the coast was clear. Another cruiser pulled in, and waiting at the receiving entrance were four linebacker-sized police officers standing like gunmen in front of an old-west saloon. He fought well, that angry cholo with XIV tattooed on his shaved head, but eventually he was no match for the bruisers. They carried him inside, suspended and hogtied, like a trophy carcass.

I was processed, questioned, fingerprinted, and sent to receiving to await my one phone call. Since my crime was minor, relatively speaking, all signs pointed toward easy release. I was told to call my parents and have them pick me up.

My father answered the phone, and the automated message began for collect calls from the incarcerated. I waited in an unsteady silence. Finally, I heard my father's cold voice.

"Hello," he said in a muted tone.

"Dad, can you pick me up? I'm in juvenile hall."

There was a long, silent pause as my father deliberated.

"Why?"

"Stealing alcohol."

There is no silence like that of an empty telephone and a desperate heart. I waited and waited, and I began to notice the volume of my breathing.

"Call your mother," my father finally commanded with stinging frost.

"But she's in Korea for work."

"Well?" he said, then hung up.

I couldn't believe my ears. I knew he disapproved of my behavior, and I knew my parents fought over me, but I never thought he would leave me in that place. He left me, and he didn't even flinch a muscle in deliberation. I told the correction officer he was not coming, and a slight look of surprise fell over his face before he ushered me through the rest of the process.

A mandatory shower was followed by the delightful experience of a rectal contraband search. Spread your butt-cheeks with your hands, slightly bend at the waist, and offer a satisfactory cough.

Then I was given white underwear, brown pants, a white t-shirt, and a green sweatshirt—standard issue. After that, he handed me a pillow and bed covers and told me to follow the painted white line on the concrete floor toward the metal door.

"Go through the door and keep following the line until you reach the next officer at the central booth. They'll tell you where to go from there."

I didn't know how to feel. I was scared at first, but that quickly faded away. It was anger that consumed me, and it was in anger that I found solace. Four days later, a corrections officer came to my cell with good news: I was to be released. Following the line on the floor back down the hall through the sequence of metal doors, I was back in the processing hall. As I looked out in the waiting hall, I caught a brief glimpse of my mother pacing in front of the small window through the metal door. My heart sank. I had all the anger in the world bottled up for my dad, but for my mother, an endless pool of guilt stirred in my gut. Back in my own clothes and processed out, the buzzer rang to release the electronic lock on the intimidating door, and I stepped back out onto the side of freedom.

The moment the door shut behind me and the latch smacked closed, I saw for the first time the eyes of everything I hoped I would never have to face. My mother's eyes were gruesomely bloodshot, and her cheeks sodden and reflective. I could tell she had been crying for a long time. When I first looked at her, and she looked into me, I could feel the weight of her broken heart shatter every story I had or angle I could play. She hugged me and started to cry for what must have been the hundredth time that day.

By the time we sat in her car, she had stopped crying long enough to regain a slight sense of composure. She started the car, turned to look at me, began sobbing again, and uttered:

"Anto, how could you do this?"

21

I didn't know what to say except, "I'm sorry."

Over and over she asked me questions, and over and over I offered hollow apologies. There was no logic behind this that I could share with her. How do you tell your mother that you hate your home, you hate your father, and you hate yourself? All I could do was backpedal into more lies for a while before giving up, going silent, and hanging my head in shame.

assault by attrition

I was always the fat friend, and I watched with great interest as the eyes would pass over me and land on a more attractive option. The smiles seemed similar enough, but the eyes were always so transitory, so brief, and reserved at a safe distance, like the space between a handshake and a hug. I learned to live with it, but it was hurtful to be so unwanted, especially during those early years of teenage exploration.

I was on house arrest, again. No ankle monitor this time, so I had the nights free to sneak out once my parents had fallen asleep. I waited in my room anxiously. My heartbeat was dense, and it seemed I spent the majority of my time in this hyper-tense state—always something to watch out for. I snuck out the side door and cut through the elementary school behind my house instead of going down my street, which was too exposed. I didn't get on my skateboard until I was well past earshot of my house, then I jammed down the corridors like a marauding Khan on horseback.

The school was empty at midnight, but that increased my paranoia tenfold. The field looked like an eerie swamp as a low moon cast baleful shadows through the high redwood trees standing guard around the perimeter like sentries. On the blacktop, a slight wind slithered through the open space, just enough to sway the chains on the tetherball poles and give them the appearance of a row of nooses, eagerly awaiting their royal performance. A soft clinking was heard as metal kissed metal. I stayed tight to the buildings where orange high-pressure sodium lights guided my way and the wheels of my skateboard created a rushing echo down the corridor.

Justin was waiting for me in front of his apartment, smoking a Camel in the shadows, with a backpack full of Old English stashed close by. He told me we had a place to hang that night instead of our usual loitering ground on the railroad tracks, and it happened to be in the apartment complex where he lived.

Justin was dating Lindsey, who lived with her sister, Haylee, and their mom. Their mom wasn't home that evening, and the sister, much to my surprise, was a year older than Lindsey and cuter than I expected. Haylee had short, straight hair down to her neck, and the color was always changing in keeping with the grunge scene look of the early nineties. At present, it was jet black with blonde roots and her bangs had recently been trimmed. The hair framed her soft face with a gentle accent; her cheeks were a little puffy and her skin was Scandinavian pale. Haylee didn't look at me for very long at first, but eventually I saw her bright blue eyes, magnetic and luminous, a stark contrast to the forceful black hair surrounding them.

The party was in full swing. One of the sister's friends was also there, and everyone was drinking from the supply Justin had brought over. Everyone except me, that is, because I was being piss-tested every other day by my suffocating probation officer. Eventually Justin and Lindsey made their way back to a bedroom, the friend fell asleep, and Haylee and I were left to chat the night away.

We were talking about my current predicament of house arrest, and our general distain of authority, when Haylee shared her heart-numbing history. She looked down at the floor when she spoke.

"Up until two years ago, I was a good student. I was always top of my class, I took ballet, and my dream was to go to Stanford and

24

become a doctor. In sixth grade, my house changed. My parents' marriage became toxic. They were never home, and my dad became angry and moved away. During that time, a neighbor would look after us a lot. He did things to me, nasty things, and I was too scared to tell anyone. I tried running away a couple times, but I had nowhere to go. I didn't want to tell anyone because I thought it wasn't fair to ruin anyone else's life. My grades fell off, everything fell off, and eventually I tried to kill myself. I was hospitalized, but I still couldn't tell anyone about what happened. I came home from the hospital and the neighbor had gone on with his life and smiled when he saw me. He was dating someone, looked happy, and he had a new job, so there I was feeling all fucked up and alone. "

The sadness was heavy when she let it pour out, and I sat there in silence as she opened up.

"I made a friend when I was in the hospital. She was planning on running away with her boyfriend, and I thought I should go with her just for support. The boyfriend was another nasty guy. For two days, I was locked in a garage. I don't remember a lot. I remember it was cold. Someone gave me a jacket. I remember the sound of a car pulling up outside the garage. I remember his glasses and him laying on top of me."

After a pause, she shook her head and laughed, then dismissed the moment as overly-depressive and changed topics with her teenage pseudo-confidence. We went back to more digestible topics of conversation for a while.

A little later, with her friend fast asleep on the couch, Haylee looked at me with a devilish grin and those wide blue eyes.

"Hey!" she said with her pointer finger to the corner of her mouth, as if expressing deep contemplation, then giggled a bit. I looked at her and waited. She asked me a question that I had never been asked before, a dirty question, one I never expected to be aimed at me. It was said so nonchalantly that I wasn't sure I had heard her correctly, but emotion doesn't need assurance. I blushed.

"Uugghh. What?" I stuttered.

She laughed again and focused in on my eyes.

"You heard what I said. Yes or no?"

The real answer was a resounding NO, but I tried to play it cool enough not to explode with nervous laughter. Of course I'd never done that with a girl. Was she looking at the same person I knew myself to be? I was the fat guy who waited patiently as his friends explored sexuality and pretended it didn't affect him.

"Uughh. No." I mumbled under my breath with my eyebrows standing high at attention.

She smiled with flirtatious eyes. There it was; there they were. Interested eyes. It was the first time I had seen that look directed at me. She stood up, grabbed my hand, and led me back to her bedroom.

What had started innocently enough with young Haylee offering me my first sexual experience quickly turned into something else down the road. I didn't know what was appropriate in that new one-sided relationship, so I just kept going to her house hoping for status quo. Conversations quickly become vapid when boys are only after one thing, and you can hear the same thread of banal pretext all the way through adulthood. We would labor through small talk until I worked up the nerve to ask her for another blow-job. The conversations afterwards were even more abysmal as I tried to disregard the truth.

I could see the difference in her eyes after the third time. Gone was the silliness of two teenagers innocently exploring, and all that was left was a sense of forced obligation—but I didn't care. I kept going back. Eventually, she would casually avoid me or try to change the subject when we saw each other. Still, with a sense of entitlement and determination, I saw those passive rejections as a reason to convince her until she acquiesced.

The last time I saw Haylee was at a place called Blackberry Farm. It was a picnic ground in the middle of a trough that cut through Cupertino. In the summer, the pools were crowded with children and the barbecues were smoking late into the long days. Adjacent to the communal area was an open space reserve, and between the two was a small wooded section where we used to hang out to drink and smoke in seclusion. A small creek guarded three sides, and towering oak trees provided us with enough cover to do what teenagers did. A blue tarp was left next to a massive stone, and an unkempt fire pit still held the rock circle originally positioned.

I took her there because her mom was home that day, along with the mom's boyfriend, so the prospect didn't look favorable for a lewd little boy and his lecherous intentions. Haylee didn't feel comfortable out in the open at Blackberry Farm, or maybe she was tired of being used, or maybe I had become a predator and couldn't register the hesitation in her eyes as stemming from the fear in her heart, but the end result was that my blowjob was looking less and less likely. I implored and I persuaded, and we kissed as I tried to reduce her apprehension and get her to sit with me on the blue tarp. I sucked on her neck and gave her hickeys. I sat down and tried to pull her with me. When she tried to leave, I held on to her hand and continued my coercion. She walked away briefly a couple times, but I refused to join her, choosing instead to be petulant until she returned. Finally, she capitulated and gave me what I wanted.

We walked back in the same direction, then veered our separate ways as I headed for my place and she went home. Two hours later, I was home alone. The doorbell rang. Two officers were at my door, and they questioned me about my whereabouts that day and my relationship with Haylee. They said her neighbor had called the police because Haylee came home with bruises on her neck and

27

arms, and when the police pressed her, all Haylee said was she had been hanging out with me. She didn't say I had caused the bruises, choosing instead to stay silent yet again.

I told the officers we had been hanging out at Blackberry Farm. Naturally, I left out the part about my pressuring her to perform fellatio. When they asked me if I had hurt her or forced her against her will, I answered with an overly dramatic "No. Of course not." They believed me.

Haylee had been taken to the hospital to undergo a rape kit procedure in which they swabbed her and took pictures, and all the while she stayed silent. She changed schools shortly after because the anxiety had gotten so bad, but her only reward was then to drive by the house of the man, the original neighbor, who had assaulted her years before.

perfect harmony

P.E. class, as a fat 14-year-old, was a glaring reminder of how much I jiggled. I was on the cusp between obese and just really fat. The standard-issue red cotton shorts and light grey t-shirts for Kennedy Junior High School physical education did not help my cause much; snug in all the wrong places. God did I hate fourth period.

The sports field sat above a slight ridge to the blacktop and each of the four corners were anchored with a backstop for the great American pastime. The west and south sides of the field were buttressed by a residential fence line, while the north side was left unguarded, parallel to Hyannisport Road, with only a chain-link fence separating the school from the sidewalk.

After our stretches and jumping jacks, the whole class took a long lap around the field to warm up, beginning at the north end and circling counter-clockwise. The herd began its migration fairly cohesively, then thinned out as the fatties lagged, and the spry galloped in front. As we passed the first backstop, I noticed two figures looming on the sidewalk of Hyannisport, just beyond the fence.

One was wearing grey Dickies sagged well below his ass, a black and white checkered flannel with only the two top buttons fastened, a white t-shirt, and a flat-brimmed, black baseball hat with white old-English letters stitched across the front that read "SJ"; his head was cocked to one side with his eyes fixed on me, and his thumbs looped in his belt line as he assumed an arrogant stance. The other guy leaned against the chain-link with his forearms, fingers hooked through the openings for support, and a malevolent grin spread across his face. He was wearing a blue sweatshirt with the hood pulled up over the back half of his head, black jeans six sizes too large, and gleaming white boxer shorts which were left nearly fully exposed from his sagging waistline. They both seemed a few years older than me, and I noticed the kid with the flannel proudly displaying his coming-of-age mustache. Not only could I tell they were tough kids from a tough neighborhood, but the kid in the hoodie was black, and not the kind of black you typically find in white suburban Cupertino. He was black with all the attributes that set off racist warning bells within all the soccer moms in the area. I knew these kids could kick my ass, and I was nervous.

"What are you lookin' at, fat boy?" the white kid shouted out. The other, with his head still leaning close to the fence, said nothing, but he nodded with an upward scoff and menacing smile.

I could have chosen to look away, shut my mouth, and continue my languid jog like the rest of the kids were doing, but that would have left a glaring hole in my résumé. The role I had been playing for the past two years was that of the bad kid—skater, stoner, and a mix of wanna-be thug all rolled into one.

I responded with the customary mindless retort one offers when trying to act tough in such situations, "You got a fuckin' problem?"

We exchanged expletives, and I tried my best to feign confidence. There were kids jogging and walking by, some even stopped to watch the calamity, so I performed with the fear of pending humiliation at my back. Gambling on the assumption that they would not jump the fence to fight, much less risk teacher or police intervention, I boldly stood my ground in the verbal scrum. All was well, and my reputation remained untarnished. I even bragged about the incident in my remaining classes that day.

After school, my path home took me directly by the location of the earlier incident, but for reasons beyond my comprehension, it never occurred to me to avoid the route. The two guys seemed to come from nowhere, and before I knew it, they were on either side of me.

"What up, faggot? You still wanna pop off?"

I started back peddling both with my feet and a slew of apologies. My back was to the fence, and they stood in front of me at slight angles, each protecting possible escape routes. I begged them not to hurt me.

"Then bow down to us bitch, and we'll let your sorry ass go."

"Yeah, punk-ass mothafucka. Kiss my fuckin' feet bitch."

I was scared, and the thought of fighting them didn't even cross my mind. I wonder sometimes how kids develop that instinct to face fear or take a beating. All my favorite characters have all taken a defining stand, and most learned that principle somewhere during childhood. I had only learned how to lie and manipulate thus far, so I took the coward's way out. I got down on both knees and stared down at the ground. One of them smacked me upside the head and told me to bow lower and kiss his shoes. I lowered my face all the way to the ground. A black Nike Cortez flicked up and gave me a little rabbit kick to the lips. They were both laughing, mocking me as I cowered below them. I felt the tears stream from my eyes and watched them darken the dirt below me with each drop. Humiliation creates quite the vacuum. Time stops, sound goes away, thoughts crawl into slow motion, and whatever chemical is being released at that moment, that's one hell of a drug. Is that the result of a bundle of misfiring synapses, or is it actually a point of perfect harmony?

By the time I looked up, they were already walking down the block away from me, jostling with each other, replaying the story between them. I was humiliated, dejected, hollow and alone. I picked

31

myself up and dusted off my knees. The walk home was only a block, but it felt like a hundred miles. I didn't want anyone to see me, so I ran the whole way. When I got home, the front door was locked, and my father wasn't there, so I went around to the side gate and made my way to the backyard where I spent the next hour crying and waiting for someone to come home.

pilfered wine

A new Italian restaurant opened in my neighborhood run by an eclectic group of degenerates I would quickly befriend. A weathered old man sat on the patio most of the day, sipping a bottomless glass of wine, while the restaurant was run by Mexican cooks and a manager filling the role of lead quasi-gangster, gold chain and Kangol hat to boot. The lead henchman would eventually become one of my sources for considerable quantities of marijuana. One of the cooks, who later took over for the henchman as manager, would end up supplying me cocaine during my college years of self-employment. But it was the old man, posted outside for hours, drunk on gratuitous wine, who had the greatest impact on my life.

The restaurant, sitting on a major road of a small, up-and-coming suburban town in Silicon Valley, circa mid '90s, was one of four businesses in a one-story commercial structure built 20 years prior. Across the street from this newly-launched dining experience was the town post office, and to the right, a family-owned video rental store. At the far end of the structure was a quiet notary business, but directly to the left of the Italian joint was the real gem on the lot. Curtains were drawn over any discernible vantage points into the mystery, and the only identifying mark was a neon sign in the window that claimed the bold notion of being "open" for business. Late into the evenings, that sign remained lit, attracting its prey like a mosquito zapper. Beyond the neon, there was no sign of identifiable business branding, and no hours of operation were posted, but once in a while, usually with their eyes focused on the ground and hands in pockets, men would scamper quickly into the door. Strangely, I never noticed anyone exiting.

A group of us were eating outside the restaurant one night, a make-shift patio set up under an overhang, and the old man was lobbing one-line intrusions into our conversation from his perch at the next table. His skin was flaky, voice raspy, teeth stained red, and his belly sat on his thighs, halfway to his knees. When he spoke, the wattle under his chin would cluck and jiggle, the skin loose from years of one-sided conversation. He was lonely and wanted to tell us all his clever punch lines on life. On the topic of love, which was arrived at tangentially during a diatribe concerning the wonders of tits, he concluded the idea to be grossly inappropriate; an out-dated manmade concept. He boiled down the issue to a mere bio-chemical urge to ejaculate which he solved by enlightened means of business transaction and skipped any of the additional bother-some complications.

"I don't want to give a bitch half my money when she gets tired of my shit. I'd rather just pay one of those slants next door whenever I need their services and keep the rest all to myself."

He chuckled, then sat back smugly in his chair, pleased with him-self, and sipped his pilfered wine. I couldn't quite make them out, but words kept being mumbled under his breath for a full cycle of what should have been awkward silence.

All bitter men have the same predicable argument against women, and all bitter men die regretful and lonely. I couldn't possibly know that then, but I did know enough to ask one fateful question:

"What is that place next door?"

One week later, a friend and I had worked up the nerve to visit the massage parlor. I didn't know if he was as nervous as I was, but I remember feeling extremely anxious as we walked up the railroad tracks on the way to the brothel. The repetition of railroad tracks, as you walk on top of them, can be either soothingly meditative or explosively unnerving. This experience was the latter.

A coating of invisible slime saturated me as I stepped through the door, thick with secrets and regret. A bell attached to the door rang to announce our presence while simultaneously sending off bells in my head. I should not have been there, I could feel it, but my mind was hyper-focused on sex and the allure of perversion. There is no greater loss of mental command than a man's mind obsessed with sex. The place smelled of incense and disinfectant.

What we entered looked like a small waiting room for a doctor's office, with a counter and sliding opaque window concealing what would be the receptionist area. We stood and said nothing, not sure what to do. Sports Illustrated, Newsweek, and People magazine lay on a small, black coffee table in the center of the room with four chairs arranged neatly around. A black bookcase in the corner of the room held a bonsai plant; a splayed fan with writing on it, which I assumed to be Japanese; and a small, electric, recirculating water fountain letting out a tranquil sound. Finally, a shadow appeared behind the window, and slowly, the glass slid open. A very short Asian woman, somewhere in her mid-fifties, stood behind the counter and giggled immediately when she saw the two of us standing there.

"We want to get a massage," my friend said with an obviously fake muster of confidence.

"Oh no. So sorry. You go now. No massagy. You go now. "

She pointed to the door and repeated the choice words in broken English.

I'm sure we didn't look like her typical clientele of businessmen and guilty husbands, but I found her discrimination perplexing and mildly insulting. My naïve assumption was that they, the business of massage parlors staffed by droves of illegal immigrants

35

from Asia, were in no position to dictate terms of business. That it was in fact us, the paying and documented customer, who held the upper hand in that situation. Prostitution is like any other business: whoever is more desperate will maintain leverage and bargaining rights. This can be expanded to relationship theory as well. Whoever is the lonelier will be more desperate, and the desperate reek of vulnerability.

In order to show the madam we were indeed serious customers, both of us pulled out wads of money, and her objections quickly faded away. We were allotted one girl between the two of us, and I kindly allowed my friend to venture inside first. I have never felt more uncomfortable in my life, before or since, than I did for those 30 minutes in that waiting room.

My friend eventually walked out with a big grin on his face, and I was summoned inside by a young, pretty Chinese woman, no older than twenty-five, wearing a royal blue kimono, with amber eyes and fair skin. I remember being struck right away by how kind and gentle she seemed. She could tell I was nervous, and she did her best to make me feel comfortable.

Through the door from the waiting area was a hallway with three doors on either side. She led me into the second door on the left, gave me a towel, and pointed to the shower. On the left side of the room, behind the open door, was a massage table topped with white linen. Behind that, there was a small, open Jacuzzi built into the structure. In the back of the room was a stand-up shower with a built-in sitting ledge, gracefully tiled a dark turquoise and framed by a glass enclosure. I didn't know what to expect going in, perhaps just a worn mattress lying on the ground, but these were five-star accommodations as far as I had experienced.

I took off my clothes, laid them sloppily over the single chair in the room, and made my way into the shower. It's intriguing when you engage in routine activity in a non-routine setting. Going through the motions of rinsing off felt very ordinary until I remembered that a prostitute would soon enter the room and serve me. I felt calm while letting the water run over me, but as soon as I stepped out, I was a nervous teenager again. I did a poor job off drying off, then lay down naked on the massage table.

Time slows to a crawl when you wait awkwardly on the verge of sex. My face was sticking through the hole in the table, and my sinuses were already building with pressure, clogging my nose; clumsy mouth breathing ensued. My heart was pounding, reverberating off the table and back into my chest, making it feel as if I had a palpitating heart banging away double-time, a death marching pace.

A soft knock on the door and words barely audible were heard. I remained silent. The door creaked open and she entered the room. I didn't dare look up. My only visual queue at this point was seeing her tiny bare feet through the face-cradle opening as she stood at the head of the table. A fresh coat of red nail polish had recently been applied.

"Heyro. My name Cindi. How yu rike maasagy?"

"Uh," was the only description I could think of, but as I said it, I felt embarrassed. Wasn't I there for sex? What does the massage matter? At what point do I see your vagina? So many voices all having separate conversations in my head, but when all else failed, I just said what came to mind: "Strong."

She put a small towel over my bum then proceeded to give me one of the best massages of my life. My face stretched through the opening in the table, and my eyes followed her tiny feet around the perimeter, until they disappeared from my line of sight. She worked tirelessly to dig into every possible pressure point. She crawled on my back with her knees, then stood up on her feet and walked along my spine, taking a pause at each critical juncture, telling me to breathe out, then executing a slight bounce in order to crack my back, vertebra by vertebra. After 30 minutes, I was complete jelly.

"Preese turn ova," she told me, so I flipped onto my back.

As the massage proceeded up my legs and toward my thighs, thoughts of lust danced back into focus. For a minute there, while she was working so diligently, I had forgotten the carnal reason for my visit. Her hands went further up, and deeper between my thighs in swooping motions, as professional massage turned into erotic foreplay. The feeling was absolutely mesmerizing. I had little sexual experience to this point, so my only notions of intimacy were aggressive teenage kissing, groping, or the occasionally persuaded blowjob. She systematically played and teased, while touching me in places that sent little shock waves throughout my body; woman teaching boy about the art of seduction. I kept my eyes closed because I was still a scared teenager with no idea what to do. Inner thighs and lower abdomen, then a hand glided gently over my member once, as if by accident, en route back to the previous erogenous areas. I could feel the surge swell, and I was already close to climax.

What's my move here, I wondered, as I swooned in and out of ecstasy. I had never been touched like that, in those places, and I was certainly excited, but I could not understand what proper decorum would dictate in such a situation. Do I simply rise and do with this woman as I please, or is there a proper set of questions to be asked first? Perhaps a code word to signify the beginning of fornication? I could not contain myself any longer, so I rose from the table, sat up, and took her hand into mine.

She smiled and giggled, bowing her head slightly, and said to me: "Sixtee dorra teep you geeve me okay?"

I nodded in agreement.

"I be back," she told me, then slipped on a kimono and promptly left the room.

The sense of disappointment was fairly high while waiting for the woman to return while watching my erection fade away. I forced dirty thoughts into my mind and fondled myself in hopes of sustaining the valiant stance but, at 14 years of age, concentration in such moments was inconceivable.

I was sitting up on the massage table, legs dangling over the edge, when she came back holding a towel with both hands as if presenting me with a royal gift. On top of the towel was a single condom with blue label. I had previous experience with condoms, as I had attempted their use several times in prior efforts at intercourse. To say the events were not fruitful would be kind. For me, sexual experiences to that point were new and very unnerving. I was scared and anxious to begin with, and the process of putting on a condom only added to my anxiety. I tried multiple times to have sex previously, but each time would end in one of three ways. Usually, I would lose my erection while applying the condom or manage to get it on, only to prematurely ejaculate en route to vagina. If I was lucky, I would actually engage in 5 seconds of intercourse, but to call that sex is like calling a stick-figure drawing a work of art.

It is astounding how powerful fear and anxiety are to the mind and body. I was scared to death. Again, the concubine was experienced in such matters, and remarkably graceful, as she sensed my nervousness and gently guided me back down the path of arousal. She untied her kimono and let it fall to the floor, then touched me lightly, and guided her bare breasts toward my face. I held her close to me and ran my hands along her smooth skin. As she rubbed my shoulder and neck with one hand while the other hand commanded my sexual attention, a sense of calm settled in, and I felt at ease.

I was ready. Somewhere, while I was lost in the moment, she had put the condom on me with minimal commotion. She put her hand on my chest and guided me back to lie down on the massage table. With a dancer's grace, she climbed on top and straddled me, the entire time looking gently, but passionately, into my eyes. She sat there for a moment, looking at me, feeling my heart with her left palm, and shined a friendly smile. I smiled back and put my hands on her breasts. She rotated her weight slightly forward, applying more pressure on her left arm which was still planted over my heart, brought her face close enough to mine to let her hair fall over me, and raised her hips a few inches into the air. With her other hand, she reached between her legs.

When she found her mark, she sat back and let me glide slowly into her. As soon as I felt the depth of her warmth, it was all over. I grabbed her by the waist and tensed up like a seizure victim. When I opened my eyes again, she smiled brightly. I slowly slid my hands around to her shoulder blades, as I pulled her down to me. For a minute we lay there, a big grin across my face, with only the sound of my panting between us.

Slowly she dismounted, making sure I didn't move a muscle, and covertly sneaked the condom off in one easy motion. She told me to stay still, slipped on her kimono, and left the room for a brief moment before returning with a hot towel. I flinched a bit when I first felt the towel being laid over my privates, but after a few seconds, when she wrapped her hand over it and began cleaning me off, I realized how wonderful that warm towel felt. She wiped me thoroughly with the hot towel then took a dry towel to give a final run through. The level of service dumbfounded me. I had never experienced such royal treatment before.

When I was getting dressed, standing there shirtless, I reached into my pocket and held out three 20-dollar bills as we had previously agreed. Assuming she discounted for my conservative performance time, she plucked two of the bills from my hand, smiled, bowed her head, and thanked me.

in the kitchen

It happened on a Saturday morning and began with the usual cacophony from the kitchen downstairs. My parents were in the throes of an argument. I was under house arrest, again, so I spent most of my time secluded upstairs in my bedroom. That meant that often, far too often, I would be within earshot of the arguments between my parents once the volume rose past civil. They were pretty good at raising decibels in a hurry.

Nine times out of ten, the arguments were on the topic of me, their delinquent and ever-defiant son. My father wanted to take my freedom away permanently by sending me away to military school, forcing me into some kind of reform program, or leaving me in juvenile hall for as long as the law allowed. As all mothers do, mine fiercely protected her cub. I sat and lamented, plotting how to more effectively conceal my illegal activities so I didn't end up in the clutches of the law again.

My father would chastise my mother, blaming her for the disobedience of my sister and me. Their children became her children, which in turn became her problem, since she didn't want to abide by his gritty version of reform. But he would be damned if those ungrateful offspring of hers would jeopardize his freedom or the integrity of his household. They argued in the kitchen, always in the kitchen, and I could hear every word. My headboard leaned against the hallway wall. The words would thunder from the kitchen and festoon the entire house. As I leaned against the headboard,

41

I could feel his malignant anger swelling, and with it, my blood boiled. Fifteen years old and I sat there brooding like a bitter drunk in the corner of a shanty bar.

My mother had always been a strong woman, a leader, and never shy to give her opinion. My father would yell, and my mother would do her best to retort with confidence in her voice. This particular argument was different, however. In this dispute, I heard my mother's voice change by an octave. Like most arguments, there comes a point where the power dynamic shifts as one party feels victory slipping away. Pitch, cadence, and intonation convey power and threats in ways words never can. I didn't catch what he said, but suddenly, she was pleading.

"Please. Please don't do that!" she implored.

A cascade of dishes fell to the floor. I could hear glasses shattering on walls.

"I won't live like this! You can do whatever you want, but I will take care of myself. He won't have that shit in this house so I can go to jail for him!" my father shouted.

I scurried downstairs to witness the commotion firsthand. As I turned the corner to look into the kitchen, my mother was anticipating my arrival and staring in my direction. She had both palms to her cheeks in an over-exaggerated, confused manner. She was scared, and her wide eyes held me frozen. When my mother was uncomfortable, scared, or caught in a lie, she would use the same defensive maneuver to deflect attention. She acted dumb and confused, as if an event completely out of the grasp of known reality had occurred, and she just witnessed the impossible. She stood just in front of the kitchen counter, barely out of range of the flying dishes, looking bewildered.

My father was ducked behind the counter, the small divider between kitchen and hallway, with his head buried in the lower cabinet. He continued to take dishes out and throw them haphazardly behind him, the way a dog throws dirt when digging a hole.

"What are you doing?" I asked.

My father stopped for a moment and pulled his head out from the crevice to glare at me with toxic radiation.

"I'm looking for your drugs!" Conviction and enmity heavy in his words.

"In the kitchen? With the dishes?" I scoffed.

The hubris of a teenager is always thickest when he thinks his opponent exemplifies stupidity. I thought the idea of hiding drugs in the kitchen seemed obviously foolhardy, so I took the opportunity to mock my father with a snide undertone and a whimsical grin. It only served to enrage him further. I had seen those eyes before. Deeply focused into the apex of my soul, he glared at me with the rage of countless generations of angry, domineering men accustomed to total control of their households.

Seeing the tension between us, my mother stepped in and urged me back to my room. Standing there only served to provoke my father further, and, by Croatian standards, he had every right to tear the entire house apart if he deemed it necessary. I was comfortable in my small victory, knowing he would find nothing. Fresh off of my arrest, well-versed in the routine of probation, and serving house arrest again, I chose to clear my room of the usual paraphernalia, but even that knowledge wasn't my ace. The kicker, in my opinion, was his obvious idiocy and, by default, my consequent cleverness. My eyes mocked him loudly. He was looking in all the wrong places and making a fool of himself in the process.

Back upstairs in my room, I blasted victory music, Cypress Hill's first album. I could still hear the peaks of argument bobbing over the music, the way you might catch glimpses of the shoreline when treading water out at sea. I thought about my life and was pleased, at least, to see clearly divided sides. My father was obviously the enemy, and I, the noble, persecuted hero. The police and court system served as his standing army, willing to wage unholy crusades on those deemed sinners. My mother was caught in the middle, unsure how to mediate peace, and I was the valiant Robin Hood, confident of a cause but never being able to articulate it.

The shouting suddenly stopped. I turned the music off but still heard nothing. It was an eerie silence; my heart picking up tempo as my mind raced through possibilities. I opened the door and stuck my head out. It was faint, and I could barely pick it up, but the muffled sound was unmistakable. My mother was crying, and I could hear the whimpers escaping through her attempts at concealment. I leapt down the stairs and into the kitchen hall. My father was now in front of the master bedroom door, adjacent to the dining room, ten feet in front of me. To my right, my mother stood in the same place I had left her, in the kitchen, broken dishes all around her feet. She was holding her mouth with both hands and crying. I remembered the feeling and look of dismay in her eyes because it was the same I had elicited from her each time she picked me up at juvenile hall. She had been betrayed by those she loved most, not by our actions, but by our blatant disregard of her heart.

By the time I turned back to look at my father, he was already behind the bedroom door. Only his head stuck out around the edge to watch for danger. Fury rose from my belly and infected my mind in a flash. I was diseased. I didn't know whether my father had hit her in reaction to her defiance, in the heat of argument, or if he had done it as a secondhand retribution for my actions. The moment I took a step in his direction, the bedroom door locked shut, and my mother pleaded and shouted my name. She was wailing, and her words became unclear through the gargle of tears and panic.

Demands for battle and curses at God permeated through the door as my shoulder rammed into the barrier between my father and me. I pounded, and I rammed with full fury. My mother was quickly at my side pleading, crying, and dying inside.

My father yelled from inside the room. "Stay away from me! Don't come in here!"

"Please, Anto, stop it. You will go to jail, or he will kill you," my mother begged.

The wood around the lock crackled as it began to give way to my ramrod. Adrenaline was thundering through my veins. Sound became white noise, sight became monochrome, and the only sensory perception left was an undefined awareness: The gravity of rage. In the throes of my insanity, a gentle hand grabbed my arm. It squeezed with compassion and mercy. She didn't say a word, but her touch conveyed everything.

As my senses came back online, my mother pulled me away with the assurance of her voice and a flood of tears. It wasn't a dramatically violent scene, her physically wrenching me away, but rather a somber one, with my submission coming more voluntarily than I would have cared to admit. Deep down, I didn't want to fight my dad; I just wanted him to go away. My mother calmed me down and reminded me of my recent troubles, my current stint on house arrest, and the likelihood of another arrest should any fighting break out in the house. Her tone was soothing, and her logic sound, so I took the opportunity to recuse myself from the case of avenging her abuse.

My mother's bottom lip had a small swell to it, slightly off center, and she focused on it by poking her tongue at the sore. I knew it wasn't anything serious, and I chose to stay quiet and simply console. Even as a 15-year-old, I knew the implications of that look in her eyes. The tough character of my mother could have endured a dozen busted lips, and a black eye to boot, but her tender heart couldn't absorb the weight of such betrayal. After 15 minutes of calm, she finally said something.

"I'm going to the doctor to get this checked out. Just to be sure. Can you please promise me you'll stay in your room if I leave?"

I agreed.

As I stood in the kitchen, staring out the window, watching her pull out of the driveway, torrents of emotion flooded my heart: relief, anger, confusion, loss, and something somber lurking deep in my belly. Would this be enough for my mother to leave him? Would we be forced to run from our home and flee from my father? One thing was sure: I was officially part of a dysfunctional family now.

Up to that point, my rebellious nature had been something of a mystery to most outsiders. School officials, probation officers, and community parents all scratched their heads at my blatant disregard for rule and law. I was from a nice home, in an upper-middle-class neighborhood, yet the chip on my shoulder would lead people to believe I was raised with something to prove. But why? What was I trying to prove? And why did I so desperately cling to the outlaw persona behind which I was hiding?

Nobody understood the feelings that brewed inside me as a child, and I had no proof to present in my defense. So my dad was overly authoritative and controlling in the household; whose dad wasn't? Especially dads that were within the Croatian community or any old-world immigrant culture. My dad was no different from the majority of stubborn men who hid their insecurity with dominance and assertive control. I couldn't explain the fear and isolation I felt because I didn't feel justified by my mild level of suffering. Surely there are more substantial reasons in the world to claim victimization. My father didn't throw a baseball with me, boohoo, and he had a temper that caused me to walk on eggshells, big deal. So what if I felt I missed out on the basics of innocent childhood because my father simply didn't know how to engage in a comforting, loving manner? There are millions of children more deserving of a sympathetic ear than I. But now, things were different. The truth would be known, and I would be vindicated.

The anger was far in the background, but I tried to focus on it because I assumed it to be the appropriate response in this situation. Tough guys get angry, and I would rather pretend to be holding up the vale than admit the deep hollow I felt in my heart. I lost something dearly important that day, and I would spend the next 20 years trying to find it.

The truth was I knew exactly what I was doing from the start. When I was ten years old, I began playing the game: I started lying deliberately. I stole money from my parents so I could buy candy and play video games, and I knew I could get away with it. The lies grew as my appetite for instant gratification increased, so by the time I was 13, I was arrested for possession of marijuana at school. The tension in my house became sinister. I kept lying and manipulating my mother to stand in the way of my father.

Now, sitting back in my silent room, it was the first time our house had been void of sound in years. Since my recent arrest, the house had become angry with noise, even if no words were spoken. Our house had squeaky floors and hollow walls, so I could always tell where my parents were and what kind of mood they were in. It was the footsteps that caught my attention most, always fearing the impending march of authority. Many times I would sit, listening to my parent's conversations for hours; their voices easily carrying from the kitchen, up the stairs, and through my closed door. Discussions about me would end in one of two ways: either my father would yell in anger and berate my mother for her part in the civil collapse of his life, or a quiet tone would precede my mother's footsteps as she climbed the stairs up to my room, demanding my attendance at the kitchen table for discussion. Yes, it was the footsteps I feared most.

Discussions at the kitchen table never ended well for me, as my grasps at freedom always slipped just a bit further out of reach. I usually sat silent, listening to the lecture and punishment, with as little emotion as possible. When I did speak, I only offered apologies and lies in order to escape the interrogation as quickly as possible. I told them what I knew they wanted to hear, with no real intention of reform. I never once truly listened to what they had to say.

My father always sat in silence, smoking a cigarette, staring off into the abyss of his mind. If it were up to him, I would be shipped off to hard labor somewhere or kicked out of the house, forced to learn the realities of life through difficulty. But he never managed to get his way, and my mother always succeeded in saving her son with one more opportunity at redemption. My father never said a word during those talks at the kitchen table, but he knew every sentence I offered was a lie. He absorbed everything I said without ever looking at me and offered no additional commentary when my mother asked his opinion. These kitchen-table lectures had become a frequent occurrence over the past few years, ever since I began immersing myself into the derelict lifestyle. Anger boiled in my father and resentment brewed in me, but now, sitting still in my silent room, I felt the first moments of relief in years.

An hour or so later, I heard the doorbell ring. I waited for the sound of footsteps to indicate my father was going to answer the door, but I heard none. The doorbell rang again. I reached the bottom step, just in time to see my father heading back toward the same door to his bedroom he had hidden behind a short while earlier. We locked eyes just before he shut the door. As I approached the front door, I heard chatter outside, a combination of a deep male voice and a squeaky feminine sound funneled by something I couldn't quite make out.

Not bothering to look through the peephole, I opened the door to see a police officer standing a few feet back. My heart rate doubled by the time I exhaled. He was big, I remember thinking, standing higher than I was even though our entryway allotted me an additional six inches to his lowered position. His hair was short on top but full, black and combed back to produce a slight wave in the hairline. He was powerful, Latino, and his eyes were stern and dark. His jaw had muscle tone and his stare commanded authority.

He wore his uniform snugly, probably a size too small. The veins on his biceps were noticeable, crawling up under his short sleeves like worms. My focal point shifted to his silver name tag, and I saw the one name every delinquent in my neighborhood feared most: LOPEZ.

Officer Lopez had arrested nearly every single one of my friends at least once. The mere mention of his name incited fear within any group of stoners, skaters, taggers, or truants. Having only a few arrests under my belt, I had not yet had the pleasure of meeting the fabled arch-nemesis, but I knew the stories well enough.

"Is your father home?" Lopez asked.

"Uuhhhhh," was the only sound I could manage to let out.

"Are you Anto?"

"Yeah," I responded.

"I've heard about you. We haven't met yet. I'm Officer Lopez."

I turned my head back and shouted, "Dad! It's for you."

My dad came around the corner, into the hallway, ten feet back from the front door, and looked at the officer standing outside. My father never once looked at me.

"Mr. Lajalick, please step outside here for me."

Normally my father would take the opportunity to correct the mispronunciation of our last name, but that day he said nothing, and his eyes were wide. He moved with small steps, almost a shuffle, toward the door. The officer spoke into the radio clipped to the shoulder loop on his uniform.

"10-4. Suspect at residence."

It was at that moment I realized the officer wasn't there for me; he came to arrest my father. Lopez told me to stay in the house as he took my father toward the police cruiser parked at the curb in front of my house. As I stood in the doorway, I looked out to see a second officer waiting near the cruiser and my mother's car pulling around into the driveway. Dusk was approaching, and in the background, across the street, I could see our neighbors standing in front of their porch light, just outside their door. The light was at their backs, faces shadowed, but I could feel the condemnation of rumor being whispered as the heads leaned toward each other.

My mother was talking with the second officer when Lopez led my father toward the two to join the conversation. I couldn't make out the words, but I could see the typical mannerisms. My mother held most of the conversation in her usual animated style while my father stood silent and still. When Lopez turned my father around and began handcuffing him, my mother's voice rose in volume to desperation. The only word I heard was "please."

Turned back around and now handcuffed, my father stared at the officer blankly as Lopez began reading the Miranda Rights. The second officer escorted my mother back toward me. She was distraught, but she seemed much more lucid than earlier when she left for the hospital. In the face of adversity or challenge, my mother could always shift gears into business mode. She was explaining to the officer the unnecessary nature of my father's arrest and very succinctly outlined justification for his release, but to no avail. The cruiser, with my father in it, pulled away as I shut the front door.

"What happened?" I asked my mother.

By law, doctors in California are required to report cases of domestic violence. My mother was not aware of such facts. She had gone to the clinic to have her lip looked at and, through the normal course of conversation with her doctor, it was mentioned that the swelling was inflicted during a domestic argument. The doctor calmly left the room, called the police, and came back to finish the rest of his medical examination without saying a word. The police were waiting for her outside when she left and, in her words, forced her to report the crime.

I didn't know how to react when my mother told me what had happened, but inside, I felt a growing sense of victory. My father was going to jail, and I was finally free from the reign of the evil king. At that moment, I thought my father would never come back. I thought this event would create enough momentum for my mother to push for divorce and my father never to return. I felt vindicated. All the anger, suspicion, fear, trepidation, and guilt I had lived with for years would now be gone, and I would finally get a chance to live what I considered to be a normal life. My mother was strong enough to stand on her own without a husband. I had my revenge. Things were going to change.

In the weeks that followed, my mother and I spoke often and she confided in me the long hidden truths of her marriage. This event was not the first of its kind, just the first during my conscience memory. The stories were both unbelievable and perfectly predictable.

I felt an amazing sense of connection with my mother after hearing those stories in the weeks that followed my father's arrest. We spent hours talking, and I felt the creep of maturity crawling up my spine as I realized the severity of the situation. My father had been released from jail a week after his arrest but was not allowed to come back home due to the mandatory restraining order placed on domestic abusers by the state. My mother openly discussed the possibility of divorce with me and the realities of that decision should it come. Things would get ugly, and we would have to settle in for tough times, requiring a great deal of sacrifice and responsibility on my part.

The ask wasn't anything one imagines in such a difficult situation. It wasn't like my mother was dependent on my father for income. She was a powerhouse in the corporate world, and she could easily

51

provide on her own, so my required contribution would not be a financial one. Her ask, directly and frankly, was that I knocked off all the shit I was doing. The attitude, the arrest, the disobedience, the drugs—they all had to go if we were going to make it.

The house was calm and quiet, peaceful, accepting and friendly, comforting, warm and safe. I had never felt this way about my home, ever. I had never wanted to be home before. We talked a lot in the first few weeks, but as time went by, the conversations be-came less frequent. There was only so much detail one could offer before repetition invited dullness. And so, as with many climactic moments in life, much of the awe faded and people returned to routine. Two months passed.

One day I came home from skateboarding to see two cars parked in front of our house that I recognized immediately. The first I identified as belonging to our close friends, a Croatian family we often had over for the long, loud, drawn-out dinners that turn into political conversations. The other car set off alarm bells, jump-started my heart, and I quickly felt the anger rising from my gut. My father was home.

I stormed into the house, announcing myself as I entered the front door more as a warning shot than a courteous declaration. Immediately, I could smell the cigarettes. I turned the corner toward the dining room to see our family friend, Miro, standing near the table with his typical friendly smile.

"Hii guy. Vat's up?" Miro rolled off in a thick Croatian accent. The H was too heavy, and the smile far too manufactured, but he was trying his best to convey a sense of calm.

I took another step and saw my mother sitting at the kitchen table with folders and documents scattered in front of her. On the table was a plate of homemade apple strudel with a silver serving fork leaning on the edge, a glass bowl of shelled hazelnuts with silver cracker on top, a small saucer with sugar cubes pyramided neatly, a milk serving cup, and three porcelain coffee cups with bits of grounds at the bottom. The dishes all matched in white china base with black and gold trim; the set reserved for formal occasions.

Why is there such a sense of civility being displayed here? I thought to myself.

My mother looked at me and played dumb, using the masterful effect of one inorganic word: "Hi."

I had seen that look on her just a couple months prior, in the kitchen hallway where I now stood, with broken dishes surrounding her feet. It's the look of a proud woman trying to hide a sad truth from an angry son. She quickly looked away from me and began shuffling papers.

To her right, farthest around the corner from my initial line of sight, near his usual place at the head of the table, stood my father. His right arm was hinged at thirty degrees as he held a cigarette close to his face. His left arm was limp, unthreatening by his side, and his stance was meek, the way an intellectual might stand unconcerned with posture or poise.

"Hii. Hhow arr yu?" my father asked with slow, heavy, Slavic words.

All I felt was betrayal. My mother had betrayed me, and I caught them in the act of reconciliation. My father should have said more, but he didn't know how. He was raised in a place void of expressed emotion, so he, too, learned to internalize anything resembling sorrow or pain. It was awkward. I didn't know what to say. Standing there, I felt a terrible sense of loneliness wash over me.

"What are you doing here?" I asked.

My mother jumped in and started flooding the room with vague terms and loose concepts. My heart sank further. At that moment, my home became the house of old, and I wanted to run away as far as possible. I walked away from the table while my mother was still spewing lies, grabbed my skateboard, and ejected myself from the house.

I didn't know where to go but, more importantly, I didn't know what I was going to do now in the larger sense. Before that fateful day, I had direction, purpose, and meaning. I was a broken child ready to help fix a broken home with my broken mother. Now, I was free falling with no bearing on up, forward, or safe. All I knew for sure was the way down.

I made it as far as 7-Eleven, a mere five minutes from my house, and bought junk food, stole a pack of cigarettes, and shoulder-tapped for beer. Behind 7-Eleven was a small plot of land, a groundwater recharge lake and railroad tracks, where I learned about many truths of life. It was where I first got high, and the place I had my first real fight. Sitting in the back, hidden by the cover of bushes, I looked out across the water and brooded over what had just happened at home. My father was back, or he would be soon, and that left emptiness and resentment in my heart. A few months ago, I felt vindicated because the world would now have proof of what I knew all along: my father was cruel, and my family was a sham.

Although the arrest and pending divorce would secure our label as a broken family, I felt confident in our ability to rebound and, more importantly, in my ability to care. But now, with my corrupted father being reinstated as the head of the household, the title of broken family seemed something to strive for, something sane compared to the charade being perpetuated. I wasn't broken anymore; I was completely shattered.

When I came home later that night, I asked my mom to explain what was happening. She never came out and admitted she was allowing him back into our lives, choosing instead only to mention they were discussing the details of the restraining order. It was never mentioned again. The restraining order was dropped, divorce talk faded away, and within a few weeks, things were back to old.

My father moved back in and for a while, the energy was different in the house. His tone was soft, his eyes gentle, and he made an effort either to stay out of my way or say little to me when we did cross paths. But it was the dinners I remember most.

My mother was vice-president of a large corporation, but she still managed to come home nearly every night and cook dinner. I was not impressed by her determination to feed her family. Instead, I was astounded by her uncanny ability to step right back into the groove and pretend nothing had ever transpired. We never spoke about what had happened, neither separately nor as a family. Instead, my mother served dinner, and we ate in silence or with the malaise of small talk to cover our emotions.

The scene was always a derivation of a flashback to the origin for me. I was five years old, and we were living in Switzerland at the time. It was dinnertime, and my mother hurried in the door, finally home from a long day at the office. She quickly flung her purse and coat on the sofa and began rustling in the kitchen. The house smelled of cigarette smoke, and I was playing on the carpet, hiding action figures behind the furniture, while my father was in his office.

Dinner was ready, and my mom made her announcement. I ran into the kitchen and hopped up in my chair. As she was serving me, my father walked in, and there was a presence about him. No words were exchanged, but none were needed. Anger fumed from his essence and covered every inch of the kitchen. The anger was from an old world, from a generation not accustomed to female disobedience. I have seen this old world, once, when driving by a city named Zenica, deep in the mountains of Bosnia, where the sky is dark for miles around. At the center lies an old steel mill, built during the height of the communist regime and left unchanged for

50 years. Soot is continually thrown from the central smokestack and covers the people in a haze, bleak and heavy. My father's anger was like that.

His cigarette burned in an ashtray on the kitchen table as he sat and brooded, still as a leopard stalking in high grass, with only his eyes following his prey. My mother shuffled back and forth from stove to seat, constantly in flux and only managing to consume food in quick, hurried mouthfuls. Something had happened, something was not done according to plan, and my father was trying to force her confession with his silence. A plate of spaghetti was left untouched in front of him, and a vein on his left temple, the color of deep ocean death, swelled as if looking to breech. He fired a verbal jab, a question of foment, and she slipped with sass. Like a horse before an earthquake, I had felt it coming for some time now. The moment before the fury is the center of all creation; everything stands still and no sounds are heard. Then, with the immediacy of waking from a dream, sound is blaring and everyone is voluble. As he rose suddenly, the chair fell behind him, and he grabbed his plate of food and sent it flying across the room. His hand was stern, with one finger pointed sharply out, as he delivered a trembling speech with the conviction and fervor of the great dictators of the twentieth century. I began crying and pissed myself. My mother took me in her arms and began bouncing me, trying to comfort me, while the two of them continued shouting, and I wailed in the middle. When it was done, I was placed back in my chair and told to eat. Eat my boy; all is well.

I remember wondering how many more versions of that same looping movie I would have to sit through during the course of my lifetime. My mother buried the truth, and I hid my emotions, under mounds of food while I uncomfortably retreated to the corners of my mind. It was always the kitchen table that brought events to their confusing conclusion. I ate with silence, or I ate with lies, all the while stuffing the festering emotions further down into my viscera with each bite.

the silence of a freeway

As we headed out for the night, we took care to stick to the shadows. It was just past one in the morning, so it was in our best interest not to be spotted frolicking in the streets. There were three of us that night. We were all wearing dark clothing and carrying backpacks full of spray-paint cans. The suburbs were quiet at that hour, and any headlights we spotted caused us to veer toward some version of camouflage like a bush or a dumpster. Shadows next to shadows don't stick out as much to the passing car. We walked together but covered separately. As soon as we could, we got off the streets and used the railroad tracks to slice through town undetected. Conversations were kept to a minimum and senses were on high alert.

There were few moments in life that gave me a total sense of freedom—the kind of vast invincibility that truly allowed me to feel the expanse of the universe. One of the best was found when combining teenage recalcitrance with the allure of committing crimes in the middle of the night. We were the barbarian hoard that invaded under cover of darkness. We were the last initiates of anarchy who defaced the Queen's garden under penalty of death. We were the filthy artists who spray painted vile truth in plain sight for your children to see.

Every major maturation event in my teenage years happened near railroad tracks. Everywhere I went, I navigated by using the tracks as my main artery. Railroad tracks were my territory, my natural environment, and your chances of winning plummeted when I was in my setting—like an alligator in water.

Just before two o'clock, we reached the first shot. As it turned out, the railroad tracks in my hometown curved through the city and followed the freeway wall for a good two-mile stretch. This meant we could pop back and forth between the freeway and our escape routes fairly easily all night. The only thing to be wary of was confronting a homeless person who lived in the bushes, but having a group usually gave us the advantage.

We started out with an easy one: a wall visible from the freeway but with enough distance and bush cover to make us comfortable while spray-painting our marks. We hopped one fence and walked up a steep brush-covered hill until we reached the wall. Freeway walls always had overlapping sections, where one wall ran behind the other, to provide access points for maintenance workers. The gap between the walls was usually closed off by a chain-link gate and secured with a combination lock, and there was nothing easier to hop than a corner-sectioned gate with ample toeholds. If we were lucky, the bottom corner of the fence would have been kicked out already, perhaps by homeless looking for a nook to crash in along the freeway. Sometimes, the gate was just left wide open.

We were already on high alert walking up the tracks, but when we took our first steps past the walls and out into the open edge of the highway, it took us to a whole new level. The first thing that always struck me was the sounds. Any car that passed our location had an echo of speed chasing it from the audible tunnel created by the two-opposing sound-barrier freeway walls. Also, I could hear a car from what felt like years away, when it was just a speck of light far off on the horizon, and the increasing volume carried with it a sense of awe as I stepped carefully along while machines whizzed by at 70 miles per hour. The shadows along the bushes carried my heartbeat like a maestro conducting an orchestra. Headlights cutting an angle created a scene of monsters prowling about the wall as I tried to focus on the outline of my letters. Everything moved and stopped in unison; shadows, lights, sounds, and heartbeats. Then, out of nowhere, we were left with eerie silence as the freeway lay motionless for 20 seconds like a swamp with frogs that all go silent in one croak. I focused on the sound of the spray paint as my center for grounding, and the smell of the paint fumes always reminded me that I was doing the only thing I knew how to do: Live.

When I finished, I made my way back toward the gate and waited for my crew to be done. I watched them as they were completely rapt in their art. Both of them had been writing for far longer than I had, so I stared at them with fascination. Their letters were crisp, and the shadowing was perfect. I saw them take two steps back, absorb the whole, and then walk back in for a few minor finishing strokes. When they were done, they turned the spray can upside down and pressed the cap until only air came out. If they didn't clear the cap, the paint would harden and clog and leave them with a sputtering tip.

As I hopped back over the fence, I caught the baggy crotch of my pants on something and heard a small tear as I forced my way over. No matter— only a small hole. We were back out on the tracks in no time and each of us lit a cigarette to puff on as we strolled toward the next shot. We walked in the darkness and kept our cigarettes cupped in our hands to hide the cherry. My heart felt booming compared to the sound of our footsteps. The moon looked like a spotlight, far too vain for a situation that called for stealth. We walked on.

The next spot was going to be an all-out blitzkrieg. We came up to a major freeway interchange: 280 and 85. As soon as we hopped the gate, I could feel the energy. This access point would spit us out directly on the freeway shoulder; no bushes and no dirt. We had to sprint along the shoulder of the freeway for about a hundred yards before we reached a little pocket of shadows and shrubs. From there, we could start our attack. The catch was that the initial stretch of asphalt was on a blind sweeping junction, and motorists driving at this hour certainly weren't expecting to see people running along the shoulder. Also, there were usually a lot of drunks driving at that time of night, so we hoped they were not nodding off as they punched it on that racetrack turn of a junction.

We were facing traffic, hugging the sound wall, waiting for a break. When we felt it, all three of us turned the corner, turning our backs to the flow of traffic, and began sprinting across the stretch of pavement that was our no-man's land. My friends were small and quick, I was not. Ten seconds into an all-out sprint, and I heard a car coming from behind us. As the headlights swept around the bend, a sense of terror rose in my chest. Holy fucking shit, it sounds like it's coming straight at us, I thought to myself. Cars sound ferocious when they pass you at high speeds, especially when they come from your blind spot. I sprinted with gasping breaths, and even with a backpack that was clumsy, I moved as if a lion were chasing me. The car whizzed past us, then the scene went from movie set bright to midnight dark in one stride. Holy fucking hell, where is this cut-off? It felt like I had been running for hours. My insides were on fire and my pants were slipping down around my ass.

Finally, I reached safety. I cut a sharp right and veered my way back to the corner of the sound wall behind a large, unfriendly bush. My friends were squatting and panting and looking inside their backpacks for the right colors. I hoped we would stay in that spot forever so I could catch my breath. I didn't want to do that again, but before I could steal five panicked breaths, our leader was already sneaking away in a low crouch along the shadows. Fuck it. Let's go.

There was a nice open stretch of wall in the recess we were in, so all three of us hit it up. I did my best bubble-letter throw-up and focused hard on getting the shadows right. I always fucked up on the shadows. My partners were doing more elaborate work—smooth mini pieces with multiple colors and even a character. When we were done, the leader pointed to a lush patch of grass and trees across the freeway.

No lights and no sounds coming from our left, so we booked it across the two lanes of freeway and made our way to cover. Now we were in the heart of the beast; no more sidelines. In front of us were eight lanes of interstate freeway. Above us were six additional lanes of perpendicular concrete.

"If you get stuck out there, straddle the center divide," were the only words of guidance offered before both of them dashed off like gazelles.

I quickly followed as best I could. We hopped up over the railing above us and stayed crouched for a moment. The sound of a car could be heard approaching, so we waited like sprinters on a starting block with a spray can in hand. When the car zipped past us, we sprinted across three lanes of freeway and got to the center divide. It was quiet for a moment, and it felt like I was in the middle of ancient ruins. The orange glow of the freeway lights added a sinister sensation, and the freeway appeared to go on forever in each direction.

We squatted down five feet apart from each other in the middle of the freeway, at arm's length from the center divide. Our faces were stern, and our arms glided long fluent strokes of paint. The only sound was the hissing of aerosol. We finished the quick shots and hopped the center divider. The concrete was about waist high, and when I kicked one leg up on the top lip, I heard the sound of my pants ripping again from the crotch. No matter. We ran across the other side and into the safety of a construction loading site. Plenty of cover there.

Things are different on the freeway than one might expect. For example, the potholes one experiences while driving over them at 70 miles per hour don't seem as massive as when you are running for your life and accidentally step into one. Also, everything is farther apart than it appears from the interior of a car. Four lanes of grid-lock traffic from inside your car gives the feeling of a sardine can, but those same four lanes become a distant horizon when you're trying to run across them in the night. And the yellow buckets full of sand—you could hide a whole family inside one of those.

The freeway was an echo chamber for full-throttle engines. On the plus side, this afforded us an early warning when cars were approaching, but on the flip side, we couldn't hear shit from one another unless we were talking face to face. Shouting across four lanes was pointless, as the vacuum stole sounds with an effortless malaise the way a flooded river takes with it anything that comes near.

For the next hour, we ran back and forth across the freeway and bombed everything we could: center divides, center blocks, sound walls, carpool signs, sand buckets, overpass gaps, and sometimes we even tagged the freeway itself. I hopped over the center divide more times than I can remember, and I spent a lot of time catching my breath in the bushes. A few times, I thought I'd lost my friends and then, all of a sudden, they showed up out of nowhere.

It was the last shot of the night for me. I planned to do block letters and shadows on the center divide, so it would take some time. I ran out and got started. I was squatting down and slowly duck-walking the length of my shot. I was in the zone, and all my letters had a perfect tilt to them. Dope. As I got going on the shadows, I felt a strong breeze swirl by and then felt a tremendous chill surge up into my stomach. I looked down to see that my pants were ripped from the crotch down to both knees, and I could even see my balls hanging out of my boxer shorts. As I stared for a moment, I zoned out just enough to forget about the car that had been approaching. By the time I snapped out of it, the headlights were already glued on me. I turned to look, and the light blinded me. I heard the car horn begin to sound, and I froze.

The wind vacuum nearly knocked me over as the car flew by in the fast lane, no more than three feet between us. Dust and debris flew all around, and I was left with watering eyes. As I tried to regain sight, I could still hear the car horn as it faded out of earshot. Of all the times I expected to be panicked, I was not. A sense of calm filled my spirit, and soon, my sight returned. I looked around at the empty freeway and smiled. Then I looked down at my pants and laughed. I finished my shadows, cleared my cap, ran back across the freeway, and plopped down in a soft patch of grass surrounded by bushes. Clouds were covering the moon, and a sense of relief stood guard over the land.

The three of us found each other and started making our way back toward our exit point. There was a water-drainage tunnel along the freeway wall that would let us out near the railroad tracks, so we squeezed through the rebar grate and crouched through the narrow corridor. A rat scurried past us in the dark, and a single bird chirped in the distance. Once we were back on the railroad tracks, we sparked up a blunt for the last leg of the journey.

The last stop was a freeway overpass. We called these heaven shots, and it was the top of the pyramid in terms of respect from peers. No fucking way this fat boy was pulling that off, but at least I could be a lookout. We were off the railroad tracks, making our way through the neighborhoods and backstreets until we found a main street—but not too big—that crossed over the interstate running underneath. At either end of the short bridge were apartment complexes, so we had solid escape routes in case we had to run. The sidewalk across the overpass was shielded from the road with a two-foot concrete wall on top of which was a tubular metal guard. This meant we could lie down flat on the sidewalk and not be seen by a passing car from the road, as long as it was dark. Two of us lay down and kept watch as the leader went over.

He scaled the chain-link fence then carefully grabbed the back of the freeway overpass sign. I was lying flat on my back, watching him scale the obstacle course like a monkey. The freeway sign backing angled away from him, so he had to gently hang over a naked lip and then manage his way down to the platform somehow. If he slipped, he would fall 50 feet down onto the freeway. He cleared the lip and then disappeared out of sight. The concrete was cold on my back, and the giant hole in my pants didn't help the situation.

Finally, the lights from the freeway sign went off, indicating he was safe and had found the electrical control box. Now we just had to wait in silence on the cold concrete and hope a cop didn't drive by and notice something odd about the freeway sign being dark. I stared at the sky and lost myself.

Three minutes later, the lights came back on, and I could hear my friend call out:

"Is it clear?"

Two of us sat up and swiveled our heads around to check for any cars.

"You're good," I shouted back.

He was back over on our side of the fence before I could even stand up, then we were running to the end of the overpass and into an apartment complex, apartments to backstreets and backstreets to the park where we split up. Two of us headed south toward my friend's mom's apartment and the other went north back to his place. Everything ended perfectly, and the night was a success.

The mood was festive as we walked down backstreets and relived the night's events. My friend was telling me how he slipped in a big mud pit between two trees and ended up falling on his ass right into the mess. I hadn't noticed it until then, but when I glanced at his pants, I saw the big smear. It looked like he had shit himself. We laughed together as only two people who had survived something could. We were laughing hard as we rounded a bend in the road and started to see his apartments come into view. The sky was pitch dark except one tiny sliver of shaded sky over the peaks of the nearby mountains; the day's first light. It would be another hour until sunrise, but here we were, witnessing the daily miracle.

The apartments were a hundred yards in front of us. To our left, we were approaching the YMCA, which ran adjacent to the apartments' perimeter. We were still bantering, walking down the sidewalk, when we spotted a car pulling up to the stop sign on a perpendicular street, just before the apartment complex and directly in our path. The car stopped for a long time, and my insides went to knots. It was a cop, and there was no way he didn't see us.

As my jaw tightened up and my anus constricted, I did my best to keep walking. I could feel the tension from my friend as we both went mute instantly. We kept walking toward the cop with backpacks full of cans and paint all over our fingers, not to mention we were minors out walking around at hours that could only imply criminal activity.

As we continued to walk, the cop started moving, but surprisingly, he didn't make a left toward us. Instead, he made a slight right and then a quick left into the apartment complex. As soon as he began entering the driveway, I said to my friend:
"YMCA on three. One . . ."

The cop pulled his car up slowly but still had a straight line of sight at us.

"Two . . ."

As he pulled forward, and just barely went past a wooden fence, he lost his angle of sight. Then we saw the brake lights come on, followed quickly by the white back-up lights.

"Three!"

We sprinted across the street and into the YMCA parking lot as we watched the cop back out of the apartment entrance. We quickly ran down the long face of the building, around the back corner, where we both knew there was a perfect dumpster up against the fence for us to use as a springboard to safety. We were both in a

65

full sprint and took one great leap onto the dumpster, then jumped head first over the fence and grabbed onto the top as our legs came flying over last. We landed in perfect dismounts and continued running. Just as we cleared a corner into the maze of apartments, we saw the beam from the searchlight barely missing our trail. Ten seconds later, we were at my friend's apartment, heaving for air as he tried to steady his hand to put the key in the door. We did our best to tiptoe into the place so as not to wake his mother. Then we scurried into his room, closed the blinds, and kept all the lights off.

We were both panting for breath, but trying to do so quietly. The room felt extremely claustrophobic and a little bit of light sneaked past the blinds from the outside walkway. We both stared at the window like victims waiting for the murderer in a horror flick. Then we saw the slow crawl of light as the officer drove by and shone his searchlight through the walkways. Eerie. Ghoulish. We stopped breathing and waited.

The light passed, and we started breathing again. Thirty seconds went by and nothing happened. We stared at each other with owl eyes. Two minutes more, and still nothing. Nobody knocked on the door, and we hadn't woken his mother up. After five minutes, my friend turned to me with a gigantic grin on his face.

"Holy fucking shit," he said in a whisper.

I started giggling and covered my mouth to keep the sound down.

He started giggling, too, and we both stared at each other with hands over mouths and heavy, sporadic breaths coming out of our noses.

"That shit was hella sick," he said and snapped his fingers.

I nodded and smiled and didn't dare take my hand away from my mouth.

66

the greatest teacher

Vista point between High Meadow Trail and Wildcat Loop, Rancho San Antonio Open Space Preserve. Summer. It was clear that day, and the smog was light enough to allow for a glorious panoramic view of the San Francisco Bay Area as far as the eye could see. Directly below me was the South Bay, Silicon Valley, and I tested my brain to identify landmarks. Shoreline Amphitheater was always where I started. To my left, off in the distance, I could see the high-rises of San Francisco and Oakland, and the engineered vein between them. Fog sat atop the city as would a mother hen covering her brood. I took a deep breath in through my nose and shook out my legs one at a time. Clean, crisp air filled my lungs as I struggled to catch my breath.

It was just over two miles from the parking lot, but the climb in elevation was brutal. That summer was particularly warm, and I was soaked; still, I was proud to have made it up the hill again. I spent my days running the trails of Rancho because legally, it was the only place I was allowed to be other than the confines of my house. I was under house arrest yet again, this time for graffiti. Or was it a failed drug test? It didn't really matter because I had lost track at that point. Regardless, I was arrested again and given house arrest instead of spending my sentence in juvenile hall. So how did I end up running trails during the day?

A few points to consider here: First, sometime the year before, one of my old friends took me running for the first time. He had turned his life around and found exercise, particularly long-distance running, to be a great alternative to the hooligan lifestyle. I was playing high school football, so I had a mild interest in exercise. I was still quite fat when we started out and far more interested in the drug culture, but exercise became something my friend and I could bond over, and we ended up jogging the hills together. Like many other positive seeds planted in my soul, it took at least a year to establish roots; but when the shoot finally did poke through, it dominated the canopy.

The second point of note is my arrest record: "Lengthy" would be an accurate description to start. So there I was, arrested again, given house arrest again, but something happened, and I asked my house-arrest officer a random question, not expecting much from it.

"Is it okay if I go running in Rancho San Antonio during the day?"

She was surprised by my question and thought about it for a moment.

"Yes," she replied. "Yes, running in the hills would be a positive outlet for you. You can go running as long as you don't go anywhere else, one of your parents drives you, and you call before and after so I can have a log of the times you are not at home. If you fail your check-in and you have not called to indicate a run or a doctor's appointment, I will violate your ass in a heartbeat, and you'll do the rest of the three months in the hall. "

So there I was, on top of a hill overlooking San Francisco Bay, with the sun burning my shoulders. It was in the nineties that day, so I was drenched in sweat, but I felt something coming alive inside of me for the first time—and I was starting to like it. Because I had lost some weight already, I ran without a shirt. It seemed I was starting to catch a little momentum in something.

In the same way erosion will allow rain to find a path down a mountain, my constant defiance had softened my father by some

68

form of attrition. He stayed home during the day, managing a few properties in which he and my mother had invested over the years. I would have thought my confinement to the house would have caused hostility to rise quickly between us. But as I've come to find along my life's journey, often it is from the most improbable situations that a glimmer of light sneaks through.

Besides managing rentals, my dad was completely consumed by remodeling the entire house. With a stubbornness that can only be described as Bosnian thick and immigrant cheap, he took on every task himself with little to no hired help. The backyard was just about finished after a grueling set of projects that had lasted many years past reasonable. My dad began by tearing out the old backyard, which was an overgrown shit box, using only his two children as unpaid day laborers. He never threw a baseball with me, but he put a shovel in my hand when I was ten and told me to work. When I finally cried enough for my mom to notice, he dismissed me from my duties with a backhand wave and minimal eye contact. Years went by, and slowly he made progress, inch by backbreaking inch.

Now, every morning, my father stood at the lip of the sliding back door, one step higher than the plane of the yard, smoking a cigarette and admiring his masterpiece. The sun had just crested over the neighbor's roofline and the tops of my father's trees caught the first morning shine as they and my father seemed to smile in unison. From behind, as he exhaled smoke into the early morning sunlight, it looked like rivers formed where the fumes met the sunbeams. Right then, I saw a connection between my father and the earth; it was the most tender moment I had ever witnessed with him.

The perimeter of the yard was enclosed by a wooden fence, with a lattice crown, all made of western red cedar and stained thrice for a deep hue. Along the fence line, on the north and west sides, stood a conclave of fruit trees, all spaced symmetrically, giving the appearance of a cabinet meeting in a presidential office. We had apricots and plums, apples, pears, persimmons and pomegranates, cherries, oranges, and lemons. On the east side was a non-raised garden, per my mother's request, where she grew vegetables such as tomatoes, peppers, cucumbers, and half a dozen more of the usual suspects. Covering half the patio was a metal lattice that had long since disappeared into the thicket of grapevines that now provided perfect shade during the summer. The rest of the yard was covered in sod—immaculate, vibrant, lush, neatly-trimmed green grass that would give Augusta a run for its money. In the center of the lawn stood a king—a weeping willow sitting proudly on his throne for all to see, his crown so large and flamboyant that its shadow forced you to look up in amazement, squinting toward the sky.

"Vell. Vat's new in the yard today?" I called from the kitchen, feigning a heavy Croatian accent.

"Oooohhhh, vel. Son of a bitch. I guess I can't vin no matter vat I do," my father replied with enthusiasm, his genuine accent bending the pronunciation.

"What's going on today, Dad?"

"Come, come. Loook at vat they do to my ahpricot."

I walked over to join him at the sliding door and looked out at the scene.

"Can you see vat is happening?" he asked.

I scanned the backyard and immediately spotted his source of vexation. At the rear of the yard, along the top of the fence line, sat three apricots in various states of undress. All of them had chunks of flesh missing from their portly stature, but none was eaten more than a third of its total offering. I chuckled out loud as I figured out who the new enemy would be that summer. My dad took a long drag from his cigarette and stared at the crime scene while running scenarios in his head. I reached into the front pocket of the green Dickies shirt he was wearing, the same work shirt he had worn for seven years, pulled out his pack of smokes, and lit one up.

It was tense before. It was always tense in the house, especially when I started getting arrested. To say my father and I didn't get along would be understated at best. One time we were driving, my father having picked me up from a two-week stint in juvenile hall, and the car ride was quiet and ominous. His gaze was a thousand miles away, stumbling over his own thoughts to try and understand why his son behaved the way he did. I sat in the passenger seat of his two-door Isuzu pick-up and tried to breathe quietly. We had just gotten on the freeway, a few blocks from juvenile hall, when traffic came to a gridlock. I stared out the front window, hoping a meteor would fall from the sky, when I noticed a car in front of us with a unique bumper sticker. My father couldn't help but see the same thing. For a moment, the man I had rarely seen drop his austere performance put his hand to his brow, shook his head, and allowed a few solid laughs to escape.

"MY SON WAS INMATE OF THE MONTH AT SANTA CLARA COUNTY JUVENILE HALL."

I laughed as well, cautious not to let too much out, and I saw him look over at me in a way I had never witnessed before. For the first time in my life, he wasn't a parent or dictator; he was just a guy who looked at me and was as confused about life as I was.

We began talking a little about what it was like to be locked up, and somewhere along the way, I asked if I could have a cigarette. He already knew I smoked because I had been stealing cigarettes from him for years. But this was the first time there didn't seem to be a big game of deception around it. He told me to go ahead, and we drove home while sharing a cigarette together for the first time.

So now my father stood there, looking out at the backyard, and I took a cigarette from him and joined in his morning ritual. We

71

didn't have much in the form of laughs or joyful memories from my childhood, but we had these moments—two guys sharing a smoke, shooting the shit—and I wouldn't have wished it any other way.

"So what's eating your fruit?" I asked.

"Veeelllll. It's the squirrels, but that's not the problem. Those sons of bitches just take a few bites and then waste the rest. I have no problem sharing my apricots, but they take the very best, eat a little bit, and then leave the rest for me to see how smart they are. Son of a bitch!" he exclaimed, half serious, half kidding.

I took a slow drag while squinting one eye and offering an affirmative nod.

"What are you going to do?" I asked.

He bent his left elbow to 90 degrees, pointed one finger to the sky in philosophic fashion, and raised his eyebrows.

"Eehh! This is where you will help me. What do you think? Will you help?"

"Sure, Dad. No problem. How?"

"I will buy you a BB gun, and you will practice so you can shoot them."

It was the coolest thing my dad had ever said to me. My father and I spent that summer closer than we had ever been before. He would drive me to and from the trails of Rancho San Antonio during the middle of the day and at sunrise and sunset, when all the critters seemed to be scampering about, and I would take aim at the squirrels with the pellet gun he bought.

House arrest comes in two different flavors. The Cadillac of house arrest is electronic monitoring via ankle bracelet. A coaster-sized, black plastic box is secured to your ankle, and a transmission device is plugged into your phone line. If the ankle monitor goes farther than the allotted radius, a signal is sent, and the authorities are alerted. The Pontiac version of house arrest is electronic voice-recognition software. After supplying the county with a baseline recording of words, specifically the names of American states, I would receive phone calls intermittently throughout the day to verify my presence at home. Even though this was Silicon Valley circa late '90s, Santa Clara County seemed to have an ancient form of software, probably due to budget restraints. The voice sounded choppy and simulated, like you hear in every cheesy science fiction film to date. The first prompt is for the speaker to say "continue." This would then take me into the next sequence of words to repeat such as "California" or "Nevada." My father found great amusement in my recitals.

It seemed like every time we had company, the phone would ring, and I could be heard in a distant corner running through the names of America's great states. My father chuckled every time he explained the situation to our guests, and my mother covered her embarrassment with feigned denunciation of my father's lighthearted attitude. Sometimes I would be in the shower, or on the toilet, so my father would try to buy me time by initializing the sequence. On some attempts he would make it past "continue," and other times he would just repeat the word so many times that he would end up cursing at the telephone. We laughed together, my father and I, about his accented English and the fact that not even a computer would let him get away with such biased timbre.

By the time summer came to an end, I had gone from 283 pounds to 209. I began my senior year of high school enrolled in a program called Middle College, where I attended classes at the local community college as an alternative for kids who felt high school life was no longer serving their interest. The core Middle College classes didn't start until nine a.m., so I continued to indulge my passion of running in the crisp morning air, with the birds and the dew, as I followed the railroad tracks that looped around Cupertino.

My runs ended at my high school, Monta Vista High, where I ran the bleachers as a finale. As I came around the tennis court fence that separated the parking lot from the football field, I slowed down to a walk. My hands were buttressed on my hips, and my breath was heavy as I reveled in the feeling of accomplishment and let the runner's high take over; little flashes of light going off everywhere as my endorphins were in full release. With warm September air still dominating the climate, I had managed to work up quite a coating of sweat on my bare torso and the waistline of my shorts.

I walked to the water fountain for a quick sip before hitting the bleachers, but as I drank, I heard some noise in the distance. A quick look around didn't reveal anything, so I took another drink. As I bent over, I heard the noise again, so I looked toward the school and saw a couple faces peeking up over the stairs that led down to the main level of the campus.

"Oh my god, it's Anto," I heard them say.

I stood up and started walking toward the intruders. As I gained a line of sight, I saw the culprits running back into the P.E. building, and recognized the bunch as a group of senior girls I knew in passing but certainly didn't claim as friends. They were part of a group from the opposite spectrum of my social circle, me still known as a source of illicit substances and they as the cute do-gooders I would occasionally see at a party but never in the thick of the mob. As they ran back into the building, I saw a couple of them peeking out from behind the door. One girl in particular, the most attractive one, was looking and giggling with astonishment. Those eyes— those big green eyes of hers—glanced for a moment then disappeared into the shadows. And so it was that I tasted my next favorite drug at the age of 17. Instantly, I was hooked on vanity and became obsessed with working out.

The rest of the year was nothing short of miraculous. Not only did I become a new person physically, I was also inspired by a teacher who unlocked something inside of me that changed my life mentally. He challenged me in a way that was kind but direct, a form of respect and encouragement I had never felt from a teacher, parent, coach, or any other authority figure in my life. He saw through me, yet he didn't choose to abuse that privilege. Instead, with a pious gaze and a humble tone, he led me to water with an argument that implied I could do better; I drank like an elephant tasting the Nile for the first time.

"There are many people out there who have pushed the boundaries of provincial lifestyles," he told me. "Why don't you read about what they did, and then get to work on your own path? Do the work."

With that, I threw myself into academia, and my grades never dipped below the top ten percent of the class. I was on an absolute roll. Look good. Feel good. Good-looking girlfriend.

My ego was, and still is, the greatest antagonist from all worlds, across all millennia. This change in behavior, this slight shift in consciousness I experienced, began innocently enough. But eventually, what I thought was righteous confidence turned out to be toxic hubris, and all that was came crashing down.

House party, senior year, two kegs, game on. I was one of the first to arrive, and I began putting down beers immediately. As the backyard filled in and the party got into full swing, in walked a friend—a buddy, an acquaintance. It's difficult to describe male relationships sometimes because of the way we interact with each other, so let me try to paint the picture in the proper context.

Kyle was a junior and arguably the biggest and strongest kid in his class. I held the same title, only for the senior class, thus giving me a slight edge in dick-bragging rights, but the pecking order certainly wasn't agreed upon in any democratic fashion. Kyle and

I played varsity football together, so one must incorporate archaic male logic into this social structure, much the same way one might observe pack animal phenomena. In the pack, one alpha stands noticeably above, and all the rest tend to nip and play and fight with each other in constant little skirmishes. Well, in true western fashion, no mentor was established as alpha, and we of the pack were left to constantly provoke each other as teenage boys so often do. As such, Kyle and I were friends, but not direct friends. We played ball together, but we didn't run in the same circle. We talked to each other at parties, but we didn't call to make plans. We knew each other, and we certainly weren't enemies, but we did nip verbally the way dogs do physically. Underneath it all, I still considered myself superior because I was a senior and he my underclassman by one year.

Kyle walked into the party, and I was already in an aggressive mood. I lobbed a few glib remarks his way and sipped from my red Solo cup with satisfaction. Kyle offered the standard retort: a mix of pompous disregard and feigned amusement before delivering his own callous insult. The backyard was dimly lit, and I was considerably buzzed, so my frame of reference and ability to accurately gauge intonation was dull. Kyle stood six foot three and a lean 210 pounds. His stance was all swagger, like a bull rider at the rodeo. His speech had the cadence of a professional wrestler a la Hulk Hogan or Ric Flair. Something about him that night was really getting under my skin.

It seemed appropriate, an almost cordial impetus, when I suggested to Kyle that we stop wasting our time with these verbal pillow fights and raise the stakes to full impact. With a convivial grin, he agreed, and very quickly the party started clucking like a ruffled chicken coop as word spread around: Kyle and Anto are going to fight. The two biggest kids in school were finally going to fight, and a spectacle was on the horizon.

In order to preserve the sanctity of the party, it was agreed that we should hold the event at the park down the street, so the entire audience packed into cars and ventured off to the arena. I was driven by a friend who offered a composed disposition as he calmly asked me if, indeed, I wished to proceed with this ill-conceived idea. Yes, yes my friend. Forward and only forward.

The grass was damp and the park was empty at that time of night except for the salivating mob we had brought with us. Kyle and I chose a spot toward the rear of the park, farther into the shadows, where the park's backside came up against a freeway wall. A circle formed, and we stepped inside as Kyle took off his shirt, and I stared across into the fray. It was only his eyes that I remember because they came alive in a split second when he stepped toward me and cut through a beam of light from a metal halide lamp burning bright toward the entrance of the park.

"Are you ready?" he asked me, and I nodded in response. I stepped toward him with my hands in a boxer's position and swung.

When I woke up, I was looking into the face of the friend who had driven me to the park. Behind him was a bright night's sky full of stars.

"What happened?" I asked.

His grin was neutral, teeth clenched together, and brows squinted downward as he shook his head slightly from side to side.

"Not good man," was all he said.

He helped me to my feet, and I noticed there were barely any people left at the park anymore.

When he drove me back, he told me I had swung once, missed, and taken a straight shot from Kyle that knocked me out immediately. What an engrossing mix of emotions to face, and what an opportunity for introspection and growth. That was it. Such are the moments that can open up new worlds if we only have the courage to sit in the mire and absorb the embarrassment and fear for what they truly are: the greatest teachers of all time. This is the secret language of the universe, the songs of freedom, and the fire from which the most beautiful swords are forged. All we have to do is listen. I didn't listen.

where the hollow grows

There were ten of us inside a three-star hotel room in South Lake Tahoe, somewhere around the turn of the millennium. I had left my girlfriend for the evening, so I could have a night with the guys, and she could have some fun with her girls. The walls of the room were an obvious veneer of log-cabin rustic. The window shades were drawn and the carpet, once a vibrant celery green, was now faded into wilted vegetable dross.

I had taken a poster-sized, framed picture off the wall, a quaint bouquet of summertime flowers, and laid it down on an ironing board to serve as an operating table. On the glass, I dumped out two eight balls of mediocre-grade cocaine and began dissecting, chopping, and segregating. I held a plastic card in each hand. One was my AAA membership; the other, a Blue Cross health insurance ID. I prepared the evening's entertainment with the skill of a Benihana chef.

We were a group of hometown buddies in our late teens and early twenties. It wasn't quite New Year's Eve, but what the hell did we care? I'd had the foresight to bring more than an ounce of blow for the festivities, so that night we all agreed to get the party started a couple days early.

One by one, they came to the station and helped themselves to my customary, wildly oversized lines of blow. Snorts, grunts, and coughs filled the air. Quickly the energy in the room changed;

cocaine has the ability to do that. The guys started yammering about completely irrelevant topics, overly attentive and emotionally connected to each statement as if a cancer survivor were sharing the details of his journey. High school football stories should not have drawn this level of compassion from people.

We came into the room boisterously, and now that my beak had been packed full of Charlie, I was racing through thoughts to find a suitable outlet. I consumed beers in four movements or less. Like most processes on cocaine, one tends to find his thoughts in the narrow alleys of sexual deviancy fairly quickly. Narcotics grant temporary clemency from the absorption of guilt. God help you when sobriety returns and the self-loathing begins.

"Let's call a stripper over!" I declared to the republic.

The senate mumbled and conferred, then nodded in agreement. Someone behind me snorted a line, gagged, coughed, then smiled at the avoided heart attack.

Calling a stripper made me nervous. As I began calling the services, I hatched a devious plan inside my rotten head. The initial fee was somewhere around a hundred and fifty dollars, just to get the woman over to the hotel, and any potential "extra" services were negotiated thereafter based on tips. Well, said the sinister darkness pirating my soul, I have enough cash on hand for the entrance fee but not much left after that to entice her into making immoral decisions. After all, if I hired a stripper in order to feed the dark monstrosity that is ten coked-out guys crammed into a medium-sized hotel room, then I wanted this party to go into the furthest depths of the unholy.

With the courage of the cowardly lion, I squeaked out over the phone:

"Hi. Ummmm. I'm looking for a stripper?"

"It's a hundred and fifty for the hour for dances, and anything above that I accept tips."

"Great. When can you be here?"

"I need about an hour to freshen up, but first I have to ask, are you a police officer or working with the police somehow?"

The audacity she had to question my integrity! My voice raced to a higher pitch, and I rubbed a little bit of cocaine on my gums.

"Oh, hell no. I'm not a cop. We're just having a little party over here and looking for some company."

"Okay, sweetie. Give me your address, and I'll be there soon."

Forty minutes later, I was snorting my tenth line of cocaine of the evening when my cell phone rang. My heart was beating aggressively as the combination of stimulants and anxiety ripped through my system. Each step of the process reminded me of the mistake I was about to make. Each time I was reminded, I almost soiled my pants. She said she was outside the hotel and would like me to come out and get her.

I opened the door and stepped out of the safety of drawn curtains and drug indulgence into the cold Tahoe sunset. In the parking lot, I saw a cute girl stepping out of a worn Nissan 4Runner. She was wearing a thick winter jacket with a fuzz-lined hood pulled over her head. Did I look suspicious because I was in a t-shirt? For that reason and many others, I am certain I did, but that was not the time for epiphanies.

"Hey. Are you Adam? My name's Megan."

I confirmed I was indeed the fake name I had given over the phone, then invited her to come inside. As she stepped in and saw the pack of trolls waiting for her, I could feel her reluctance. Imagine the feeling a sheep must have walking into a den of wolves who all promise to be on their best behavior. I handed the cash to her right away and offered a beer and shot of whiskey, which she graciously accepted.

As we sat and discussed the evening's entertainment options, I mentioned my idea for tips. I had an additional hundred dollars to throw in for extras, but the bulk of my generosity I hoped to show by offering an endless supply of cocaine for her to consume while she danced. The moment was tense as she pondered the merits and clarified the fine print.

"Just dancing and stripping?" She asked while taking a big pull of Coors Light.

I assured her our only intent was to watch her float around the room while we all continued drinking, snorting, and having a generally agreeable time. I led her to the ample mound of cocaine I had previously dumped out on the picture frame and showed her my reserve stash, which was enough to choke a full-grown donkey.

"I'm not sure. I used to, like, have a problem and just got clean and, like, my brother, he's like 6'7", and he would be really pissed if he found out I was doing this."

"It's your call," I said as nonchalantly as I could with a heart rate of 147.

With expert precision, she picked up the straw and inhaled a pile of powder I had set off to the side as the re-supply mound for chopping personal lines. She easily put over half an eight ball up her nose without flinching. She looked at me, smiled, took a swig of beer, and asked for another shot of whiskey.

The party got started, and everyone seemed to be having a good time. We arranged a lopsided circle between the beds and a couch so Megan could dance from one rabid monkey to the next, as is customary for stripper shows. I stood by the picture frame and continued to handle the cocaine preparation, waving over one friend after the next to come blow lines. The need to control a situation had always been paramount for me. I learned to cover up my insecurities by always clamoring for alpha male spot among a group. I brought the cocaine. I had drug dealer status. I monitored who snorted what. And I had an unofficial leash on Megan, and her now naked body, as she glided lap to lap and rubbed her ass firmly into everyone's crotch.

There was no music playing to help her with the rhythm. She was completely naked and being groped at will as she straddled each of us. Those not within arm's reach stared with the gaze of hungry jackals waiting for the lions to leave an opening. When a mind on cocaine latches on to the idea of sex, the soul has absolutely no recourse.

Markers of time passed were cigarette butts and beer bottles. Ashtrays overflowed. Counter space became scarce. Everyone in the room was intoxicated enough to fail a sobriety test two days hence. Slurred speech turned into 30-minute emotional diatribes about childhood and heartbreak as the two substances battled for dominance inside our systems.

For the crescendo of her act, Megan sat on one of the beds, legs spread akimbo, and swirled a lollipop inside her vagina. The guys were all huddled around with rapt attention—think med school students watching their first open-heart surgery. She didn't seem to mind the cluster of hands reaching to grab a piece of her soul. Without any warning, she took the lollipop out, held it up for the group to admire, then stuck it into the mouth of the deviant sitting closest to her.

It took me a good five seconds to process what had just happened, and the reactions varied among the group. Some nodded in approval of the lewd act. Others snickered and mocked the man who'd been publicly defiled and now faced a list of sanitary questions

83

demanding clinical answers. Eventually, the whole group banded together in unified derision. Uncontrollable laughter filled the air. Someone shouted the moniker "Sweet Tooth!"

Hours passed, and it was apparent Megan was now more of a guest than an employee. We sat and talked, opening up about our lives, as most cocaine encounters go. A couple of the guys had left to go to the casinos, but most were still going strong—drinking, snorting, confessing.

Megan and I were by the cocaine station, each doing a line, when I felt we had enough privacy for me to say:

"Hey. I want to ask you a question, and I totally understand if you're not into it."

She took up a line and looked at me, "Sure. Go ahead."

"Would you want to go to a different hotel, with just me, and I can pay you for your time?"

There is a moment right after offering an illicit proposition that stops a man's heart dead in its tracks.

"Yeah. Okay," she replied nonchalantly.

She began packing her things. A slow rumble rose as, one by one, the guys figured out my plan to steal the only woman in the room. They were not happy. I doubt any of them would have ventured as far as I had by propositioning her for sex, but there was a mental outlet I was taking away from them, not just physical. We had all been mentally fucking her from the moment she walked in.

As we walked toward the door, I tried to avoid eye contact with my betrayed friends. When I did catch a gaze, I held a placid expression and callous eyes. One friend, Matt, fixed a gawky stare on me. He was stunned by my cavalier demeanor and almost embarrassed by my reckless indulgence in prostitution. Why would a good-looking college kid need to hire a prostitute? Insecurity and loneliness, not drugs, bring out the worst in people.

We walked out of the room, and a bitter cold was in the air. Megan got in my car, and we slowly made our way through the snowy streets of South Lake Tahoe. It was two in the morning, and we were the only car on the road. I concentrated with every available brain cell; half drunk, half yakked out on coke. All the while, my heart beat like a war drummer leading the charge for Custer's last stand; impending doom, yet I continued to march. Quick stops for alcohol, smokes, and cash, then we pulled into a dingy looking motel based on her recommendation.

I gave her money to pay for the room, then sent her out into the cold to handle the face-to-face interaction. The attendant spoke through a security window as Megan shivered out in the open cold. I sat in the warm car with the engine still running. She gave the thumbs-up signal, and I grabbed all the essentials: 24-pack of Coors Light, one pack of Camel lights, one pack of Newports, a box of Trojans, and a rolled-up brown paper bag of pre-measured cocaine.

Inside the room, we sat down on opposite beds and looked at each other with uncomfortable smiles. Was there proper decorum for small talk in that situation? I suggested we just hang back for a bit, drink a few beers, and wait for the heat to fully defrost our bodies. It's amusing how a man thinks he needs to make the woman feel comfortable in this situation, as if he has the upper hand somehow. I tried to make the mood as light as possible, but it was more for me than it was for her. No doubt she had seen hundreds of men just like me: nervous and intoxicated while trying to be cool or funny as they skip heartbeats between fleeting breaths.

An hour passed, and we had reestablished a solid buzz. I was snorting cocaine off her tits. That was where I felt halfway comfortable again. The apprehension of knowing I was about to do something illicit had passed because now I was in the middle of it and it didn't feel unnerving anymore. Anticipation of guilt is worse than the act itself. I was lost in the moment. Somewhere hidden among the thicket of self-indulgence, there was innocence. Somewhere between the beers and the lines, we talked as only two strangers who knew they would never see each other again could.

Her real name was Kristi not Megan. For obvious reasons, she used a fake name at work. She was tall, about 5'9". Her skin was white, the pale skin of German and Polish heritage. Her auburn hair still held a slight wave from the curling iron she used before she came to the hotel. She was above-average pretty with a slender waist and naturally perky breasts, B-cups, with large puffy nipples the size of silver dollars. We both sat in our underwear, topless.

She was about my age, early twenties, and her world extended only as wide as the perimeter of Lake Tahoe plus two outliers: Sacramento and Reno. She was raised there in the mountains, where everything grows wild, and she enjoyed the simple life. After high school, her plan had been to attend community college while holding down a full-time job. Her parents were split, and neither had the means to pay for school, so she had been working since the age of 14. Her main line of work had been as a waitress, but somewhere between high school and dropping out of community college, a friend told her about being an escort. She was tired of working for minimum wage plus tips. Tired of truckers leering when they thought she wasn't looking; tired of them blatantly gawking when they knew she was, and tired of seeing families sitting together at her tables. She hadn't sat down for a family dinner since grade school.

She made a thousand dollars her first night as an escort and quit her waitressing job the next day. The work wasn't that bad, she said. Half the guys were too drunk or nervous to get it up, and, even if they did, they didn't last very long. So it usually ended up being a 15-minute house call for a couple hundred bucks. She had run into her share of men who scared her, got a little rough, or asked to do really nasty things to her, but she always managed to get out of the situation somehow. She told me she drank a lot, and judging by her ability to keep up with my pace, I believed her. The drinking became standard each night for work she said, you know, just to loosen up a bit. That turned into always having vodka disguised as water in a Crystal Geyser bottle in her purse, and that turned into a few bumps of speed or coke to level off the haze from drinking too much.

Encouraging how even after spending hours, or years, or a lifetime numbing your feelings and burying your soul, the spirit manages to climb its way back up and gasp for a few life-sustaining breaths of air. I looked straight into her eyes, put my hand on her knee, and asked in the gentlest manner I could muster:

"Why do you keep doing this? Why don't you stop?"

Her eyes swelled. Tears rolled down her high cheekbones, and she let out an exhaustive sigh.

"I don't know. What else am I supposed to do? "

Easy for me to extend the guise of wisdom from my complacent perch. Easy for me to hold the mirror up to her. She was crying now with her face in her hands. I put an arm around her shoulder and grabbed a box of tissues with the other.

"I'm sorry. Oh my God. I'm so embarrassed," she whispered.

"Don't be. It's okay. I don't mind."

She grabbed a tissue and filled it with thick, honest snot the way you do when no one is watching. We both laughed. In that silly moment, I almost felt human again.

"It's going to be okay. Everyone has parts of themselves they want to change."

She looked at me with soggy eyes and smiled.

"We're both fucked up, and we both need to work on things, but now that we're here being this honest, might as well let go and just have fun tonight." I suggested.

Beer, cigarettes, and cocaine—and lots of each. The mood was loose again. Two lost souls in a motel room at four in the morning.

After snorting a haphazard pile of blow off the crease of her pelvic bone, I lay my head on her abdomen and listened to the echoes of her racing heart. She ran her fingers through my hair. Slowly, I turned to look up at her then climbed to meet her face to face.

We kissed, and we held each other tightly. Some men talk about all the women they have slept with in all the most exaggerated situations, and this would certainly be a moment to which I could add my stories. Unfortunately for me, I have a kill-switch; if there is even one variable out of harmony, my brain will not allow my cock to work. When I combine illicit behavior with alcohol and cocaine, I get a recipe for embarrassment. Yet, through the miracle of infected pride, I always managed to try again. I tried for arousal, and she tried for me, but nothing seemed to work. Now, I was thinking about not thinking about it, and that only made it worse. Half limp, the cowering sidekick simply wouldn't join the fight.

Is there any embarrassment heavier than not being able to perform with a woman you've already paid for sex? I haven't found it yet. She said what every guy hates to hear:

"It's okay. Don't worry about it."

Oh, I was worried about it all right, but I tried my best to play it off.

"Why don't we take a shower and relax?" she suggested.

Every time I smell Herbal Essence shampoo, whatever flavor
the pink bottle is, I still think of Kristi. She brought her cosmetics
bag with her, and inside was everything she would need for a
quick rinse and reload while out on the job.

In the shower, we shared the hot water gracefully like a couple in
a long-term relationship. She scrubbed my body with a loofa and
held me with a lover's embrace. She was on her knees, washing
my legs, when the rush of excitement hit me. I stared intently
down at her face the entire time while she took me into her
mouth.

After a while, the water began to get cold, and I knew I had
no chance of reaching climax. I pulled her back up to me, kissed
her, and told her she didn't need to finish.

I got out first, quickly dried off, and got dressed. She lingered in
the shower for a bit then took her time in the bathroom drying,
brush-ing, and reapplying makeup. As I leaned against the
edge of the doorframe, and watched her going through the
motions of normal life, a deep panic hit me.

It was in that strange moment that I decided it was all a mess and
I needed to flee immediately. I told her I was going to the car for
an-other pack of smokes, but my eyes gave me away. I could
sense her disappointment. I turned away and scampered out of
the room. The cold stung my face and the sun was just letting
out the first traces of morning light as I stumbled into the
parking lot.

I drove back to my original hotel, as carefully as I could, while
sucking down a cigarette. In front of my hotel, as I walked toward
the door, I did the customary pocket tap, checking for all things
important: Wallet, check. Cell phone, check. Bag with a thousand
dollars of cocaine inside? Oh shit!

I turned the car inside out and stripped down all the way to my

89

boxers to make sure the bag wasn't hidden in some obvious place I could have stashed it. No luck.

Back in the car and back on the road toward the dingy motel. The sun was up now as respectable citizens began their morning commute. Each person I saw sipping coffee was a swift reminder of my hollow soul. I was certain they all knew what I had been doing for the past ten hours. The glimmer of turpitude is far easier to hide under the shadow of night.

To this day, I still wonder why she didn't leave. She knew I wasn't coming back when I lied straight to her face and walked out the door. The bag of drugs would have been perfect penance for my behavior yet, when I knocked on the door, she opened it.

"Hi," she greeted me, then immediately looked down at the floor as if she were the one who should have been embarrassed.

Shame stings the guilty most poignantly when the innocent try to jump on the grenade. My heart sank into my stomach. Somewhere between the grime and the smut of the previous night, we shared a moment of innocence. We both let down the veil and admitted to being lonely and insecure, lost and vulnerable, and we were comfortable with ourselves, and each other, in that brief break from the great act. But I left her there, naked and afraid. I left her when my ego slithered back around and whispered original sin into my ear. I left her because I didn't know what else to do.

"I think I left my bag here."

"Yeah. It's on the bed."

Neither of us looked near the other's eyes; odd angles, nervous gestures, unnecessary scratching. I walked in, put the bag in the front pocket of my parka, and walked out while she stood silent. I could feel her crying on the inside, but she stood stoic.

"Bye." I barely managed to say as I slid past her.

That moment, like so many others, could have been a wonderful mark of benevolence in my life. The universe offered me a perfect setting. I had the option to apologize. I could have told her I was scared and didn't know what else to do but run. We both could have used that moment as the foundation for a pact to stop drinking, stop doing drugs, stop drowning our souls, and start facing the mayhem of emotions we had been burying for years.

The feeling of disappointment was toxic as I walked back toward my car. I had my drugs, but all I wanted was for that day to be over. It's riveting to look back at moments like that when you come to see the blessings for what they are. I was so angry with myself that I could only think about not wanting to exist or somehow erasing the scene in which I had just participated. It is in the darkest moments of life that I have found the greatest levels of truth.

Sometimes, it takes the breaking of a man before he becomes desperate enough to surrender. Through surrender, one gains the capacity to open their heart. And only an open heart is capable of absorbing the truth that the universe is so patiently trying to share. You may think it is malady that causes you to make the same mistakes over and over. But it is merely fate knocking on your door, yet again, to get you to open the locked vault in your mind, that place where you hide all the monsters, so you can realize you have been living in a prison your entire life. Until you become free from the bondage of ego, time will spin in a loop, waiting for you to awaken.

Somehow I managed to drive back to my hotel, once again, and not kill anyone on the way. As quietly as I could, I slid the key into the lock and opened the door to my hotel room. On the couch, in the fetal position, was a mound of a snoring friend. On the chair next to him, with feet propped up on the coffee table, blanket askew, was Matt, doing his best impersonation of someone trying to be asleep. Breathing rhythm and tensed eyelids gave him away.

I took off my winter clothing and oozed into bed next to my girl-friend. There was so much cocaine in my system I thought I might have a heart attack. I lay flat on my back, head poking out above the blanket, hands folded across my chest, staring straight up at the ceiling, listening to my heart stomp. My girlfriend rustled next to me and pulled my arm over her. As I turned to hold her, I caught a glance from the corner of the room. Matt's wide-open eyes were slicing through my soul. It was the same look of amazement he couldn't suppress when I was walking out the night before with my freshly propositioned escort in tow. I looked away, shuffled around, and squeezed my girlfriend's body tightly into mine.

steroids

Clenbuterol is a non-FDA approved bronchodilator that also doubles as a thermogenic. Thermogenics raise internal body temperature a touch, thus allowing bodybuilders to cut off those last few stubborn pounds of fat when they are shredding down for competition. Winstrol is the brand name of the steroid stanozolol with low androgenic properties, meaning it will not bulk or saturate the user with water while providing powerful performance enhancements and an extra edge to keep solid muscle while leaning out. The combination of these two is a blast.

I wanted to look good, and I spent enormous amounts of time and energy working out. I had made changes to my physique that most people couldn't even begin to imagine. The confidence I gained from looking the way I did had permeated into all facets of my life. I felt I deserved to play on the edge when it came to adding a little pharmacology to take me from the 95th percentile up to the 99th.

I was in Tijuana, shopping at different pharmacies for Clenbuterol and Winstrol. Some had one and not the other. Others had Winstrol in a bottle with a metal top. No good for me because I had to walk back across the border through a metal detector. What I was looking for was bulk Clenbuterol in a plastic bottle and single-serving Winstrol that came in little glass ampules. I bounced around from pharmacy to pharmacy until I found a place that had exactly what I needed.

It was the middle of summer, and Tijuana was arid. The pharmacy had a non-enclosed front, so the only mode of temperature control was a rickety old fan that coughed in the corner every time it reached the extent of its oscillation. The woman who ran the place was Aztec dark, maybe late twenties. She never quite closed her mouth all the way. She sat on a tiny, blue stool and stared at an even tinier, monochrome television. Next to her, a child slept on the floor curled in a ball.

The woman and I spent some time fumbling through broken versions of each other's languages until we finally caught a rhythm and started smiling a bit more. She went into the back, behind an old bed sheet hanging as a door, and returned with rectangular cardboard boxes of manufacturer-sealed pharmaceuticals. Bingo.

I paid in American dollars and asked if she might let me go in the back to conceal the glass ampules in my underwear. She didn't mind. Behind the bed-sheet partition, I took out all the glass and handed her the cardboard to throw away. I had about 40 glass ampules to hide. I always wore compression shorts under my underwear with baggy shorts on top. I took my time to distribute the glass evenly but kept the contraband centered near my genitals in case of a pat-down.

I repackaged the Clenbuterol in an old 500mg ibuprofen bottle because the border guards didn't give a shit about us coming to Mexico to buy legal pills for cheap. Better to have something to show them than to pretend I was just coming back from a sightseeing trip. With everything set, I thanked the woman for her help and walked out the store.

I made my way down the congested sidewalk, weaving through the chaos that is Zona Centro Tijuana. I was offered the usual surplus of goods and services as I proceeded, but I did not make eye contact with any of the merchants. I had what I came for. I crossed the street, made a turn, and then saw a van pull over just in front of me. The passenger jumped out and stepped directly in my path.

The man was fit and his hair was well-kept. He wore tight designer jeans and a fashionable collared shirt with the front unbuttoned down to his sternum. A large, platinum cross reflected the sun uncomfortably into my eyes. He came right to me, put his hand on my shoulder, and held up a badge. Behind him, the driver moved around and stood guard near the van.

"Hello, my American friend. Tell me, what are you doing in Mexico today?"

"I'm just, uuhh, I'm just doing a little shopping."

"Si, Si. A little shopping. Please show me what you have in your pockets."

I took out the bottle marked Ibuprofen and handed it to him. He read the label, shook it, then opened it and poured out some tablets onto his hand.

"These look like steroidas to me, my friend. Do you have a prescription?"

"Uh no. I thought they were legal here? That's why we come down here."

"Mmmm. No, no, my friend. You need a prescription and you cannot just come and buy whatever you want. What else do you have?"

"Nothing. Just my wallet and cell phone."

I took both items out to show him. He looked at my wallet, which was pregnant with American cash, and motioned for me to open it. I removed all my money, a couple hundred in small bills, and handed it to him.

"Is that it?"

"That's all I have. I swear."

He put the money in his pocket then gestured toward the man behind him. The second man opened the sliding door to the van, and I could see it was a form of paddy wagon full of young men roughly my age, all Mexican, tightly squeezed together. I was ushered into the van where I forced my way onto the bench; one of the younger guys ended up sitting on the floor. The door slammed shut, and all the guys looked at me. Then the van started up, and we were driving through Tijuana.

The inside of the cramped van was boiling. We all sat leg to leg and arm to arm. I was sweating all over the young man next to me. The guys looked worn down, tired, as if they have been fucked with by the cops their whole lives and were numb to it by now. One guy was wearing acid-washed jeans that were soaked all around the crotch. Another one had a face so swollen that nothing moved when he talked to his friend. The air smelled of sweat and piss. The floor was covered with a large, dried blood stain.

There was a metal grate between the officers and us. Mexican music was pumping in the front cabin. I raised my voice to shout over the mariachi sounds.

"Where are you taking me?"

The passenger looked back and smiled.

"Shut the fuck up gringo. You are under arrest."

Fear washed over me as I stared at his malevolent smile. Through the windshield, I could see we were leaving Centro Tijuana, and I felt the panic rise. As I began to realize I was in serious trouble, something clicked and everything felt natural and calm. I had an idea.

I took out my cell phone and punched in some numbers, but I

never pressed send. I put the phone to my ear, waited a few moments, and began the show.

"Yeah, hey, it's me. Listen, I'm in trouble man. Call the lawyer and have him reach out to the consulate right away. Yeah, I'm in Tijuana and the cops are fucking with me. I'm in the back of a van, and they say I'm under arrest, but the whole thing is bullshit. They took my money, and now I don't know where they're taking me. Okay, thanks. Tell them to hurry and call me back."

I put the phone back in my pocket and beamed a look at the passenger who was watching intently the whole time. The two cops said something to each other in Spanish, then the van made a u-turn, and we headed back the way we came. I stayed silent and watched the roads.

A few minutes later, the van pulled over and the passenger opened the sliding door. Sunlight forced everyone to squint as we all waited to hear the verdict. The cop pointed at the guy who pissed himself, the guy who was beaten, and me. Then he pointed toward the sidewalk and whistled at us. I sprang from my seat, saying nothing and looking at no one, and walked out into the foot traffic on the sidewalk as if I had never missed a step. I quickly found my bearings and made my way back toward the border crossing.

The line to cross was obscenely long that day; half the time I was standing in the blistering sun. Nothing worse than being in a herd of people, shuffling in little steps, in the blistering sun. I put my hands in my pockets, reached through the material to feel around my groin, and patted around to check on the rest of my contraband. Not good. Through all the commotion the ampules had pooled together into two large clusters.

I walked through the metal detectors safely, then waited to be called up. It was hot, I was sweating, and I stuck out among the crowd. Two months ago, I had ended my last steroid cycle—a combination of Sustanon and Deca-Durabolin. Those are powerful androgenic compounds that stacked on 30 pounds of bulging muscle, so I looked like a gorilla among chimpanzees.

The officer called me up, looked at me, and laughed.

"I hope you're just coming over here to take your shots and not bringing any of that shit back with you," he said sarcastically.

Oh dear Jesus, fuck. Come on. Could I really be having a day like this?

"Yeah. I just take my shots right at the pharmacy," I replied, offering an exaggerated chuckle.

The officer looked over my ID and back up at me.

"Be careful. Make sure those syringes are clean."

"Will do."

As I took my first step toward the exit, I heard a sound that imploded my heart and nearly released my bowels: glass tinkling in my shorts. The cluster of ampules shifted and bounced ever so lightly off each other, just enough to give my position away to the enemy.

"Hey!" I heard the officer call to me.

I was looking at the exit doors, which were all propped open. Only one portly cop was anywhere near them, and he was sipping coffee and reading a newspaper. A bead of sweat slid from my hairline down the crook of my nose.

I stopped and turned around and walked back up to the booth.

"You forgot your ID," the officer said and handed back my license.

A little smile outside and a huge smile inside.

"Oh. Thank you," I muttered as I tucked my ID back in my wallet then walked out the front door.

another day at the office, part 1

The alarm went off at four in the morning. On days like that, my dreams were anticipating the intrusion. The neighbor's dog was awake as well. I leaned over and silenced the alarm. Alicia shuffled a bit, then scooted her booty back into my lap. It didn't matter that no one else could see my prideful smile, I still stretched a wide smirk. I reached over, grabbed a generous handful of her perfect 23-year-old breast, and nibbled the rim of her ear.

"Sorry. Gotta hit the gym before work." I declared with a rascally tone.

She held the back of my neck and moaned.

"Mmmhhhh. No fair teasing like that," she whispered.

"You started it," I said playfully.

A few more kisses to confirm my exit, then I slid out of bed, grabbed my gym clothes, and quietly exited the bedroom. I didn't need to turn on any lights; I had this routine memorized.

The checklist was already running through my head as I rushed. Timetable benchmarks needed to be hit. I flipped the switch in the kitchen and allowed the lights to surprise me. Clock on the oven read six minutes past four. On the counter, amid a bouquet of bodybuilding supplement jars, sat a small plastic bottle with a picture of a yellow jacket on it. I reached for it. Ephedra had been outlawed a few months prior, but I wisely hedged against such a possibility.

I took out one capsule, untwisted the ends, held the contents upright, and poured the brown powder onto my tongue. A little bit of water to slosh in my mouth, gulp down my throat, and almost instantly, I was wide awake.

The clock in my Honda Civic read 4:15. The streets of Pacific Beach were empty. It was a quick three minute drive down Garnett Ave to the gym. Leg day this early was usually brutal, but there was inspiration behind my movements that morning. Only three other people, all women, were in the gym that early. Two were middle-aged and draped in layers of oversized sweatpants, but the third was an attractive blonde, early thirties, climbing the StairMaster in tight shorts and a sports bra. I flashed her a friendly smile, silently conveying my wanton intent. Her eyes informed me that she knew of my intentions and didn't mind.

Rage Against the Machine played on my portable CD player. By the time I got to heavy squats, it was ten past five and a few more people began filling up the cardio machines. I wore a baseball hat pulled low to my eyebrows, an oversized t-shirt ripped down the sides with the sleeves cut off, and shorts that ended well above my knees. The shorts were reserved specifically for leg day. The brim of the ball cap provided cover for my leering eyes to find angles in the mirror. I scanned for spectators.

At six foot two and a solid 240 pounds, I was a spectacle to observe in the gym. The blonde was paying attention. I allowed pride to wash over me for a moment before stepping under the 405-pound barbell. I grunted loudly on the tenth and final rep like a silverback declaring his territory. By 5:45, I was walking out the door.

The sun was just piercing the horizon, and the air was already warm. Seagulls and saltwater were nearby. I peeled the wet shirt from my torso and drove home bare chested.

Five minutes shy of six, I was back in my kitchen blending protein powder, ice, water, and peanut butter. I stood in the kitchen, shirtless, drinking the frothy shake directly from the blender. Alicia came around the corner with squinty eyes. She was wearing one of my workout shirts with the sleeves cut off, so I got a generous view of the side of her breast. It never failed—I was always fascinated. She mumbled and wiped her eyes, then leaned her head on my chest and wrapped her arms around my waist. With the hand not holding the blender, I reached down, pulled up her shirt, and held her by the butt cheek.

"Good morning," she murmured in a groggy voice.

I finished taking a three-gulp chug of protein before responding by way of two firm squeezes to her butt.

"When are you going to be back?" she asked quietly.

"Tomorrow. Early evening," I assured her.

"Be safe, please."

"I will."

Alicia was gorgeous, and absolutely neurotic. Half Mexican and half Caucasian, her skin was the perfect shade of olive. She was tall, and had a figure made for sex. Long, brown flowing hair down to the middle of her back that she insisted be pulled hard when I fucked her from behind. There was a need in her to be noticeably submissive; a proclivity I had never experienced with other women. It felt like she was trying too hard to give me what she thought I wanted. She spoke about her family often and how badly she needed to get away from them. I could tell something nasty had happened to her in the past, but I didn't want to get too involved. She was looking for a source of safety, and I certainly would not

103

be the one to provide it. I planned to keep her around as long as she didn't mind coming over when I called and not complaining when I didn't.

I finished the shake and put the blender in the sink. Alicia was cutting peppers for an omelet, slightly bent over the cutting board on the kitchen counter. I watched the side of her breast ebb and flow with each movement of the knife. With pride comparable to an owner watching his prize filly run the track, I stood and admired. When I stepped behind her and pulled up her shirt, she looked back at me, smiled seductively, and arched her back to accentuate her perfect heart-shaped ass. I dropped my shorts in one motion and wrapped her hair around my hand. We were loud in the kitchen. The neighbor's dog noticed.

It was 6:30 by the time I got in the shower. The timetable was now in jeopardy of collapse. Within seven minutes, I managed to accomplish everything required of a civilized member of society. Then I grabbed a backpack and quickly stuffed in the basics: shorts, t-shirt, underwear, flip flops, and a toothbrush. It was casual Friday in the corporate world, so I was wearing the standard jeans and polo shirt. I took a large gym bag from the closet, opened it, and was satisfied to see the stack of banded cash and four gallon-sized, Ziploc bags full of weed. I counted and measured the night before to make sure everything was on point. Bags in tow, I scampered through the apartment, grabbed Tupperware from the fridge, gave Alicia a kiss, and ran out the door.

I worked at one of the largest computer companies in the world, and this was my first real job out of college. The campus was vast, and the reminders of mundane existence were everywhere. Two kinds of cars dominated the parking lots: minivans and symbols of midlife crisis. I took the back entrance into my building in hopes of avoiding the early birds. I had memorized the schedules of everyone working near me along the paths to and from the exits. I was lucky that morning; Bob's computer was on, but he was not sitting in his chair when I scuttled by.

104

I made it to my cubicle seemingly undetected, so I turned on my computer, cascaded a few spreadsheets across the screen, and felt satisfied with my efforts. If anyone asked, I had been there since six. Time to get coffee and wander a bit.

There were coffee stations and communal snack areas all over the buildings, but I always chose the ones farthest away and most likely to afford an opportunity of bumping into a cute girl from a different division. Some days I spent entire afternoons sampling coffee from various teams. I had been working at Hayes/Palmer for seven months and still felt clueless about what my job entailed. As engineering coordinator, my main tasks had been fetching lost files and filling in large spreadsheets, which made for an extremely boring existence. Usually the work took me down longwinded, tangential conversations with engineers who had serious deficiencies in the most basic levels of social interaction.

Walking through the labyrinth of cubicles sent me past Esther's desk. Esther was the admin for the big cheese in my group. She was in her mid-forties, good-looking, black, proud, convivial, and married to a Navy Admiral. Conversations with her led into such fanciful gems as Jesus, how Jesus can save you, divorce proceedings of team members, the latest Fox news exposé headlines, and her desire for me to take her 17-year-old daughter to senior prom. I'm not sure why, but for some reason, I played along with all of it. Esther was on the phone when I walked by, but she beamed a big smile at me and offered a chipper wave.

In an effort to begin the day in sporting fashion, I decided to walk to an entirely different building to partake of morning coffee there. Near the front entrance of my own building, I saw the doors open, and in walked my manager, Rakesh. I passed by and gave a big, fake "Good Morning, Boss." I tried my best to look like I'd been at work longer than I had, whatever that was supposed to look like. As soon as I passed Rakesh's line of sight, I let my stomach relax.

The morning process went as I'd hoped—quiet and mostly

105

unnoticed. Back in my cubicle, I slowly sipped coffee and read through the morning headlines, website by website. When I first started my job at Hayes/Palmer, I would never leave non-work related websites on my screen; but by now, I simply didn't care. I took an ample two hours in the morning skimming through articles, engaging in small talk with cubicle neighbors, and generally not doing any real work.

My manager had assigned tasks I needed to accomplish, but they had been completed to a point of relative exhaustion. The remaining ten percent of the work would require hours of meaningless file mining on the topic of paper: active SKUs, extinct SKUs, paper thickness, gloss content, retail name, mill roll requirements, lead engineer, and on and on with details on the paper my division engineered and manufactured. Once I got this deep into the weeds of paper specs, my mind simply could not take much more.

By 10:00, I felt satisfied at having reached the halfway point of the workday. Claiming to have been at work since 6:00, and engaging in a slack ten minutes of actual work, I felt content with that story. Before I came to work in corporate America, it was easy to see how the activities of the day filed into order for the machine in my head to create a sense of importance with my life. But here, in the slow-paced corporate malaise of email chains and neutral tone conversations, I had a difficult time. I wanted to be productive. I wanted to contribute and build a reputation as a hard worker, but it all seemed like a bad dream.

When I started, the first three days of my new job were spent watching mandatory HR training videos on such enlightening topics as OSHA, drug-free work zone and non-disclosure basics of a publicly-traded company. One's first exposure to a docile, impersonal, politically-correct message can be overwhelming. Did people really talk like that? Three days I spent forgotten in my cubicle while voluntarily ingesting big brother indoctrination and taking a multiple-choice test after each vignette to make sure I had paid attention. Never before had I felt my eyes so heavy. Not since I was

106

a child had I fallen asleep sitting up. In college, even for courses of lesser interest, I still listened, I engaged, and I was moved by whatever effort professors were able to put forth because it was still within the gravity of human spirit. But this was something altogether different. I spent three days having the soul force sucked out of me by something pretending to be human on a computer screen. Once a day, my manager would stop by to check on me. During those visits, he promised to have more meaningful tasks after my acclimation was completed. But the purpose never came. The fulfillment only diminished.

Days and tasks became lived permutations of the human resources videos; slow, grueling days spent floating in worthlessness. Everyone to whom I reached out told me to stick with it and the fulfillment would come. Just keep your head down, persevere, and eventually you'll get promoted or transfer to a better group, I was told. I was supposed to feel fortunate to have landed in such a strong and reliable company. Now the trick was finding the right fit within, then building a career out of that. Can this be real, I wondered, this acceptance of the hollow? Twenty years spent on my fat ass in front of a computer would surely drive me to blow my head off.

After about a month, I realized I wasn't going to make it. My days became focused on cutting corners and finding angles in which to hide. How to get through the day became how to get through the meeting. My mind was conditioned to run on sensory stimulation, but nothing about that place was stimulating. I felt languid and retarded to the point that I would simply tune out entire events. Hours spent in meetings not listening to one word, just floating in my head on some low-power idling mode. I changed my working hours from the usual eight-to-five to six-to-three. Soon I discovered no one usually came in until 6:45, so I could come in 40 minutes late and claim to have arrived on time. Forty minutes sliced off a level of hell is a monumental victory.

My manager once took me to an adjacent building where the quality engineers had impressive labs for testing specs of paper products. I was told to stop by, introduce myself, and ask to be shown how the process worked. I did so once, then considered hanging myself in the restroom as a more enjoyable alternative. What I did find useful, however, was the connection to a different part of the campus and a readymade justification to be away from my desk. Sometimes I just went to the restroom, pulled my pants down, and sat on the toilet for an hour.

Three months into the job, I couldn't take it anymore. Even when I was doing something, I really wasn't doing anything. The days all ran together to make one big disappointing blob. Finally, I decided I'd had enough, and it was time to take out the old costume.

Ever since junior high, I had sold some kind of illicit substance, off and on, and I'd always kept a heavy interest in the soft science of criminal conspiracy. It began with a desire to fool my parents and evolved into a compulsion to fool the world. My house was tense, to say the least, and inside of a lonely little boy grew a malignant anger. Parents, schools, jobs, and anything else that claimed to have a verified path for success or happiness became a target for my scheming. In my eyes, my parents were liars and frauds. As such, I rallied against anything they suggested, any rules they tried to enforce, direction they offered, personal beliefs, all religious inclinations, anything at all for which they stood.

So off I went on my crusade, with no messiah to guide me and no holy land to reclaim. I initially sold drugs because I enjoyed the feeling it engendered. I became important overnight. I was someone desired, feared, or at least spoken about, but with the increase in pseudo fame came a heavy increase in anxiety. I never lasted longer than a year.

The process was always the same. Things were great for the first three months while I built the business. Days were spent delivering bags, networking, and passing out free samples to attract more clientele. Around six months in, the machine would start humming practically on its own. Most of the sales came from guys who themselves had a small operation. I became a wholesaler, or consignment front, sifting through different friends and references until I had found the ones hungry enough to push weight to. At this stage, pride would start infecting the mind. Nothing I did seemed to be a wrong move. Somewhere around nine months, I would wake up in a cold sweat, convinced somebody must have known by then.

It didn't matter what level I was selling at; there was always a splinter of fear in the mind. Suspicious parents became glaring neighbors, then paranoia turned everyone into police and feds. Somebody was bound to have spotted the pattern, and collapse was on the horizon. On top of that came paranoia of theft. Nobody better to rob than a person who couldn't report the crime. White suburban marijuana trade was the perfect industry to loot because it fell in a grey zone of consequences.

Thus I could never keep the business going for more than a year. The paranoia always became too great, and too many nights were spent without sleep, so my only option was to pack it up and hibernate for a while. But I always kept a map back to the chest where I had buried my secret identity, and I always put away enough cash to get back on my feet when the time came. Off and on it had gone like that since I was 14.

Back at Hayes/Palmer, it was time for another coffee break, but this time, I would venture off campus. Ten o'clock seemed to be when some people made a quick Starbucks run, so I co-opted the idea. I left a spreadsheet up on my screen as camouflage.

Instead of actually going to the coffee shop, I cruised into the parking garage of a shopping center and headed to the top level. The mall was barely opening up at that hour, and the top floor was usually empty. I parked in a secluded corner, reclined my seat as far as it would go, turned the sports talk radio down to a hushed whisper, and dozed off into half sleep for 30 minutes or so. I took a nap at that hour three to four times a week.

At 10:45, I was back in the building with an empty Starbucks cup in hand. I kept cups in my car as props for the performance. The next hour was spent working, my definition of the word being rather loose. Around noon, the grazers slowly began stirring and a new energy filled the air. Everything the majority did, I—more often than not—did the opposite. When asked by several co-workers to join them for lunch, I politely declined. I had tried joining the group during lunch hour previously, but it was far too crowded. After wasting most of the allotted meal break waiting in line, or driving somewhere to get food, the actual eating part was usually rushed and replete with small talk. Sometimes, when in the throws of small talk, I found it soothing to picture the person drowning as I watched from safety and did nothing to help.

The Tupperware I brought from home was full of chicken, brown rice, and broccoli—the bodybuilder's standard. From 12:15 to 12:35, when I was certain everyone had gone to lunch, I scanned the personal ads on Craigslist; not the escorts, but the women looking for relationships. Anything I found interesting was copied and pasted into a document and saved for later. Once I had collected enough ads, I switched to perusing bodybuilding forums.

When people returned from lunch and the cubicles filled back up, I pulled up my work email and began crafting brief introductions. The document I had stocked earlier was used as a base station. Each personal description was skimmed for pertinent information; then I adjusted my prewritten opening paragraph to give the appearance of a personalized touch. I sent out introductory feelers from my work email for two reasons. One, it allowed me to have a work-related window up on my screen so passersby would think I was actually working. The second reason was the implication of financial stability and the social status I assumed was attached to the corporate email address and signature block. Surely women will think me important, I told myself, and of strong breeding stock, if I was able to get a job with a Fortune 500 company.

Almost two in the afternoon, and the clocks all trickled down to slow motion. I stared at a spreadsheet; my eyelids were fighting a losing battle. I stood up to keep from falling asleep and decided to take a lap around the office. As I walked, I was called to take a seat with my two favorite admirers, Claire and Jean. Claire claimed to be a fortune teller. She was holding Jean's hand, palm up, while giving a dissertation on the state of her future regarding love, money, and all things pertinent to a single mother of two. Both women were in their mid-forties, kindhearted, motherly, and appreciative of a little flirting from the good-looking bachelor on the team. I accepted the invitation and sat.

When attention turned to me, I offered the usual assortment of rehearsed lines and witty banter. Single mother Jean appreciated the devilish grin and charm, but the clairvoyant looked at me dispassionately. Claire's smile for me was held with the same disposition most produce when passing the homeless; guilt hidden by pity. She offered to read my palm and, purely for the sake of amusement, I obliged.

"Your lifeline is long, but there comes a point where you must choose to live that life or sink into darkness. You will lead and inspire, but be wary of those who offer themselves as mentors; they can see the hole in your heart. Your heart searches desperately to feel loved, but you won't find it sleeping next to another broken soul. Things will get better for you; but, before they do, they will get much, much worse. "

My palm was sweaty in her hand as I tried my best to keep a fake smile plastered across my face. I chuckled, and both women could feel the waves of insecurity ripple out from me. Obviously, something hit a little too close to home. She knew. In that moment, I knew that she knew everything. Her tone was softened to accommodate for impact, but her eyes shattered me with one glance. We sat there, silent for a moment. I stared down at the desk and considered the impossibility of fortune-telling. Nothing is easier in life than dismissing intuitive truth with logic. Smiles and witty banter came bubbling to the surface as I faded back into character.

111

No harm done.

Finally, the hour was upon me. At four minutes to three, I opened my desk drawer and carefully lifted my keys with ninja-like silence. I didn't bother to take anything else with me because leaving signs of settlement, like my docked laptop, may serve to confuse people as to the actual time of my departure. Even though technically the team knew I worked six to three, it still didn't sit well with them when I left before everyone else. Nothing would flush my face faster than hearing the "must be nice" cubicle grenade tossed at me just as I was attempting to flee the scene. So I made my exits as covert as my late entrances.

I stood to take a peek down the escape route. My neighbors were staring at their computers, backs to the aisle, so I took the opportunity to initiate the plan. The shortest distance to any exit would take me directly past my manager's cubicle, so naturally I went in the opposite direction. I planned to take an old, trusted path I had used many times, one that was disguised to the enemy by a coffee station. If people thought I was just going to get coffee, then guns would be drawn down, and I could slip by unnoticed. My heart beat loudly as I took the first step.

Ten brisk paces and I made it beyond the perimeter of my direct team. I made a pit stop at the snack station to pour myself a quarter-full Styrofoam cup of cold coffee.

"Oh, hey there handsome."

Curse the gods! My cover was blown. I turned back to see Esther standing behind me and, judging by the angle of her smile, I knew she had a doozy for me that day.

"Um . . . sooooo . . . you know I told you about Michelle's senior prom and how I just wanted to throw it out there . . . that it would be nice to have a responsible, good-looking gentleman, such as yourself, take her so her mother would know she's safe? And, you told me you would think about it and . . . well . . . it's four weeks away now so, I mean, we have to start thinking about the dress and corsage, and . . . anyways . . .I was just wondering if you thought about it."

"Yeah. Hey, thanks Esther. I really appreciate the offer, but I just don't think I'd feel comfortable at a high school prom."

"Oh no, you'd be fine. Listen, all you gotta do is dance a little and then just enjoy the limo and dinner that my husband and I are paying for. I really think you would have a good time."

Stepping out from the row behind Esther, I noticed my modest manager, Rakesh, walk by and look in our direction. I knew better than to lock eyes with authority while on the verge of mutiny, so I kept my gaze securely focused on Esther, adding extra nods to really sell the idea of being transfixed in a deep conversation with not just a fellow co-worker but, more importantly, a fellow human being. These are matters of importance we are discussing here, kind sir, and I must give this lovely duchess nothing less than my full attention.

Rakesh was still holding his gaze tight as he walked around Esther, demanding a courtesy glance from me, or at minimum a no-look wave, but I stood firm. When one is this far involved in the role of a lifetime, there are no moments when you break from character. I took a fake sip from my almost empty cup of cold coffee. Once Rakesh disappeared down another tributary, I focused in on my last hurdle.

"Look, I'm sorry Esther. I just don't think I'm up for it. I'm sure she can find another date."

I pointed to my watch and exclaimed: "Oh, wow. I'm late for a meeting."

Then I made my final break. I walked to the opposite end of the

113

building, taking the most roundabout yet highly-calculated route, and found myself skipping down an unguarded stairwell. Like an escaped convict, once out the door I closed my eyes and angled my face to the sky, letting the sun shower me in the sweet bliss of freedom.

I always parked my car as far away from the building as possible. Vigilant eyes from the building's windows would have a more difficult time identifying suspects from a distance. Once I reached the safety of my trusty car, I took off my shirt and hopped into the driver's seat. I shimmied off my pants and slipped into the shorts and flip flops I packed for the trip. As I left the campus, I offered a backhanded peace sign to the guard manning the security booth.

another day at the office, part 2

A large, muscle-bound, shirtless man drove a small Civic up I-15 north at 3:15 in the afternoon. A cigarette dangled from my lips and bounced up and down as I sang the words and drummed the steering wheel to Foo Fighters blasting through my blown speakers. All the windows were down and ash was swirling around in a vacuum, but I didn't mind. If being locked up under corporate fluorescent lights was akin to depression, then this blast of energy qualified as mania. I felt invincible, and every sensory expression reaffirmed how alive I was at that very moment.

Interstate 15 to the 78 to I-5 north. My first stop was in Anaheim. Woo worked as a bartender at a hotel adjacent to the calamity that is Disneyland. The place was usually half-filled with the plump and the fanny-packed, but never as husbands and wives together. One half of a couple fueling up, or winding down, from a day of sensory overload while the other half corralled their offspring somewhere away from the booze. I never knew this was how adults got through their visits to the happiest place on earth until I started selling weed to a friend who happened to work behind the curtain.

In the parking lot, I pulled into a secluded corner. I kept a hamper full of unfolded laundry in the back seat for the drive up north; under the seats were a few paper grocery bags. I took a half-pound from the gym bag and placed it the bottom of a grocery bag. A few shirts from the hamper were thrown on top of the plastic, in haphazard fashion, to make it look simple, dirty, and college-like. For the sake of civility, I slid on a tank top before crossing the parking lot with a gingerly step. I walked in through the main entrance, across the lobby, and into the bar while swinging the light paper bag like a pendulum. My demeanor even seemed playful.

The seat I always hoped to get was always open. People usually didn't like to sit by the servers' entrance to the kitchen, but the floor space and constant traffic provided good cover for a quick hand-off. Woo spotted me as I walked in and gave a slight nod. I placed the bag on the floor, on the side of the bar, and sat in my seat. Immediately, Woo reached around, took the bag, and pushed it into a safe cubby under the bar and out of view.

"You want anything to drink, or you driving all the way up tonight?" Woo asked with his usual expressionless face while wiping a wine glass for fingerprints.

"Making the run. Just water."

Woo filled a pint glass with water and grabbed an envelope that was propped against the register. Both were put in front of me at the same time.

"I still have a couple zips out floating, so it's short two. I'll get you next week," he explained.

"No problem. Half elbow in the bag. Call me in the middle of the week and let me know how you're looking," I responded as I observed the lounge patrons behind me by way of the bar mirror.

Woo nodded approvingly while holding a wine glass to the light for final inspection.

"Will do."

I downed three large gulps of water, slid the envelope in my pocket, and left through the side exit. In the car, I wrote "W" on the envelope and threw it into the gym bag. No sense counting the money in a parking lot full of soccer moms. Plus, I was back on a timetable. I could get right with Woo later if the count was off. Back on the road.

Back on I-5, I headed south to the 22 to the 405 north. Traffic was appropriately heavy for a Los Angeles freeway, but I didn't mind the congestion. There was a sense of safety that came with being buried in the middle of a herd. Predators and police officers usually go for the outliers, lames, and stragglers. I watched the other drivers, with their angry or defeated faces, and rehearsed their biographies in my mind. They had submitted to the preprogrammed lifestyle and now felt the full weight of their own insignificance. The rebel spirit in me fanned its wings.

My next stop was Pablo in Long Beach; always quick and preferred to pay up front. Every time we met, I tried to bump him up in weight, but Pablo never accepted. I secretly respected the decision, even though it went against my bottom line. Half pound sold then I was quickly back on the 405 north.

Dillon represented Manhattan Beach at its finest. Surfboards hung on the walls of his apartment, and a different version of The Dude was usually sleeping on the couch every time I cruised by. Dillon ran consistent volume that came with heavy risk, but it was worth the gamble.

Although Hawaii was known for having some of the kindest weed on the planet, the island state could not escape the fundamental laws of economics. They had pot, but not a lot of it. And what they did grow for themselves was subject to the same high prices as every other commodity on the island. Seizing the business opportunity, Dillon shipped two to three pounds every couple of weeks to his surfer buddies in Oahu.

The principles of shipping pot via a major freight-forwarding company were rather simple. First, don't ship too much in one box.

117

Three pounds, shrunken down and vacuum-packed by a food sealer, fit comfortably in a large box with enough room left for the required accessories. Dillon shipped to Hawaii what everyone else shipped to Hawaii: non-perishable food, clothing, and various run-of-the-mill products that cost half as much in California. It wasn't usually the smell one needed to be concerned about, or fear of drug-sniffing dogs, because a triple-layer food seal did the trick to contain most odors. The real concern was the dreaded pin-probe of would-be drug pirates disguised as courier delivery employees.

Everyone in the business of selling drugs had a friend, who had a cousin, who once worked for one of the big companies, who told them what they did inside of shipping warehouses. Boxes moved and changed hands all the time, so workers became fairly skilled at guessing what might be inside by weight and distribution of contents. Like children on Christmas Eve, freight workers shook and listened to packages all day long, hoping for a jackpot. If a box was suspected of containing drugs, they probed it. An extremely long and thin pin was used to poke through the cardboard into the guts of the mystery prize. Corners were good places to use as entry points because they got so much wear from normal handling through the delivery chain. The pin pierced all contents, even thick plastic, and left no real sign of intrusion. What it did do was accumulate just enough residue to give the inquisitive honey badger a chance to detect a winner. Certain drugs would leave visible signs on the pin, others left an olfactory clue, and some required a taste test. In any case, the average warehouse employee was usually able to determine whether someone was trying to sneak a shipment of drugs past him.

If it was determined that a box likely did contain illegal narcotics, the box was opened and checked. If drugs were found, they were embezzled. The box was then filled with enough miscellaneous content to match the weight posted on the label, resealed, and thrown back onto the heap for delivery. If no drugs were found, the same procedure—minus embezzlement—was applied. Either way, the box was delivered without raising any red flags for upper management. Customers who received packages usually did not know what the box looked like when it started the journey, so an extra layer of packing tape across a seam didn't draw much attention. Customers who opened their packages only to find their illegal drugs were missing did not have much leverage with which to file a formal complaint. All in all, it was usually a bad idea to conceal drugs in a stuffed animal, throw it in a box, and send it through the gauntlet of thieves.

A true professional had to put in more effort to avoid detection. Dillon layered his bags and surrounded them with cans of soup, jars of mayonnaise, jeans, and magazines. Plus, in order to leave the package in the hands of strangers for the least amount of time, he took the box in twenty minutes before the store closed and paid for overnight delivery. As such, all his shipments had made it through safely.

I spent time counting out stacks of cash in Dillon's apartment. It took about twenty minutes to verify the accuracy of $12,000. I left three pounds of product in the care of my trusty surfer colleague, then hopped back in the car and into the slow crawl of the 405. At 5:30, I was passing Santa Monica Boulevard and putting in a mixed CD of Creedence songs. I tried to keep up with the mighty pipes of Fogerty note for note. Two generations removed, but I still found an odd pull to the classic rebel soul of a movement long past.

Traffic opened up as the Valley became the Grapevine. A cool breeze whipped over the summit and found its way into the car. As I hit the flatlands of central California via I-5, I was overflowing with excitement. Everything felt just right. I flew up the freeway, topping one hundred miles per hour, when I managed to catch open pockets of road and came dangerously close to 18-wheelers when passing congested groups of cars. Legally speaking—with only undeclared dollars left hidden in the car, no narcotics, and the peace of mind that comes from not looking like a minority—I gambled on breaking the speed limit in order to reach the Bay at a decent hour.

Ten o'clock. The Silicon Valley Hotel. My good friend was usually the manager on duty, but he was gone for the weekend. In his place, he left cute, little Allison to staff the desk. I walked into the lobby carrying a backpack and a gym bag, and looking like I just spent many hours in an uncomfortable car. Allison looked up and smiled playfully. I caught her eye with mine and smiled back.

"You must be Anto. Alex told me you'd be coming tonight. I'm Alli."

"Hey, Alli. I don't think we've officially met before, but I've seen you around the other times I've stayed here," I stated playfully, then reached out for a handshake.

"Well hello. It's good to officially meet you," she replied.

We shook hands and smiled at each other for a few seconds longer than the standard greeting.

"Just the one night again?"

"Yeah."

"How come you always come up for only one night?" she wanted to know.

"Can't tell you. CIA shit."

She rolled her eyes flirtatiously and cocked her head to lightly mock me.

"I'm sure," she countered.

She was cute, young, and surprisingly confident. Allison was wearing black slacks and a white collared shirt unbuttoned down to her neck line. When she leaned over to write my room number on the envelope of the keycard, I looked down her shirt and almost let myself get caught—close enough to let her know I was nibbling around the edges. Our eyes met again, and the agreement was sealed with mutual smiles.

"Are you working all night?" I asked while trying to play it cool.

"Yeah. I'm manager on duty until morning."

"I'm going to meet the guys for a drink. I'll be back in a few hours. Will you be up? "

"I should be. If I'm not here, just come knock on my door. Room 212."

She handed me my keycard, and I tried to hide my eager smile, but the color in my cheeks gave me away. I strutted down the hall, out into the courtyard, and skipped up the steps with the confidence of a movie star playing his defining role.

After a two-minute shower, I stood at the sink brushing my teeth, with a grin glued on my face as I watched myself in the mirror. The excitement was so overwhelming that I laughed out loud, danced around a bit, then pulled up my left arm and flexed my bicep to admire just a bit more. There was a pressing urge to get there, but I couldn't clearly define the ultimate destination: the restaurant full of friends, the hotel room where Alli would be waiting, or the meeting with my connection to re-up. Everything on the horizon came attached with its own unique euphoria, and the anticipation of it all was a high unto itself.

At 10:30 p.m., I pulled into the parking lot of Hanzo Sushi and saw two friends outside the restaurant smoking cigarettes. A woman in a tight pink dress had her arm sloppily draped around the neck of the tall Caucasian while pointing an accusatory finger at the Korean. Andrew was holding up the inebriated woman reluctantly as she slurred nonsensical curses toward Doman, who in return was laughing, baiting, and instigating the woman.

121

Her lipstick was cracked, and the crow's feet around her eyes picked up defining shadows from the neon light behind her that announced "sushi." Her pink dress was a size smaller than appropriate, and her jewelry was two octaves too loud for a middle-aged, dejected woman who was old enough to be my friends' mother.

"I bet it's spilling out the sides like pastrami at a Jewish deli," Doman declared as he took another drag of his cigarette. He let out an overly dramatic laugh and turned to see me walking up.

"Fuck you, you limp dick, kimchi smelling bastard." She managed to fire the insult, but at the sacrifice of her balance. Teetering on her high heels, she nearly took Andrew down to the ground as she desperately held on to his neck.

I walked up laughing and put an arm around Doman. The flapper kicked away her shoes. One landed on the hood of a nearby car. The other flew straight up, fell back down, then found its mark bouncing squarely off the top of her head. Everyone erupted in laughter. She punched Andrew in the gut, and he managed to deflect her second and third swings.

"Hey, guys. What the fuck is going on?" I asked, as if it wasn't obvious.

Handshakes were exchanged, and I took the pack of cigarettes from Doman's shirt pocket and pulled out a smoke.

"What up Toe? When did you get into town?" Andrew inquired while trying to balance the woman with his hand around her waist.

"Just rolled up. Half an hour ago."

Andrew let go of the woman and pulled out a lighter to hand to me.

"You just making a run, or you here for the whole weekend?"

"Heading back tomorrow. Just business."

"And who is this handsome man?" The pink dress stumbled toward me with her hand out to catch herself in case she tipped forward too far. I took her hand, spun her in a half pirouette, then sent her back toward Andrew, adding a light kick to her rump for punctuation.

"What the fuck asshole?! This dress costs more than you make in a month. You and your stupid flip-flops can suck my dick."

I took a long, slow drag from my cigarette as I examined the specimen before me.

"I thought they were just discussing your vagina? Now you have a dick to suck?"

I exhaled a cloud of smoke in her direction. She waved her hand in front of her squinty eyes and let out an exaggerated mock cough.

"I'll have you know my pussy looks like roses, and I'm sure you and your baby dick couldn't handle my skills," the woman sloppily blurted out in a drunken slur.

I took another drag of my cigarette before offering retort:

"First of all, the saying is: smells like roses, not looks like roses. Second, not sure if you noticed, but you don't look very enticing tonight. Third, I think it's safe to say something went wrong somewhere along the line for you to end up here, in front of a sushi joint, trying to hit on guys half your age. And fourth, I guarantee you we're dealing with meat curtains and not flower petals."

For emphasis, I flicked ash in her general direction and smiled.

She looked to Andrew for solace, but all he offered in return was a shrug and a whimsical smile. Her eyes glared back at me with the

123

anger of many divorces to come. Doman was laughing hysterically. As if it were the only logical rebuttal, she turned her back to us, bent over, pulled up her skirt, and exposed her non-garmented lady parts for the world to see. A car driving by honked its horn, and the passengers let out a round of hoots and applause.

"Did I tell you or what? This pussy hasn't lost a step yet," she was speaking to us with her face looking backwards between her knees.

Andrew tapped her vulva with his pointer finger in the same manner one might tap a stranger on the shoulder when passing through a crowded coffee shop. The woman remained in the assumed position.

I peered through squinted eyes, stopped myself from laughing, and offered my best scientific commentary: "Well, I hate to be the bearer of bad news, but from my initial examination—and, mind you, I am neither doctor nor deli owner—I do believe some Kegel exercises would not be a wasted effort on your part. "

With a restrained giggle, Andrew affirmed: "I concur, doctor."

Doman was laughing so hard he was crying.

"Fuck you assholes." She straightened herself up, pulled down her dress in a huff, and stumbled away while holding up her middle finger for us to admire.

"Hey, you forgot your shoes!"

Andrew retrieved the abandoned stilettos and trotted after her. Doman and I were left laughing and shaking our heads.

"I need a drink dude. Let's go inside," I asserted.

We flicked our half-finished smokes into the parking lot and stepped toward the wooden double doors. The thick doors were carved in a custom design with long, vertical handles fashioned into a spiral swirl. As they opened, I could feel sound hit me like a concert hall. The air was dense and heavy and smelled of whiskey.

The scene was saturated with noise and red faces. The decor and staging were that of a traditional Japanese restaurant; plenty of bamboo and black onyx everywhere. The restaurant had closed half an hour earlier, but the real entertainment was just getting started. The bar area was overflowing, so I navigated slowly through the crowd. I passed the hostess station and offered the cute Korean girl a playful smile. In the sea of close-talking and overly animated punch lines, I ran into the usual suspects and offered handshakes and brief greetings as I made my way to the bar. Over the hum of the crowd, a thump was heard.

Jack was in his early forties with a full head of black hair; handsome, like a young Wayne Newton. He ran the bar on Friday nights, and was part owner of the restaurant. There had never been a bartender who poured stronger drinks than Jack of Hamza Sushi. He stood behind the bar, shaking a mixer, occasionally looking down at the row of devotees sitting in front of him, and offered out his next call for liar's dice. He grinned when he knew he had squeezed someone into a liar's corner. Then he poured them all a shot as everyone started rattling the cups full of dice again. Bangs and thuds boomed on the wooden countertop, then the overly dramatic drunks peeked under their cups like meerkats scouting for predators. Jack spotted me walking up through the crowd and smiled.

"Toe. What's up brother!? Good to see you," he acknowledged me cordially.

Jack stepped from behind the bar, and we greeted each other with a quick hug.

"Same old, same old, my friend. Life is good. How about you?"

"Livin' the dream, brother. Same as always. You doing whiskey tonight?"

"Shot and a beer, please."

"You got it."

I stood at the edge of the bar and admired the scene. I'd never witnessed such an eclectic group of drunks, so closely banded together, by a yet-to-be identified purpose. There were a half-dozen friends I knew from high school all huddled together next to the sushi bar. Next to them were the off-duty cops, who were the real alcoholic backbone of the pack. Then there were the one-off couples and friends of friends, who had all somehow come to be accepted as part of the assemblage that was the shit-show of Hamza Sushi. Corporate managers, bikers, bar owners, former NFL players, pretty girls, and sultry ex-wives could always be counted on to form the assorted mix.

Jack poured shots for the ten people closest the bar, then got distracted by one of the servers asking for a round of drinks. As everyone held their shot glasses, waiting for the official word from the maestro, I, ever impatient, took my shot and tried sneaking away.

"Ehhhh. Whoa! I don't think so buddy." Jack shook his head in disappointment without ever looking up to see me committing the cardinal sin.

"You know the rules. You wait for the bartender when the bartender is pouring for the group. What the fuck, man?"

Jack poured me another shot, and this time, it was three fingers of whiskey in a cocktail glass.

"I'm sorry Jack. It's been a long day."

"It's all good brother. I know you think you're the only person that exists on this planet."

Jack laughed, half teasing, half serious, and raised his glass in my direction.

"To Anto. Thanks for letting us be at your service tonight. Kanpai."

The group erupted with a unified, "Kanpai," and threw the shots down their throats. I needed three large gulps to finish mine.

Forty minutes later, I was four shots and three beers deep on an empty stomach. The restaurant crowd had thinned out a bit, but the bar was still at full capacity. I caught Jack's attention from within the crowd and nodded my head slightly to the side. Jack offered his own nod of confirmation in response. I made my way to the rear of the restaurant, using the restroom route, but made a last-minute turn into the kitchen instead. I waited impatiently, leaning against a stainless-steel countertop.

Jack barged into the kitchen in his usual hurried pace, leaned behind a stack of drying pots, and grabbed a hidden sushi tray— the size used for serving large groups. Running lengthwise down the runway, edge to edge, were two massive lines of cocaine. Jack pulled a half-cut straw out of the front pocket of his polo shirt and handed it to me.

"Come on Jack. You can't be serious," I said.

"No worries brother. You just take as much as your training wheels can handle and leave the rest. I'm sure someone else will need a bump, and I'll have them clean your side of the plate. "

Jack smiled a wide set of perfect teeth, playfully slapped me on the shoulder, and took back the straw. With the efficacy of an industrial shop-vac, Jack sucked up what was easily a gram of blow, grunted a couple times, dropped the straw on the plate, and hurried out of the kitchen.

"I gotta make drinks. Put it back when you're done," he instructed as he turned the corner.

I was left in the kitchen, alone, staring at the plate in front of me. I chuckled a bit uncomfortably, then got to work. My first pass took up almost half the monster. Second pass, with the other nostril, was not as capable. My sinuses had never been willing participants in my indulgent ways. I tried my best to pull hard with my struggling nasal cavity, but I could see a rejected mist falling from my nose. A little bit of water from the sink on my pointer finger and thumb, then I snort back the makeshift rinse. It sounded like a hippopotamus giving birth in the kitchen. I licked my middle finger and rolled it across the end of the line, leaving a heavy section untouched in the middle of the plate. Rubbing my teeth and snorting my nose, the job was finally done; I was high as a rocket.

With the plate hidden out of sight, I made my exit from the kitchen. Walking back into the party after doing my first line always felt like the climax of a movie. Cocaine and whiskey on even ground, the brain processes in slow motion and injects a sense of grandeur into everything. I am important. I am successful. I am desired. I have this whole thing under control. I am everything you wish you could be.

As I slid back into the crowd, a couple friends caught my line of sight and grinned. Most of the people knew what happened when Jack and I would disappear together in the back. Some would participate, and some wouldn't, but all of them were aware of my extravagant ways.

Cocaine was now running the show. Thoughts became spastic and predictably deviant. Conversations held fabricated attention and produced over-exaggerated mannerisms. Like a honeybee flying from flower to flower, I bounced from group to group, pollinating with a few punch lines and witty remarks.

128

Social affairs are much easier when formalities are avoided; at least in the short run. I never said goodbye, preferring the Irish whisper instead. My mind was consumed by sex, and I knew I had someone waiting back at the hotel, so I slipped out the door as if to have a cigarette.

At half past midnight, suburbia was a desolate dream. Eddies of air and cigarette smoke swirled in my car as I drove with the window down. My hometown had changed over the years, but not enough to rob me of my memories: fight at the McDonald's, stealing smokes from the old K-Mart, skateboarding at the library, and running from cops everywhere. Reveling in the glow of a deviant childhood, there was a deep sense of satisfaction knowing I had made it. All the people who told me I needed to change my ways were wrong. The whole world was wrong. Most of the guys I ran with as a teenager were not so lucky. Addiction, incarceration, and death were the heavily favored incumbents, but not for this kid. I could play on both sides and pull it off.

One might guess Allison would be ravaged immediately upon my return to the hotel, but something strange kept happening in my life. Instead of walking into her room and tearing off her clothes, I found myself deep in an open-hearted conversation with a girl I barely knew. This was not a new phenomenon for me.

There came a moment of surrender—both of us naked, playing with each other's body parts—when we simply threw the script aside. We talked like lifelong friends and took down portions of armor long enough to let the other see that we were equally fearful and lonely. Is there anything we do in life that does not stem from fear and loneliness?

She was lying naked on her back and I was on my stomach, wrapped between her legs, looking up at her, hands resting just below her navel, fingers crossed to form a nest for my chin. There was no view I preferred more in the whole world. Words carried back and forth over the peaks of her nipples.

129

"Can I ask you a question?" I asked softly.

She chuckled, then replied, "I think we're past the point of being shy around each other."

"What about me made you want to do this?"

"I don't know. You're hot, and you seem like a cool guy."

I hid my bashful smile by kissing the ridge of her lower abdomen.

"Can I ask you a question now?" she said while looking down at me.

"Of course."

"So what exactly is it that you do when you come up here for only one night?"

I paused for a brief moment but found no reason to lie.

"I sell weed. I'm up here to reload, then I head back to San Diego as soon as I get my shit."

"So you're a drug dealer?"

"I wouldn't consider pot a drug."

"I guess," she mumbled unsteadily.

"What about you? Why do you work at a hotel?"

"Just trying to pay my way through school. I'm at West Valley right now, but hopefully I'll be able to transfer to San Jose State next winter."

"That's pretty noble. I never had to work in college. My mom paid for everything."

"Lucky."

"I know. And look where I ended up. Maybe I should've gotten a job in college, so I could get some sense of pride about my work. Now I have a corporate job that I hate and consider selling weed my real job. Not very noble. "

"You're okay. Don't be so hard on yourself. "

I began kissing her in a descending pattern, beginning with her navel and working my way south. She moaned and grabbed a firm handful of my hair, pulling me closer in as she lightly swiveled and glided her hips. One of my arms was wrapped around her thigh and holding her tightly to my face. The other reached up and slid gentle fingers over a nipple.

"Mmmm. Come here," she whispered.

She put both palms on my cheeks and guided my head to join her up above. I took my time, stopping at different landmarks to offer touch and taste, covering her whole body with my lips. When I did finally meet her face-to-face, we locked lips and held each other tightly; no distance between our hearts. The entire time we made love, we kept our arms wrapped firmly around each other, staying as one unified motion. We fell asleep the same way.

The phone erupted with a vile blast. Confusion. Squinted eyes. Pounding head. Allison propped herself on top of my chest and grabbed the receiver.

"Thanks Manuel," then she quickly hung up.

"What was that?" I asked.

"Sorry. I needed the wake up call. Need to be ready by seven for the next shift."

"What time is it?"

"Six. I'm going to hop in the shower."

Before she could make her escape, I grabbed her around the elbow and pulled her back down over me.

Laughter, giggles, teasing, and handfuls of flesh. Tongues wrestle gracefully between suctioned mouths. Morning sex. Hard and emphatic morning sex. Headboard banging. I watched her eyes intently. Panting. Perspiration. Hips in motion. I leaned over her arched back, wrapped both arms around her abdomen, and pulled her in tightly to me. Loud conquering roar. Exhaustion. Collapse. Sighs. Smiles.

"Wow. I'm sore," Alli confessed.

"Sorry," knowing full well I didn't mean what I had said.

"Not a bad thing. Just haven't had that in a while. I really need to get in the shower now," Allison said while sliding out of bed.

"Go. I'll keep an eye on the bed."

"Gee, thanks. Very noble of you."

I let out a half chuckle without opening my eyes, allowing an easy glide back into half lucid sleep. Allison showered, and I was floating in and out of dreams, each faded between connections of running water in the background. When my eyes opened again, she was putting on her clothes. I continued to view the show through squinted eyes and made an effort to keep my breathing soft. Watching a woman get dressed after sex always filled me with a sense of pride. Never got old.

Part of me was the little boy sneaking into the adult section of the video store. Part of me was the pompous young man looking flamboyantly at my latest trophy. Part of me felt the genuine connection our souls made and wished it could last forever. And yet another part was just thankful that someone held me close all night.

Allison caught my covetous stare in the mirror.

"Hey, good lookin'! Whatcha doing back there?"

"Just looking at you. Thinking. Any plans when you get off?"

"Yeah. I'm going to volunteer at church. We're serving food to the homeless tonight, so we have to get everything ready."

"You go to church?"

"Yeah."

"You believe everything they say?"

"No, but I find what fits for me."

"Were you raised with religion?"

"No. I found it when I was in high school. I was looking for something and felt drawn to explore different faiths and churches. I tried different places until I found what felt right. What about you?"

"No church for me. Raised Catholic and had an aversion ever since," I replied with a sarcastic tone. She looked at me for a moment and softened her eyes.

"Do you think you're a bad person?" she asked.

I took a long pause and absorbed the impact.

"I don't know. Probably," I admitted softly.

"If you feel the darkness in you, then maybe you should look for signs of the light?"

"Maybe. How do you feel about sleeping with me and going to church?"

"I don't really think about it like that. But I know that I don't feel ugly or ashamed about what we did. I like you, and I think we did more than sleep with each other. That said, I know the church probably wouldn't look too favorably on this. It's something I struggle with, but that doesn't mean I'll use it as an excuse to throw away everything I get from belonging to my church. I'll just stick with my piece of the light."

I thought back over a lifetime of excused faith. Easier to find a fault with theory and discard the whole thing than to face myself with an honest moral inventory. And what was this light of which she spoke?

"I gotta go. I left my number on the notepad. If you want, you can call me next time you come up."

She kissed me on the forehead and walked out the door. What a morning. What a start to a weekend. What a life.

I sat at Starbucks and let my mind wander through endless per-mutations of a different life. Something about Allison having faith, and going to church, pierced through my weary crown. I'd con-vinced myself of my own magnificence for years, but one little act of benevolence, from a girl I just met, sent my castle tumbling into the sea.

A hometown kid, and self-made drug dealer, sat stoically on the patio of a coffee shop watching the people buzz around in their Saturday morning rituals. This was the epicenter of everything I despised. Couples in workout clothes, and young families with newborns, were putrid reminders of what normal people did on a weekend. Coffee and bagels for them; hangover and clogged sinuses for me.

A few hours later, I was back in my hotel room counting out $60,000 in cash with my business associate. It was a tedious process, especially with a hangover. When we were settled, I took the hockey bag he brought with him and put it in my trunk. Everything went off without a hitch, and I was back on the road heading south at ten past noon.

alejandra

She looked at me from across the bar, and I knew. I knew because that feeling was unmistakable. I knew because I had spent so many years watching others play with that look. I remember the first time someone looked at me that way like it was yesterday; the girls giggling and sneaking away to come peek at me by the water fountain. Oh, what a feeling! What an absolutely essential part of human life—to be wanted, to be desired, to have the eyes of a stranger smile, amorously and playfully, and to feel the brain instantly give way to the power of the heart.

We are taught to reason. We are taught to guard ourselves from the savagery of impulse. But the carnal dance is one that has few rivals in terms of fulfillment. Our mating rituals imbue us with a sense of belonging like no other. If I am desired by one, then I am desired by the entire cosmos; and with that, I can muster the fortitude to continue playing this game even as life tries to prove itself inane.

She was leaning against the wall, and I was trying to make my way through the crowd at the bar to order a drink. The second time I turned my head to look her way, she turned toward me as well, and we caught ourselves in that moment where it was impossible not to smile. She raised her cocktail glass and held the straw with a delicate touch, looked down for a moment as she took a sip, then looked back up—directly at me—and my eyes were there to meet hers.

Black hair, black eyes, and dark Latin skin had my senses going wild. The dress she wore left nothing to the imagination, and the arch of her posture exuded confidence. We stared at each other for a few seconds, then broke the intensity with smiles. I abandoned my friends and forged a path through the crowd directly toward her, never taking my eyes away.

She smelled delicious, and she felt sultry as I put a hand on her shoulder and leaned in toward her ear. Her curled mane tickled my temple and cheek, and I was taken by a sense of euphoria just from being within her gravity. Three gold earrings swayed playfully from her earlobe, and I spoke into them the way an emperor whispers to an oracle.

"What is your name?"

"Alejandra."

"Would you dance with me?"

She turned her head slightly toward me so I could feel her warm cheek on mine. She nodded, then interwove a couple of her fingers into my hand. I pulled my face back a bit, looked into her eyes, and kissed her passionately. She took a small step toward me, so we were pelvis to pelvis, and she pulled me in tighter. We stayed where we were, away from the crowd, and kissed as long as it takes to forget about time. She had me pushed up with my back against the wall, and I held the back of her head with my fingers at the roots of her hair. My breath grew deeper as I moved from shallow breathing to long sweeping arcs; fully in and fully out. Our tongues were sliding around each other with the grace of two snakes in heat.

When we finally slowed down, our eyes opened and locked on each other as our mouths were just beginning to separate. She was beautiful, and confident, and knew exactly what she wanted. She took a deep, affirming breath in and let it go slowly, while never moving her eyes off me. Her breasts bulged from her low-cut shirt, and my erection was painful from the constricting jeans I wore.

"Where do you live?" she asked.

"I'm staying in a hotel. I live in San Diego."

Alejandra nodded slightly, and I took her hand before leading her through the crowded bar. As we made our way toward the exit, I caught the look of one of my friends and offered him a peace sign to indicate my departure. He grinned and nodded. As we walked out hand in hand, the bouncers both smiled at me. My ego basked in the attention, but I noticed they both had an odd smirk on their faces.

Alejandra offered to drive, and soon, we were pulling off the exit toward my hotel. Our hands stayed connected the entire trip.

"That's the hotel there," I pointed left.

Instead of going to the light to make a U-turn, Alejandra veered a quick left through a gap in the median, and as soon as she did, I saw the blue and red lights flash from a car coming our way. Not good. I knew I was fairly drunk, and I could not imagine her to be any better off. My heart was racing.

It was half past midnight, and we were pulled over on the side of a major street in Cupertino. The inside of the car was lit up like an operating room from the beaming spotlight now shining in. Alejandra reached in the glove box to pull out her registration, and I looked in the rear-view mirror, but all I could see were shadows moving through red and blue lights.

"License and registration, please."

She handed the officer the documents and did not turn her eyes from him. A second officer approached my window and shined his flashlight near my feet. I tried to look at him, but it was pointless;

blinding lights everywhere.

"Have you been drinking tonight?" the policeman asked her.

"No, officer."

And for some reason, I believed her. The policeman looked at her ID for a moment, then bent down to take a long stare at me. I looked over and tried to maintain my poise. The officer looked at the ID again, then back up at me.

"Is there a problem officer?" Alejandra demanded rather bluntly.

After staring at me for what seemed like ages, the officer finally relaxed and went back into procedure mode.

"We pulled you over for making an illegal U-turn. Please stay in the car while I write your citation."

The cop walked back to his car, and I finally managed to exhale. Alejandra took my hand into hers and smiled at me.

"How much did you have to drink tonight?" I ask nervously.

"Nothing baby. It's okay."

I was relieved, but thoroughly confused. I decided to stick to the feeling of relief. After ten minutes, the policeman returned to Alejandra's side of the car and handed back her registration and ID. He reviewed the citation briefly, then asked for her signature before handing over the pink carbon copy.

"Please be careful tonight, Jose," the cop said with a smirk on his face.

I didn't get it, but I didn't care; probably just another racist cop being an asshole. We pulled away and quickly turned into the hotel

140

parking lot. Relief. We made it. Nobody got arrested, and I was still going to get laid.

Alejandra and I quickly made our way to my room, and before the door could even close, we were all over each other. She kissed me with a strong sense of purpose and rubbed my cock through my pants while moaning softly. I quickly slipped off her shirt and unhooked her bra with one seamless effort, then picked her up so I could suck on her nipples. Her breasts were hard and motionless, and I could see the scars on the bottom crease of skin. She ran her hands through my hair and moaned with pleasure. I put her down on the bed and took a step back as I began undressing. When my shirt came off, she smiled and purred.

"Mmmm. Si, papi."

"Get naked," I ordered as I unbuckled my belt and slipped off my jeans.

She squeezed out of her pants, and I was left looking at dark brown skin accented by a bright white pair of lacy panties. As she began sliding her panties down, she kept one hand over her pussy. All the while, she teased me with an erotic smile. I took off my boxers and flung them somewhere, then stood there looking at her as she waited for my undivided attention. I waited with carnal thirst and a full erection.

She slowly began angling her hand to reveal the secret prize. I touched my cock and focused. As her hand moved away, I stopped stroking myself, stopped moving altogether, stopped breathing, and my jaw went completely slack. It couldn't be. I was beyond confused. It didn't make sense.

Alejandra had a dick. And not just any dick—a big, fat, uncircumcised cock. I stared at the beast and marveled. I couldn't take my eyes off it. The pet iguana looked as if it had been firmly pressed against her taint for a long time and was just now coming out of its hiding spot. She grabbed the specimen and lifted it from its slumber. Even with one hand around the base, she still had nearly two additional hands' width of cock to display. I didn't know what was worse—the embarrassment of kissing a chick with a dick or the veritable baseball bat with which she was now trying to entice me. It was huge. I found myself questioning the adequacy of my own manhood. She began sliding the foreskin and arousing herself. As she built tumescence and a carrot of vein emerged, I finally shifted my stare from her genitals up to her eyes.

Her eyes were fixated on me, and her stare was aggressive. Gone was the sultry feminine grace, as she now exuded a hostile energy with a twist of perversion. I felt a force rising from my gut as my confusion dissipated and a brutal tension took its place. Seething anger rose inside me until it filled every cell of my body. My eyes squeezed and focused, and my chest tightened. I stared at the trickster before me. Sound went down to one note—a high frequency vibration similar to what you might hear if you stood up too quickly. I was lightheaded. My hands were gripped in tight fists, and my stance was poised for sudden movement.

In my mind, I pictured tearing her apart. I pictured the look of her deformed face after I beat it down to pulp. I could feel my knuckles going numb as I imagined hitting her far too many times past the point of consciousness. Animal fury. I didn't just want to hurt her, I wanted to scream like a rabid monkey while I did it. How could she take me for such a fool? What the fuck did she think was going to happen when I found out she had a dick? That I would suddenly shrug my shoulders and say, "Yeah. Sure. Why not?" Or did she peg me as the kind of guy who liked that sort of thing? What possible modality of logic could lead her to conclude that this was okay? There was nothing that fit. All possible variables did not compute. I was going to kill the fucking bitch.

Then I saw her eyes change. I saw fear come pouring out of her with the same silent intonation I had as a child when my dad was about to burst. She saw what I felt inside, and she knew she had made a mistake. The ravenous hunger from her gaze was gone, and she was looking for a way out; but I was blocking the door, and she was cornered. She covered her crotch with one hand and raised her other as an apologetic gesture. We stared at each other for a moment as my mind spun out of control.

Genuine moments of compassion were confusing to me. I could easily understand the premeditated empathy I had occasionally displayed, but in all honesty, those acts were performed with some form of incentive dangling in front of me. But genuine compassion—spontaneous and devoid of the expectation of reward—was what I felt in that moment. And in that feeling, I found hope for myself and hope for humanity.

I unclenched my fists and slowly pointed toward the door. My jaw relaxed a bit, and now it felt as if I were moving in slow motion. An entire generation lived and died before I could manage to make sound with my throat.

"Get the fuck out. Now!" I commanded, taking care to pronounce each syllable crisply. My eyes had not blinked since I first saw the surprise.

"Okay. Okay. I'm sorry. I'm very sorry. "

She put her pants and shirt on in the amount of time it took me to draw one long, full breath in followed by a slow, seeping exhale. I was frozen like a statue, still pointing at the door. With her panties, bra, and shoes in her hands, she carefully stepped around me and opened the door, each of us being careful never to take our eyes off the other.

"I'm sorry. Thank you."

She turned her head and walked away. I watched the door slowly close, still frozen in my stance, and took a dramatic breath of air. What the fuck just happened?

I grabbed a beer and bottle of whiskey from the minibar and plopped down in one of the chairs near the TV. I stared at my reflection on the blank screen, watching myself gulp whiskey, as I sat there naked.

I drank the beer and whiskey down about half way each then looked over at the bed. I could see the outline in the sheets where she had laid with her legs spread. As I took one more long pull from the beer, I lost part of my armor. Something broke inside of me, in the part that always walked around with my chest cocked out, and I began to chuckle. Beer went up through my nose, and I spat some of it out on the carpet as chuckles gave way to laughter. Oh man. Holy shit. Did that really just happen?

I called one of the buddies who was with me at the bar and told him I needed him to rush over to my hotel.

"Yeah man. I'll come over. But what about that girl you left with?"

"It's cool man. She's gone, and I've got one hell of a story to tell you. Just make sure to bring plenty of weed. I'm gonna need some serious smoke to get through this one."

full commitment

I woke up in the middle of the night with a keen awareness of what I had to do, and I knew the time had come. But it was two in the morning, and I couldn't get into my office until four, so there I was, wide-awake, and I looked over at her.

That morning, "her" happened to be Jolene, and she was a delight to behold. She slept curled toward the edge of the bed, and the blanket was barely covering one of her legs. I sat up against the headboard and admired her body. The female form doesn't get much better than that of women in their mid-twenties. An oscillating fan created a soft white noise and gentle breeze. The breeze danced with slivers of orange accents, through swaying blinds, coming from a streetlight outside. The light painted Jolene's body like stripes on a tiger. Shadows created perfect lines of definition and wonder. I stared, lost in trance, with the eyes of a believer watching a Shaman.

I thought about her as I drove to the office ten minutes shy of four in the morning. Interstate 15 was empty, empty like my hollow heart, and the pre-dawn sky reminded me of Jolene's eyes—those big, dark, innocent doe eyes of hers. She was fragile, and she was trying to cover that up with a sassy demeanor and new fake breasts. Whenever I wanted sex, she never hesitated. She would stare at me passionately and let me know, without ever saying a word, that I could do whatever I wanted—just keep doing something, anything, and don't let go.

My epiphany that morning was simple: I hated my corporate job. Moreover, I was going to quit so I could dedicate all my time to selling weed. The business had grown to the point of demanding a decision from me. It was time for full commitment.

At my cubicle, on a Monday morning just past four o'clock, I wrote a letter of resignation. Nothing fancy, but I did manage to throw in an excuse about needing time away to deal with emotional difficulties related to family matters. My parents' marriage was blowing up again, and I was grieving. Ten percent truth, at best, but I knew my boss's boss had inside information about the state of my parents' marriage and, having gone through a difficult divorce herself, she would buy the emotional victim card I was playing. I left my laptop, badge, and letter on my manager's desk and walked out of corporate America, certain I would never return. Time to claim my destiny.

Within a month, I was running at the largest volume turnover I had ever dealt with. I picked up twenty pounds at a time in hockey bags that looked like I was carrying a body inside each one. When my normal connection couldn't score, I started branching out to different networks and buying piecemeal. I leveraged myself to the max, using cash I owed to my main connection to buy from others, but I always pulled it off. I was making up to five grand a week—cash—and that was net after I spent on rent and lifestyle. I spent freely on my lifestyle, but never on commodities. If we were drinking, I was paying. If I was taking a girl out, we usually dined somewhere with a view of the ocean. We always opted for a second bottle of expensive wine, which I had no business ordering, and waiters quickly learned that I was a generous tipper.

I worked out like a beast. I went to the gym twice a day, often three times. I was friends with all the attractive people in the gym—the ones who partied hard at night and sweated it out on the Stair-Master during the day. Every week or two, I made the drive up and down the coast to handle business: Orange County, LA, Santa Barbara, and San Jose.

Jolene still called me, but it was different now. I was dating so many women that I had lost interest in her. This time, when she did call, she asked me to come over to sell her pot because she knew I didn't really want to spend time with her. I played along because there is no better drug than desire. Those eyes, those big, brown doe eyes, made me light up inside. As soon as I walked into her place, she was looking at me with those intoxicating eyes. She stood close to me until I touched her. She had a full-length mirror facing her bed; when I fucked her, I watched the reflection, never her. She paid me for the pot and thanked me for my services.

One week, I was making a resupply run to the Bay Area. I picked up my load on a Friday night and left at four the next morning to make the drive back down south. As the sun cleared the horizon, I was just getting onto the flatlands of I-5 near Mercey Hot Springs. The sun made a royal entrance, the way I imagine an Egyptian pharaoh to have been received on his coronation day, and the sky let out a breathtaking display of the richest colors my eyes could absorb. Translucent yellow and amber orange filled the sky, and a few lingering clouds, with their edges now highlighted, were allowed to bear witness to the miracle as acolytes. As the One rose it exposed the underside of the clouds, leaving the opposite side in shadows, and so duality was shown to be interdependent and inescapable, only we are prone to forget each day and each night. Only at certain angles to the sun are we able to clearly see the great truth. The rest of the dance is for us to remember by intuition, but we must try to remember. Everything else is a distraction. Most mystic branches of the great religions all believe there to be two windows during the day when the portal is open and prayer is best served: the time from first light to sunrise and from sunset to last light. I stared at the miracle of all life for a moment but quickly let it slip by as just another beautiful scene. I have real life shit to get to. I'm in a hurry.

No better time to be on a freeway than early morning; only a big rig here and there along the road. I tried to stay under 80 miles per hour, but it was tough with all that open road. My foot got heavy

147

as I stared at the changing sky. When I saw the flashing lights in my rear view, I sank internally with deep disappointment. Son of a bitch, it's over. My time has come. As I began to shift lanes, I went through my safety protocol out of habit. I always kept one emergency cigarette tucked behind my visor for precisely this situation. I took the cigarette and lit it low underneath the steering wheel so the cop wouldn't see the spark. Then I began puffing on it and pulled over to the shoulder. In the backseat was a hamper full of neatly folded laundry, and I was wearing my college alma mater sweatshirt. Don't forget, I am white.

The officer came around to the passenger side, and I leaned over to roll down the window. The car smelled of cigarette smoke.

"Good morning, young man. Going a little fast this morning, ain't ya?"

"Yeah, I know. I'm sorry, sir. My foot got a little happy with all this open road."

"Yeah. It sure did. How about your license and registration, please?"

I handed him what he asked for, then remained quiet.

"Sit tight here for me while I write you up."

I nodded and stayed silent but held eye contact with him while he looked around the inside of my car. Satisfied with what he saw, he headed back to the cruiser as I watched intently in the mirror. All he had to do was ask me to pop the trunk, and I was toast. I smoked the cigarette all the way down to the butt while feeling my heart work double time. Ten long minutes went by. The officer finally made his way back and handed me the ticket to sign.

"Got you at ninety-one in a seventy. I recommend you slow down a might out here son. No sense risking it."

"I will. Thank you"

When I pulled back out onto the freeway, I let out a strange sound. It was a mixture of laughter and anxiety and fear, and I pounded on the steering wheel, unable to control my excitement. I was invincible.

Above the gym where I spent most of my time, there were offices for lease. Within those offices, there was a small up-and-coming mortgage company by the name of American Capital Services. I knew some of the guys who worked there because they all came down to work out during the day. Eventually, I struck up a conversation with one of them. I was sitting on the bench press waiting to execute my next set, and John was near me, finishing a set of preacher curls.

"So I hear you have a promotion company on the side while you're selling mortgages," I said as I watched him struggle on his last rep.

When he finished, he set down the barbell and turned in my direction.

"Yeah. Me and some buddies started it in college and kept it going for fun. It doesn't bring in a ton of cash, but it keeps things interesting, and it gets me into almost any club downtown."

"You guys do On Broadway Friday nights, right?"

"Yeah man. That's us. Let me know if you ever want to skip the line or need a table or something."

I nodded and thanked him for the offer. Then he smiled and asked me a question.

"So what about you? You doing anything else or just sticking to your, uh, you know?" he laughed, trying to avoid saying anything incriminating.

"Nothing else for me. Just sticking to my bread and butter, but I'm getting out soon. I should be done in a month or so."

"Oh yeah. Why is that?"

"I have a target in mind, and when I stack that cash, I'll be out. I never stay in too long. Too much risk."

"That's smart. What are you going to do after?"

"Look for something to invest in and probably front some money to a few of the guys who work for me so they can keep their distribution going. I'll set them up with some of my connections and keep a little passive income flowing."

"Investing, huh? You thought about buying a place?"

"Yeah. It's one of the things I'm thinking about. Also, looking to invest in some legitimate businesses."

"Well, have you met Meggitt yet?"

"No. Who's that?"

"George Meggitt. He owns the mortgage company I work for upstairs. He would definitely be a good guy to talk to and not just for real estate. His background is . . . uh . . . similar to yours." John chuckled, again trying to avoid saying anything blunt.

"Oh yeah? Okay," I said, then scooted down and back to get under the barbell.

"Come up whenever you have some time. He's always around. I'll introduce you."

I went upstairs after the gym, and John welcomed me in. I had to wait for a little bit while George was finishing up with a meeting, so I took the time to absorb the setting. There were two secretaries running the operation from a suite in front. One was cute and the other was a knockout model, and they both were busy with escrow papers and phone calls and a high velocity of office commotion. In the offices that surrounded the secretaries, I recognized different guys from the gym and immediately felt at home. When George emerged, he had a big smile on his face and walked with his hand on the shoulder of a newly-minted homeowner.

George Meggitt was the greatest man who ever lived. I fell in love with him right away. He had a sharp direction to his gaze and always kept eye contact when he spoke. He wore a Tommy Bahama shirt with a lightly stitched parrot on the front, designer jeans, and black dress shoes. His hair was styled in the modern motif of spiky young rebel. A silver Breitling kept catching a glare from the fluorescents as he gestured with his hands while talking. He looked to be somewhere around forty years old, but with the fitness attributes of the San Diego lifestyle.

I met George during the height of indulgence and over-extension in a booming economy built on lies and greasy deals. San Diego circa 2006 was spewing with everything that collapsed the mighty American economy two years later. Everyone and their mothers was flipping real estate, and everyone was juiced on balloon payments or adjustable rates, hoping the market would continue to cover the spread. This was the perfect setting for me to permeate the membrane of tax-paying society with all my dirty cash.

George and I talked for hours that first day, and I told him everything— everything about my life, my job, my family, and every last bit of buried truth I had been hiding for years. It was perfect, absolutely perfect, and instantly I felt a tremendous comfort with him. I had finally met the man who understood me and was willing to teach me how to play the game at the highest levels.

His stories were incredible, absolutely incredible. Houses, boats, offshore accounts, international business, and all this from a guy who had grown up in the high desert of Apple Valley, California, and was running a chop shop and selling drugs by the time he was sixteen. Before figuring out there was easy money to be made, he came up learning the trades like all the good ole boys do out there in the wastelands. He knew how to build a house, fix a car, and manufacture crystal meth, and then he taught himself to play the game of mortgage flipping. He came up rough in all the right ways, and now he played where the real money was—white affluent America—with a smirk of satisfaction because he knew how good it was not to have to do real work for a living.

I attached myself to George's hip like a puppy without a home. I would come into the office more and more to spend time with him and discuss possible ventures in which to invest my money. There was a car wash his friend was starting, or an almond distributor I could get with, or a furniture importer. Every one of the businesses he mentioned was run by people who were part of this circle, his circle of "associates" who didn't mind washing dirty money through their operations for a fee. While we waited for the right opportunity and the right timing, George suggested I wash a little money through the investment company he had trading on the FTSE market. I could pull my money out at any time, and I was looking at twenty percent returns and no charge for the wash since this was my first run with him. I invested with George and waited to invest more with his friends. Weeks turned into months, and we kept waiting for the right place for me. In the meantime, I stayed close to George and absorbed everything he had to say.

George called me one morning at six. I picked up while having sex with one of the women I was seeing.

"George. What's up man?" I said with a huff in my voice.

"Anto. Good god man, what are you doing?" he asked while chuckling through the words.

"Morning workout. What's up?"

152

"I need your help. Can I come pick you up in thirty minutes?"

"No problem. Call me when you're downstairs." I hung up the phone and quickly dismounted my lover without explanation. As I turned on the shower, I heard her ask in a salty tone:

"Um, hello?"

"Sorry. I gotta run. Business," I said cavalierly, then stepped into the shower.

Thirty minutes later, I climbed into George's oversized truck, and he handed me a breakfast burrito from Kono's.

"Here. Try that. Best in San Diego," George stated in a serious tone. He had a different air about him that day—stern and aggressive.

"Thanks. So where we going?"

"I have to go collect money from someone who is late paying me back."

"Okay. What do you want me to do?"

"I doubt he'll have the money, so I'm probably going to take his new Hummer. If I do, then I need you to drive my truck back to the office."

"Okay. How much money does he owe you?

"Twenty grand."

I continued to eat my burrito while George filled me in on the backstory. They were in Vegas together, and the guy asked for a short-term loan while they were betting high stakes at the tables. Short-term turned into excuses, and now George was going to collect. I tried not to let my smile come out too much and give away

153

my exhilaration.

As we drove up I-15, George pulled out a clear baggie that was tucked in the sun visor. It was filled with opaque morsels. He handed it to me and asked:

"You know how to chop up a line?"

"Sure do. What is this?

"Crystal. Chop me up a fat one and one for yourself, too, if you want."

"Crystal, huh? Why crystal?"

George looked at me and smiled.

"Because it's fucking rocket fuel, and it's perfect for a job like this."

I thought about it for a second, then let it go. Fuck it. May as well.

darkness and the hollow, part 1

I lived under a man's house. I dug and I dug and spent day and night under that house. I was fascinated with my job, and every day, I grew more obsessed. I had never felt so compelled to achieve and never so secure in my decisions. It had been five months since I began the project, and I had no idea when I might finish. I didn't care. I was alive, and I was building my masterpiece.

The house sat high above a 70-foot industrial retaining wall, halfway up the hill, on luxurious Soledad Mountain Road in San Diego. The driveway was so steep that it left you fighting for breath long before the front door was reached. The view always inspired me to take a long, deep breath through wide nostrils and reaffirm my place on this planet. Directly below us was Mission Bay, and a few degrees west was the shimmering Pacific. On a clear day, we could see downtown San Diego, but who cares about the high-rises when you can stare at the coastline? This was my office. This was where I spent my every waking moment.

What began as a crawlspace was now large enough to walk around in. I started digging on my knees from outside the 18- by 24-inch louvered opening. Now, I was heaving five-gallon buckets full of dirt onto a ledge above my head and out the small opening from inside that secret cave. I worked from first light well into the darkness. Sometimes, I worked all night. Other times, I managed to make it home for a shower and a few hours of real sleep. But what is sleep when you have a purpose in life? At that point, sleep was just a burden, a nuisance keeping me from my destiny.

The idea was simple: "Why don't you dig out an area in the crawl-space to build a marijuana grow-room so you can get some cash coming back in? George had suggested" Sounded logical enough. The problem was I had never built anything with my hands before and had zero experience with construction. One more minor point, I was smoking meth day and night to keep me working like a machine.

Dirt. I was surrounded by dirt. I breathed dirt all day long. It was musty and dank and dark where I spent most of my hours. Dirt becomes Earth past a certain depth, and Earth has its own presence. When I took a moment inside the cave that I had dug, and the walls of dirt on either side of me were as high as I stood, I could feel the breath of the Earth as her lungs expanded and contracted with effortless grace. There was energy down there, and I was standing in the same primordial darkness that spawned all humankind.

Dirt is fascinating because it is a great optical illusion. When you take dirt that has been compacted, break it up, and try to move it just a couple dozen feet away, it expands in volume with unbeliev-able magnitude. How could so much have come out of that small space? Where was it all coming from? It never seemed to end, and I never slept.

The slope of the grade that the house sat on demanded massive footings of concrete poured in a semi-circle spread around a cen-ter rotunda of steel and concrete. Three stories of living space rose above, secured by a steel I-beam skeleton; from there, typical wood framing was utilized. The footings were unique because of their size and impact load. Gravity wanted to send this house sliding down the hill, but man's stubbornness, and demand for an ocean view, spawned clever engineering. The footings splayed out from the apex of the load like spines on a Japanese folding fan. When viewing the blueprints from a top view, one could clearly see

156

triangles of space between the gargantuan footings, and that space was all filled with dirt. The dirt acted as a stabilizing force between concrete footings, each the size of small swimming pools, keeping the footings from sliding in toward each other or the weight of infrastructure from tipping it off center.

This was the very dirt—absolutely crucial to the engineering integrity—that I removed by shovel and bucket. In total, there were approximately 800 square feet of space to work, and I dug down so that, at its maximum, there were ten feet of height between dirt floor and wooden floor joists above.

On a concrete ledge, there was a small, battery-powered radio, and next to it, a camping-style fluorescent lantern. On the ground below me were eight orange five-gallon Home Depot buckets thrown about haphazardly. Above me ran two-by-ten floor joists that all concatenated back to a center steel I-beam and between the joists was uncovered fiberglass insulation. The corner of the cave nearest to the opening allowed light from the outside to shine in as a reminder of hope. The far corner of the cave offered a bleak and ominous void filled with darkness and monsters.

I paused for a moment and looked up at the guts of the joists. In a space where the insulation was hanging down and the plywood of the subfloor was exposed, I spotted a large predatory arachnid perched in a fighter's stance, staring down at me. Next to it, spun up in a stray-jacket, was the fallen prey, still kicking and flinching, trying desperately to escape. Can you imagine the feelings of both victor and loser—pride and fear—as they stared at each other in the eyes and faced the hollow as one? I took a smoke break to reflect.

I began gathering the buckets and arranging them for the assembly line I had created in my work space. In front of me was a pile of loose dirt, freshly dug by a Makita mini-jack with a spade bit. On either side, I lined up the buckets so I could fill them all in sequence without having to rearrange the set. I grabbed the shovel and began scooping, rotating, and pouring. Working in a small space demanded efficiency; I rotated in calculated degrees.

The next day, I worked without a shirt, and I was slovenly. My cargo shorts were covered in dirt and a sweat ring dipped from waist-line to mid-thigh. I had never been more proud to work that hard. Thrust, scoop, lift, rotate, pour—over and over and over again. When the buckets were full, I began the process of expelling. The opening to the cave was at head height for me, and below it was a concrete ledge where the footing ran around the perimeter of the block wall that served as foundation. My first step was to get the buckets to the ledge, then from the ledge up and out through the small opening. A five-gallon bucket full of moist dirt weighed somewhere in the neighborhood of 70 pounds. Seventy pounds to the first ledge wasn't bad, but that much weight from ledge up to shoulder height, then straight out in front of me through a small opening got to be a little difficult.

Every now and then I caught the bottom lip of the opening and spilled the bucket outward. Sometimes I missed the mark and spilled the bucket back onto myself. It didn't matter at that point; I had learned to work with the dirt and its temperament. When all the buckets were up and out of the cave, I crawled out through the opening and dispersed accordingly; in and out, in and out, sprawl, slide, hop, crawl, sometimes gingerly and sometimes with great pain. My knees were worn dry from the constant climbing, and my shoulders were hard as stone from all the lifting.

Outside the cave, I grabbed a bucket in each hand and walked along the top edge of the yard. When I first started, the front yard was a steep and barren stretch of dirt, not at all aesthetically pleasing. My original strategy was to pour the dirt coming out of the cave onto the already barren landscape and not worry much past that. Oh, how quickly I was surprised. The dirt turned out to be endless, and pretty soon, there was dirt all along the driveway. I had barely dug a hole large enough to kneel in, and already I was coming up against problems of concealing the dirt on the other side of the dumpsite. George had suggested that I build a retaining wall so that I could have space to dump my dirt and people wouldn't be suspicious of all the construction. Pretty smart I thought, but there was just one problem: What the fuck was a retaining wall?

In the yard, I first dug a drainage channel and back slope, filling the base with three-quarter-inch aggregate. Then I laid down my first row of block. As I built up, I backfilled with more aggregate so rain could have a means of escape and not build up pressure behind the wall. I drove down to a stone yard in Chula Vista and purchased blocks every few days. Each pallet of block I would get myself and unload myself. Each cubic yard of rock was the same routine.

Block by block, bucket by bucket, I worked to build something of permanence. I cut each block the old-fashioned way by scoring with a chisel and hammer because I didn't know any better, but I didn't care. It was a slow, grueling progress.

As a meth user, there is a certain lens through which one sees the world, and it is myopic. Every task and every interaction is an opportunity to obsess on the minutia of life because the drug takes away all perspective and hyper-focuses the brain. The proper term for this phenomenon is tweaking. I didn't think about something, I tweaked on it. I didn't do something, I tweaked out on it. Each new building aspect of the cave became a tweak for me, so let's take the tweak up to another level by trying to build hidden pieces to a secret project that is already completely out of my scope of understanding.

Upon George's suggestion, I was to build a small waterfall in the middle of the yard that would act as a distracting focal point. Why a waterfall? The idea was we would infuse the water with

159

something to give it a kind of natural scent that would mask the smell of cannabis coming up from the exhaust line I planned to bury in the yard, connect back to the cave, and end just under the recirculating waterfall. Not bad in theory. I ran a line of eight-inch rigid HVAC ducting deep under the dirt with little 2x2 wooden crosses screwed to the inside, which would prevent the pressure of the dirt from collapsing the duct.

Trial and error was manageable on paper, but when I was in the blistering sun, pouring sweat and waist-deep in dirt, it got a bit old. Days turned into weeks, and weeks turned into one long amalgamated dream, body fighting from fatigue, digging and digging until I was standing in a channel taller than the top of my head. Difficult as it was, I became more committed as months went by.

When you are tired, when you have been breaking your back all day, there is no more blissful of a recharge than smoking a fat bowl of crystal mother-fucking methamphetamine. It was the all-curing elixir, the regenerating snake oil from the Silk Road, the only substance I knew that would fix all ailments at once. I often found myself in the bathroom of George's house, smoking meth in secret. Meth is a powerful laxative so, especially for a novitiate, it was not a bad idea to combine the two activities and simply smoke on the toilet. That way, I could just release my colon and let it all come out without resistance. Meth truly is amazing in the levels of dopamine it releases for some basic human functions, one great example being taking a shit. What used to be a chore had become a mild orgasm; I couldn't help but smile. So there I was, time and time again, with my pants down around my knees, locked in a bathroom for 15 minutes at a time, just smoking and shitting, and smiling to myself about all the fun I was having.

Feeling recharged, I made my way back down to the yard, to the cave, to the dirt that had become my life. People came and went from the house. George conducted business upstairs, his girlfriend and her kids moved in part time, and all the while there was a young man working on some kind of project in the front yard. The neighbor offered a casual wave each time he passed and even stopped to thank me for doing such a wonderful job to improve the aesthetics of his drive home. Yes, yes, you are most welcome. I am here for the people.

Meth was good. Meth was fun. And when I added meth and sex together—watch out. I could not imagine ever wanting to do anything   else   again.

What do you do when you need a break from an obsession? My solution was always sexual. On the nights I would go home after having been up a few days straight, I would always find myself feeling the infection of lust stinging my brain. Meth makes you want to fuck things, lots of things, all the time.

I began with the standard relief of masturbation, and that was quite the task. I stared intently at my computer screen and downloaded several snippets of free porn so I could pop open multiple windows at a time. Free porn in those days usually limited the length of clips to one minute, and that just wasn't going to cut it for a man as high and as lascivious as I was. I needed a steady stream of film, of people copulating in all sorts of perverse manners, so I grasped for excess and got 15 windows cued up just in case my attention waned from one over-fucked vagina to the next. As I got the porn ready to go, I also took a couple hits off my pipe, then left it sitting on the table. Computer screen with porn, pipe with meth, bottle of lotion, toilet paper— game on!

I was staring at the rhythm of her tits. She was being fucked hard and his aggression rippled through the soft fill of her breasts. He went faster and harder, and I stroked my cock with equal vigor as I imagined myself there, inside her. My eyes were

161

fixated on the screen, and my grip was painful on my raging erection. Deep lechery consumed my being. The man on the screen grabbed her around the throat and squeezed just right as he stared down at the submissive woman. It looked like a ritual sacrifice, and my mouth watered. Power, rage, control, carnal fury—I stared deeper and deeper, and I related, I felt what it was to let lose all my animalistic fervor.

"Say you like it! Say you want more!"

I was shouting at the screen now, and my forearm and shoulder were burning up, full of lactic acid from the intensity of my rhythm.

"Ya, ya, that's it. Give it to her. Pull her hair."

It's building up, it's coming, keep going, I'm almost there . . . Then the screen went black. The clip was over. Motherfucker! I had plenty more cued up, but that was not the point. I was there, I was in the flow, and now I had disrupted the grand tweak. Motherfucker! I frantically clicked the mouse to minimize the movie player, found another window in the background, pressed play, and maximized to full screen while still feverishly beating my cock to a pulp. The scene began, but not with the same intensity as the last one, and I was left with a flood of disappointment. Climax rescinded, and I knew I had to start all over to work my way up to the possibility of ejaculation. Fucking meth. I figured I'd smoke a little more. Hours went by. I smoked and scanned porn sites for the perfect sequence of clips. Some nights I was able to cum. Some nights, it was hopeless.

Eventually, the thrill of porn wore off, and I graduated to grander vice. Enter Craigslist. Craigslist offered a lonely man's potpourri of peeks and promises into fulfillment. It was a gripping mix, the emotions swimming around in my belly, as I scanned the introductory paragraphs and took a look at the picture they'd posted. I couldn't go for just any call girl because some charged upwards of $500 per hour, and that was just silly

162

business. So I had to do a little research, start weighing the ratio between hourly charge and aesthetic allure, not to mention I was a bit picky about grammar and punctuation, so the opening paragraph had to have some zest. What should have taken only a few minutes led me deep into another tweak; always another tweak, a tangent, something demanding perfection, something to pull me into the vortex of my misfiring synapses.

When I finally settled on a few options, I began calling and checking for availability. Whoever could come over right away was the winner. Escorts on Craigslist weren't what you might call high-class call girls, and that meant they were usually rather callous. This was a job for them, not exactly a job they had dreamed about, and they dealt with all types of shitty customers on a regular basis. Every time my doorbell rang, without fail, my heart jumped.

They were typically surprised when I answered the door. Usually, those women had to cater to men of despair. That's not to say that I, a tweaked out horn-ball, was a great catch, but being young and relatively handsome, I was different from their typical clientele. What began as a courteous introduction quickly leveled out as they entered my apartment and saw the porn I always had queued up on my computer screen. I enjoyed playing with prostitutes and watching porn at the same time.

Then came the money exchange. I always had the money counted out and lying on the nightstand so as to remove the need for awkward pauses or fumbling through my wallet. One time, with a particularly clever little minx, I was asked to sit tight while she ran downstairs, gave the money to her pimp, then assured me she would be right back. As I quickly learned, many a scam was ripe in the escort business, and the lovely young lady never came back; she also failed to answer my subsequent 37 phone calls. The standard procedure was for the girl to call her handler, confirm the money had been received, and to start the clock. Ready, set, go.

From there, a few different scenarios were possible depending on the girl. One, I could fuck her brains out for a while, take a five-minute break, then continue fucking until she asked for a time check, at which point I knew she no longer desired my company. It is important to note that my phallic ferocity on meth was ridiculous. Most escorts were used to men who were nervous and came quickly, so when I started jackhammering, some were not appreciative of me abusing their money-maker. Scenario two was me gauging the level of comfort with said lady and, while taking a five-minute break from sex, pulling out my meth pipe and taking a couple hits on the off chance she, too, would like to engage. This was a crucial moment in the evening, for the look in their eyes would tell me everything I needed to know. Some escorts didn't like their job and didn't much like men. Other escorts were just professionals. But sometimes, if I was lucky, I ran into a girl who loved cock and liked to party. Some did, some didn't; the ones who did stuck around. That was when the real fun began.

I was sitting on a rolling chair in front of my computer. I took out my pipe from the desk drawer and looked over at the woman on my bed. She was sitting up against the headboard, smiling at me. Her hair was bushy and curly, and she wore it wild. She said she was half black and half German, and her features leaned toward her African roots. We were both naked and still a bit sweaty from the first round of sex.

"Do you mind if I smoke?" I asked with my eyebrows raised in anticipation.

"Go for it. What is it?"

I grinned as I began to hold a flame under the glass bowl.

"Crystal. You want some?"

"Sure. Is that why you can fuck me like a wild man?"

I laughed a bit, then started drawing in the smoke until my lungs were full. I held it, smiled at her, then crawled over on the bed and kissed her while exhaling into her mouth.

"It probably doesn't hurt," I said as she held in the smoke.

We smoked for a while and talked. Strangers sharing drugs. Naked. "Let me call my service and tell them I'm done here."

"Okay. You want to stay for while?"

"Yeah. That's cool."

She took a hit from the pipe then called her agency from her phone.

"Hey. Yeah it's me. I'm just leavin' now. Yeah, it's all good. Listen, I'm going to call it for the night. Yeah, I'm pretty tired, so I'll call you tomorrow when I'm ready to clock in."

And with that, we began the evening. After we smoked plenty of crystal, I started looking through porn clips and asked her if we could play along. Everything they did on the screen, we would imitate.

I didn't know which was louder: the porn playing on my computer or the escort on top of me. We were sitting on the edge of the bed, facing the screen, and she was doing a reverse cowgirl on me. We'd been going at it for almost an hour, and both of us were drenched in sweat. My cock felt raw, and my pubic area was starting to chafe. She stopped suddenly, dismounted, and put her hands on her hips.

"Daaaamn motherfucker. I need a break."

She walked over to the kitchen, turned on the tap, put her mouth underneath, and started drinking ferociously. I laughed as I looked on with pride. When she finished, she stood in my kitchen fanning her face with one hand. I picked up the pipe and started to smoke as porn was still playing on the computer.

"How the hell are you single? I'm mean, come on. You're fine, and you're fun as hell, and I ain't ever been fucked like this before. You gotta have a girlfriend somewhere?"

"No girlfriend."

"Then you must be married."

"No wife."

"Then you're taking me out to dinner tomorrow cause I wanna do more of this," she said while swirling her hand around in my direction. I laughed and took another hit.

"Sure. We can do more of this," I said, but I knew I would never call her again.

The wall was halfway done. I had deep vats of space that needed to be filled with dirt—and I had just the source. Back down into the cave I went. Now I was really cooking with gas. I broke up large piles of dirt, filled my buckets, and sent those fuckers flying out the entrance. I didn't crawl out anymore; I slid out in style and popped up from my knees like a division-one wrestler. Buckets full of dirt used to be heavy; now I could hold them out and up at any angle and not flinch a muscle. The crawlspace that became a hole, that grew into a cave, was now a full-blown dungeon. The space was vast, and I needed to start thinking about next steps—water, power, waste, spacing . . . and what about shoring up the footings somehow?

Up to that point, I had only skimmed the surface of the most basic principles of construction. Having researched retaining walls, I understood the need for footings, slope, and reinforcement, but

166

now, I faced a whole new beast. Now that I had built a structure, how would I install functioning systems? Naturally, George always had plenty of ideas, and I tried to follow along.

Yesenia and the kids all left the house by 8:15 in the morning, which was around the same time George started moving around in the kitchen. Yesenia usually made breakfast, and extras were always left for George and me. I made my way up to the house, either having been up all night in the cave, or just arriving from my apartment, and I managed to steal a little time with the man I'd come to rely on for guidance.

The kitchen and living room were located on the second story, and the view was breathtaking. Everything faced water, and the sun hadn't yet found an angle directly into the house. George and I sat in the living room and shared stories while sharing a pipe.

Those were the moments I cherished, and those were the moments that infected my thoughts ten years down the road. We talked, sometimes for an hour or two, about everything from philosophy to water pumps, and in those moments, I felt connected, loved, and willing to dig ten more holes if it meant having the respect of that man.

darkness and the hollow, part 2

If you have never felt the seduction of rhythm, the echoing boom of bass coursing through your bones, then you have not lived, my friend. There is no control, no effort, no thought; there only is. I opened my eyes and saw the flashing silhouette of my beautiful Veronica in front of me. Between the flashes of the strobe light, moments of eternity were branded on my soul.

It was midnight, and the club was at full capacity. We boogied in the middle of the crowded dance floor, shoulder to shoulder with the horde of movement. Above us, locked in adult-size birdcages, nearly naked young women danced with seductive grace. Do cobras all move in unison to the melody of the charmer's flute, or does it merely appear that way when you're lost in their trance?

The space was dark and filled with hundreds of people. Brightly colored laser beams cut through the crowd, adding wild punctuation to the crescendo of a unified pulse. Boooooooooom . . . Like thunder across the land, creatures could not help but be consumed by the sound. I was sweating profusely without the slightest hint of embarrassment. Veronica shuffled in neat little steps; her hips moved like a serpent through high grass. We danced with complete abandon. We danced for the gods.

A DJ controlled the energy from her stage, an elevated vantage point above the fray. House music offered a quick rhythm, one I could use to hide a few missed beats and glide back into synchronicity without fuss. Veronica and I had dropped ecstasy a couple hours earlier. Illicit chemicals had fully taken over serotonin output. The dam had been broken, and all that remained was the flood of endorphins.

I had never felt bass in my bones like that. The pulse carried through every cell in my body and adjusted the vibrations to match a collective frequency in an unknown dimension. It wasn't me dancing anymore; there was something larger guiding me, guiding us, guiding the entire cosmos. The dance floor was one pulse, one rhythm, and we were a congregation of cave dwellers paying homage to the coming harvest.

We were dancing close enough for Veronica to grab the front of my shirt and pull me to her. Our hips slid toward each other, and our eyes locked deep into each other's souls. She moved with perfect precision and used fine points of contact to send a current through my body every time we touched. Her breasts barely grazing me or a lock of hair falling across my face when she turned away was just enough to make me want to chase her to the end of the world. When a light cut across her face, I could see the corners of her lips creased up with intoxicating allure.

I closed my eyes and let the music take over again. Kissing felt like standing under a waterfall. Touching her hips was pure, uncut lust. This must be the Garden of Eden without the burden of sin, I thought. Sometimes my eyes saw everything in slow motion, sometimes my hearing cut out completely, but the bass never failed me. I was completely lost in the moment; right there, right then, dancing with my lover in a crease of time.

Over Veronica's shoulder, somewhat out of focus, I spotted George. He danced with the grace of a drunken monkey, but his girlfriend, Yesenia, didn't seem to mind. They both smiled in my direction and carried on.

Veronica put her hand on the back of my head and pulled my ear to her lips.

"Can we go get some water?" she shouted over the music.

I took her hand securely in mine and cleared a path through the crowd. She squeezed tightly as we slowly made our way through the mob. A feeling of satisfaction washed over me. I felt valiant when my baby held on to me tightly as I led her through danger. I'll never leave her, I thought to myself; I'll never let her down.

The bar was packed, but we managed to squeeze in and order. We both finished the bottles of water in one effort, then added a shot of whiskey at the end for good measure.

"Do you mind if I go for a cigarette?" I asked.

"I'll go with you. It's boiling in here."

A bouncer opened the door and allowed us to escape the bedlam. A vacuum of senses filtered us from one world to the next. Decibels dropped threefold. Crisp air washed over my face and stung my chest. My shirt was soaked through. The smell of sweat was replaced by the smell of downtown San Diego—smog and saltwater. Around the side of the building was a line of partygoers all waiting impatiently to get into the packed club. Girls were done up in their best cocktail dresses, and guys scanned the line with predatory eyes.

Along the sidewalk, Veronica and I spotted a couple familiar faces out for a smoke, so we made our way over. The ecstasy was strong that night. Every time I took a drag of my cigarette, I felt a wave of endorphins douse my brain and cascade down my spine, similar to having your back to the ocean and allowing the waves to surprise you. I couldn't help but smile at everything. My eyelids were lowered to a comfortable half-mast, and a sheen of glass seemed set in front of me. Everything bright had a halo or a reflection.

I wasn't sure what I was laughing at, but my friend was laughing with me. Veronica turned away from her conversation and flashed a playful smile. Her hand was on my shoulder, and she joined in the silliness. Nobody knew what the joke was, but I was in tears. I grabbed Veronica by the waist and pulled her close. She waited for a response and looked at me with a smile.

"I don't know. It's just so good," I said through fading chuckles.

"What's so good?" she asked with a laugh.

"This. You. Us. All of it." I squeezed my hand a bit over her hip bone and kissed her repeatedly with little pecks while looking into her eyes.

Veronica laughed and held my face in both her palms.

"I love you, you silly man."

"I love you, too, babe."

"You mind staying for another cigarette?" I asked. "I want to give my shirt a chance to dry out some more."

"Of course."

Veronica was chatting with a friend, and I was standing back, looking at the crowd in front of the club. Not bad, I thought to myself. Not bad at all. I had finally made it. At 26 years old, I had reached a point where I could really start making moves. I was rich and young and unstoppable. Life didn't get better than that.

"You mind if I bum a smoke, bro?" Someone politely asked me, drawing my focus back from my reverie.

High as I was on ecstasy, he could have asked me for a hundred dollars, and I probably would have given it to him.

"Sure, man."

I flipped my pack of smokes open and scooted one out with my thumb. I already knew what he was going to ask next, so before he could get the first word out, I had my lighter fired up, shielding it from the wind with my cupped hand.

I felt comfortable with him right away because he placed both hands over mine to steady the flame. Then, he gave a courtesy tap to signal his gratitude when his cigarette had caught fire, as is customary among cultures with longer standing heritages. In America, if someone asks for a light, you simply hand over your lighter. In many other countries, when someone asks for fire, you offer a ready flame; hence, a moment is created, an experience transpires, and two people share a gift, however seemingly trivial.

With his cigarette lit, the stranger took a step back, and we began riffing on the usual topics. The man was about my age, mid-twenties, with a modern sense of style and a posture that indicated confidence. A neat pencil-line beard etched his jaw, and gold accessories decorated his neck, ear, and wrist. He was a typical Middle Eastern guy dressed for the clubs, and we shot the shit like guys do.

It was his eyes that should have raised an alarm inside me, but what's the use of sounding an alarm if no one is around to hear it? I was off floating in the clouds, wading in a lake under a waterfall of dopamine, so I had no reference point from which to identify danger. His eyes focused on me with the precision of a stalking lion—deep, brown eyes as if they were made from the mantle of the earth itself. My attention was scattered, and my eyes shifted between focal points, most of the time focusing on nothing at all. I saw Veronica laughing, talking with a friend, lost in conversation, and I was moved by the innocence of the moment.

I didn't see it. I didn't even feel it. I woke up and somebody was shaking my arm trying to drag me up from the concrete. My face was wet.

173

"Anto! Anto! Get up. Oh my God. Anto!" Veronica shouted.

Floating. Blurry picture. Cold concrete. A cigarette abandoned in front me, still smoking. Two Veronicas in front of me, and both had a glow around them. A streetlight behind her forced me to squint. Single vision returned, but now I could see one of my eye's was closing up fast.

I was helped to my feet by a few friends. I looked around and saw a crowd of people staring at me, shock and pity on every face. The taste of blood finally registered a warning in my sputtering brain. I touched my hand to my cheek, then looked at the residue. Problem. I looked down at my shirt to see dark crimson droplets stained all over. My light, yellow button-up shirt made the perfect canvas against the brute color of blood. As I looked closer, I saw more blood dripping onto my shirt with increasing determination.

"Anto. What did you do? Why did he hit you?" Veronica was panicked and speaking at twice her normal speed.

"I don't know. Who hit me? What happened?" I responded in confusion.

"That guy hit you and took off. The guy you were smoking with."

I stared blankly at Veronica and offered no response.

"How bad is it?" I asked.

Four people leaned their heads forward, squinted their eyes, and left their mouths slightly ajar while assessing the damage.

"You'll probably need stitches," someone said, "but I think you'll be fine."

The group continued to stare at my eye like children glued to Saturday-morning cartoons.

"Can you go get George, babe?" I asked.

Veronica hustled back into the club, and I leaned against the wall with a hand to my eye. I pulled out another cigarette. A few guys asked what had happened, but I couldn't offer any explanation. One minute I was smoking a cigarette and shooting the breeze, and the next thing I knew I was waking up on the sidewalk. Deep, slow drags of tobacco filled my lungs as I stared down at the concrete, thinking about much more than why someone would have punched me. Drops of blood entered my line of sight as they fell from my busted eye down to the concrete. It reminded me of being a child, when my friends and I would drop small objects off a bridge and watch them fall forever below us until the smallest ripple in the water would indicate that forever had ended.

George came out of the club with purpose. Anger held his countenance in a stern scowl. I had never seen that look on him before, but something inside of me lit up. I could see he cared. Not only did he care, but he was looking to inflict damage on the villain who had hurt his loyal protégé; what a feeling. I had been in plenty of fights, and I'd had the opportunity to experience the feeling of loyal allies, but this was different because it pulled on the most tender of heartstrings of a lonely child looking for a loving father. The feeling of having someone I looked up to show himself willing to fight for me—that was an entirely different sense of belonging. When the alpha wolf shows his teeth in your support, that is a feeling of indescribable affinity.

George put his hand on my shoulder and looked at my wounded eye.

"You'll be okay. I'll stitch you up," he said calmly.

He stood erect and inspected the crowd.

"Anyone see where the guy went?" George asked in a steely tone.

"He took off running down Broadway," someone shouted out.

175

Yesenia pulled up to the curb, and George helped me into the car. Veronica sat with me in the backseat, her hand resting on my thigh and head on my shoulder. We drove around downtown for five minutes, hoping to spot the assailant, but I was in no mood to continue. I looked out the window and let the night take me away. The lights of downtown became blurs in the background as my mind faded into strange thoughts. I closed my eyes and drifted away.

When I opened my eyes again, Veronica was gently nudging me to tell me we were back at George's house. She helped me out of the car, and I stumbled in. Yesenia pointed me to a chair, and I flopped down, exhausted. George hustled up the stairs to his bedroom and walked back down quickly with a black shaving kit. He pulled a chair behind me and placed the satchel on the coffee table.

"Lean your head back, close your eye, and keep it closed until I tell you," he instructed.

Saline solution, gauze pads, Q-tips, and crazy glue; that was what I saw next to me on the coffee table before tilting my head back. George was gentle when cleaning the wound, but didn't hesitate to get into painful crevices. After a thorough scrub, he took a Q-tip and cut it to leave only the cotton swab with about half an inch of plastic, then placed it directly over my split eyebrow. With his pointer finger, George pressed the Q-tip into my laceration, then pinched the wound closed with thumb and middle finger. The wound now securely closed and held together, George used his other hand to apply drops of crazy glue in the creases between Q-tip and fresh skin. Once finished, we held the pose for another five minutes, allowing the glue to set.

I never told him how much that meant to me, but I was sure he could feel it. It's hard to hide that kind of glow when you feel loved, even if you try your best to act tough. He cared for me and put me back together. I had been looking for someone to put me back together my entire life.

darkness and the hollow, part 3

Some nights I slept; some nights, I didn't. Some nights I spent working in the cave, and some nights I was researching various aspects of construction online: concrete mixtures, electrical panels, soldering, ABS piping, grouting, waterproofing, wind tunnel theory, drainage, and on and on until my brain revolted, and my eyes no longer held focus.

Other nights I spent with her, my lovely Veronica, and I woke up with the sweet smell of my lover's hair next to me on the pillow. We made love, good love, lots of love. We spent time talking in bed about scars over our hearts—she with her ex-husband, and I with my estranged father.

I woke up one morning and lay awake staring at the oscillating fan that sat atop an IKEA faux beechwood dresser in my studio apartment. I liked to reach over in the morning, pull my lover close to me, and hold one of her breasts gently in my palm. I raised one arm and moved it toward Veronica, but my aim must have been off because instead of wrapping myself around her, I ended up bumping the back of her ribcage with my hand. It was strange—I could see what was happening in front of me, but my hand didn't register any sensation of the events. I stared at my hand while opening and closing a fist and realized I couldn't feel anything. Same thing with the other hand.

Panic struck and my heartbeat went through the roof. I sat up

177

and leaned against the headboard, with my hands on my lap, and stared. Veronica began to rustle next to me, but I just kept staring at my hands and watched them in disbelief. They moved, but I didn't feel them move. Was I dreaming? What the hell was going on?

"What's wrong baby?" Veronica asked as she turned to face me, her head barely peeking out from under the blanket.

"I can't feel my hands. They're numb. Totally numb."

One of her delicate hands emerged from underneath the blanket and held the strange cadaver of mine, caressing, massaging, and trying to bring it back to life. I was watching but not believing, I was there, but a million miles away. Was this my penance? Was this what I got for being a taker all those years and never giving anything in return? I had heard of countries where they chop off your hand for stealing, and I had been stealing, in one form or another, for as long as I could remember.

A foreign sensation started to tickle at the very tips of my fingers. Then I felt a few tingles on my palms, and within a few seconds, my entire hand was alive like a colony of ants on its morning commute. I tried pumping both hands in fists back and forth until full circulation returned. Ten minutes after I awoke, full feeling finally returned.

"Maybe you should go to the doctor," Veronica admonished.

"Yeah. Maybe."

The fear faded away as Veronica and I rested lazily in bed and did what lovers do: lie half awake and chat in a soft whisper about nothing all that important until one of us gently stroked a hand, or cracked a devious smile, or nuzzled in close and began the day as all days should.

When we finished, I offered her the restroom first because I knew my operation would take longer. I hid it cleverly, combining the morning bowel movement and a shower, but in reality, I was using the routine as cover to get high. My studio apartment was small, so this had to be well thought out. I cracked a couple jokes about stomach grumblings and advised her to make sure she had everything she needed from the bathroom because I was going to need some time. Naturally, I'd hidden a pipe in the bathroom, bowl preloaded and melted, underneath the sink behind all the cleaning supplies. Good thing most modern bathrooms had an exhaust fan, otherwise drug addicts of the smoking variety would be in a serious bind. The next problem with which to concern myself was sound. The repeated sound of a lighter flicking would certainly draw questions, so in order to muffle the noise, I turned on the shower right away for dampening. Other options included running the sink, flushing the toilet, or coughing when all else failed. Get high, take a shit, take a shower, and come out feeling like a million bucks—such was my routine. I kissed Veronica on the cheek and squeezed her butt a little before we left for the day.

Mornings like that were spectacular. It was not just the impeccable San Diego weather that got me; I had purpose, deep committed purpose. I was in a festive mood, so I went to my favorite store in the world.

There was no place I loved more than Home Depot, and I felt I was a grizzled, blue-collar working man when I was in there with the morning contractor crew. The doctor could wait. Maybe the numbing feeling in my hands was just a fluke and would pass in a few days. I smoked a little more meth on the road to get nice and geeked out, then threw in a hefty wad of chewing tobacco to give me something to clench on without giving away my tweak.

When I was on a building tweak, Home Depot was a fairytale come true. It was Nirvana, seventy-two virgins, and the chocolate factory all rolled into one. Seven thirty in the morning and the parking lot was full. As I walked toward the giant warehouse entrance, I surveyed and absorbed. Those were my people, I told myself, the ones who had chosen, or had been chosen, for a life of grit and callouses.

Eyes were all red at that hour, and kept at a difficult half-mast in remembrance of last night's twelve pack. Deeply carved crow's feet painted the corners of eyes like a topographical map of the Amazon; years of squinting in the sun doing to a face what centuries of wind and rain do to a canyon. And then there were the sounds. The Mexicans were always the loudest, fairly joyous even at this hour, but the white guys were not so resilient. Unable to keep an open heart and be grateful for the opportunity for such basics as work and food, their disposition was rather nasty that early in the morning.

Laborers held coffee cups in one hand, nothing above 7-Eleven or am/pm, and pushed a rackety orange cart with the other. Foremen held paper or torn cardboard, sometimes even a scrap piece of lumber, and stared intently at their list of supplies, mumbling lightly to themselves as they mentally navigated the job site.

Entering the gargantuan facility always put a smile on my face; the smell alone was enough to light up my endorphin sensors. Fresh cut wood, industrial solvents, cement dust, and propane exhaust mixed together produced a noxious pungency. Toxic as it may have been, it still reeked of a truth that I had not found in any other work environment across my journeys.

Mornings were busy at the Depot, so I used them to employ the many schemes inherent in the mind of any meth user. The way I figured it, there was no sense in paying for all the supplies I needed, so why not combine a little ingenuity with the order of operations. That way, I could buy, sneak, steal, and flat out ransack if I had to. Buy big and stuff the seams with small stolen goods was essentially my motto, so I purchased a couple of rolls of R-19 insulation and in the middle, I stuffed 400-watt high pressure sodium bulbs. I spotted a used, but good quality, pair of Klein cable cutters sitting out near the wire racks, so I casually slid them into my back pocket, even leaving the red handles exposed, as they went well with the measuring tape already hanging from my belt. Contractors forgot tools in their pockets all the time; why would anyone assume the wire cutters weren't mine to begin with?

I walked the aisles, pushing my cart and spitting tobacco juice in secret cubbies. A box of screws went into the cart, and a handful of micro-tubing quick connectors went into my pocket. I spotted multiple articles that would be added to my list of materials to steal. I planned to come back at night, just before closing time as the employees were winding down. I would bring a whole cart of steer manure up to the register, knowing they would only count and not lift, thereby missing the expensive sheet of EDPM rubber hidden underneath. I ended that morning's trip by spending an hour tweaking out in the tool section, drooling over Hilti and Bosch, wondering if I should spend the coin on quality tools or just get another bag of meth. Okee dokee. Over two hours spent at Home Depot and I had to pull myself out of there; otherwise, I could have gone through lunch trying to figure out a million more details of the cave. Tweak, tweak, tweak; another few hits in the car before I pulled out of the parking lot, just because.

Time is not a true phenomenon; rather, it is the best method we have for explaining the space between. Now that I had lost all touch with a manufactured concept, I wondered whether I was actually closer to grand cosmic truth during my addiction than in all my journeys prior. I was completely consumed by the project, and all other points of reference were trivial.

The wall was growing. It began near the corner of the yard and came down across the slope on a nice easy curve. In the middle of the yard, we split the wall into three sections in order to avoid building permits. One wall above five foot required bureaucratic approval, but three walls just under that height allowed us to avoid inspection.

My hands were becoming a real problem. Every morning when I woke up, assuming I hadn't stayed up all night in the cave, my hands were numb and pallid. I had been trying to avoid the subject for weeks, but eventually I gave in and went to a local clinic. That was a strange world, a world I left long ago, and when I entered, I was reminded of my isolation.

From the waiting room to the receptionist and the magazines on the table, everything was from a galaxy alien to me now. I thought in terms of cubic yards of aggregate and quarter ounces of crystal, and my clock was set to phases of the project. The waiting room was full of people staring at a television mounted in the corner, and their unified movements as I walked through the door seized me with fright.

After I explained my situation to the doctor—my demanding physical work minus the meth addiction—she suggested the numbing sensation was the result of carrying all those heavy buckets and cocking my wrists in on themselves in order to compensate for the weight. She advised me to get some industrial wrist supports to wear while I worked. At night, she instructed, I should try placing my hands on pillows while lying on my back so the wrists would be supported and not sag down, thus cutting off the damaged arteries. She also said it would be a good idea to try cutting back on the intensity of my work. I nodded and thanked her for her time.

On a beautiful day, I stood in the sun and worked on PVC lines around the perimeter of the yard. George was wandering around, working on his own things, while I squatted down and dealt with a pain in the ass T-split that just didn't want to seal and leaked every time I turned on the water. The wind blew a welcomed breeze and stopped me for a moment, just enough to look up and take a pause. I'd long ago forgotten how beautiful it was up there. Halfway up Soledad Mountain, we were afforded a stunning view of San Diego, and the day was clear and majestic.

George came over and stood near me as we both looked off into the picturesque distance.

"Not bad, eh?" he said to me.

I offered a brief grunt and continued looking off.

"What's going on with this sprinkler line?" he asked.

"Tough angle. Can't get a good seal on it," I replied.

"You should score it first, nice and rough with your razor knife, so the glue has more bite to bond to."

As George continued talking about PVC glue, my cell phone rang and interrupted his diatribe. I recognized the number. It was Katie, one of my few remaining friends who had refused to let go, who continued to call me regardless of my attempts at isolation. Though she sensed there was something wrong, her selfless heart allowed her to continue to care about me without expecting anything in return.

"Hey, Katie. What's going on?"

"Anto," she said, then choked and paused. The unmistakable pulse of fear echoed through the void and a swell of panic hit my heart. She tried to get a word out but fell back to a soft whimper. I could feel the tears streaming down her face as if she were hugging me and crying on my shoulder. Silence. Dread.

"Katie, what's wrong?"

She cried and cried, and my heart was pounding. My first thought was self-absorbed. She must have figured out I was a dope fiend. She knew. She knew like my mother knew when she figured out I was lying to her as a child and now wanted a confession from me. Paranoia. Massive psychosis. Oh fuck.

darkness and the hollow, part 4

"Katie, what's going on?"

"Anto, he's dead. Ryan's dead. He's fucking dead."

"What? What are you talking about?"

"He fucking hung himself, Anto. He's been really down, and Christie broke up with him again, and everyone's saying he's been using meth and heroin and all kinds of shit. He was supposed to do a job for Stefan's parents but didn't show and didn't pick up his phone, so Stefan went to his apartment after a few days and found his body. He fucking found him hanging, blue, and all kinds of fucked up shit. "

Between her tears, there was anger now as she searched for some kind of understanding. I offered nothing but jaw-dropping silence; silence and a sea of shame, for I knew deep in my heart I had contributed to the merchants of death who eventually came back for Ryan.

It was sometime in the summer before 9/11, and I was going through another phase in which I sold cocaine. We were at a house party one night when Ryan came up to me with that mischievous smile of his and bright, piercing blue eyes the color of shallow Adriatic water along the shoreline of a remote island. He always had a playful sense about him, and even more so around me, especially when he teased and joked about what girl I was with at the time. I was twice his size, but Ryan always had a way of loosening me up and getting me to drop the act even if only for a few moments. That night, he came up to me with a bit of a swagger and started with his best tough-guy delivery.

"Yo, Toe . . . Let me get some coke dude."

I instantly burst out laughing. Ryan was known as the class clown, the funny guy, the laid-back beer drinker, but certainly not a tough guy. That night, he purposely moved with a little bounce in his step to add a few laughs, knowing such conversations were not standard for a guy like him. I was doubled over, holding my stomach, about to piss my pants from laughter. Ryan stood in front of me chuckling, trying to stay in character, half embarrassed, half enjoying the silliness, all the while egging me on.

"Dude, it's not funny. I'm serious," he said with chuckles between his words.

I looked up at his face and could not control myself. I'd gone from laughing to crying to hyperventilating. When I finally caught a breath, I straightened myself out and looked at him.

"That's some funny shit dude. Fuck no, you can't have any coke. You don't do that shit bro, and there's no reason to start now. You don't even like smoking weed; why the fuck would you want to do blow?" I almost raised my voice to him.

"I'm serious man. I want to try it. Me and Adam are going halves on it. You guys do that shit all the time, and I want to try it."

"No, dude. There's nothing to it. It's fun for a little bit, when you're really drunk and you want to get back to level, but then it gets creepy real fast 'cause you always end up doing too much, then you get all weird, and then you're up all night and you can't go to sleep and the sun comes up and your heart's racing and it's the worst feeling in the world when you watch the fucking sun come up on coke."

"So why do you do it?"

"I don't know man. Picked up another bad habit I guess. I do it for a couple months then get all paranoid and flush a bag down the toilet. But then some time goes by, I forget how awful it feels and I see someone at a party doing lines, and I just say fuck it and start back up again."

"That sounds pretty retarded."

"Yeah man, it is. So that's why you don't need to do it."

"Okay. I get it, but I still want to try it. How much do I get for twenty bucks?"

"Dude. Seriously. No."

"Toe. Dude. Come on man. I just want to try it. You sell it to everyone else, and if you don't sell me some, then I'll just find it somewhere else. So come on man. Don't be a dick."

And with that came a response from me that signified so much about my life:

"Fuck it."

Yes, fuck it. Fuck it, I don't care. Fuck it, do what you want. Fuck it, I'm done. Fuck it, it's out of my control. Fuck it, you can't hurt me. Fuck it, I'll leave. Fuck it, I don't love you anymore. Fuck it, it's not my responsibility. Fuck it all, I wash my hands and leave you to face the hollow on your own.

I sold him his first bag of cocaine and didn't think about it again until that day, five years later, while I was working on my grand project on Soledad Mountain. I was already a full-blown meth addict, listening to one of my few remaining friends who refused to let me push her away, as she told me that sweet and loving Ryan had faced such internal torment over the years that he became a junkie. And this morning, they found him hanging from a noose.

The initial blow shook my world, but as it settled, there came a wave from far beyond the horizon, and within a few breaths, Katie's voice faded out, and I was under water. Ryan was dead. I was a junkie. How could I face any of this news without addressing the fact that I was on a trajectory toward the same outcome? I was a wasted life, a floating corpse, and I had now contributed to the death of someone I should have protected.

"Anto. Anto? Are you there? Hello?"

Light reappeared and sound became less muffled as I came back into focus, like a passenger on a train emerging from a tunnel.

"Hi. Sorry, Katie. I'm here."

"So the funeral will be this weekend. I'll let you know when I get the details."

"Okay."

"You're going, right?"

"I don't know, Katie. I'll see."

"Dude, Anto. Seriously. I know you've been M.I.A. and shit, but you've got to make it to the funeral. It's fucking Ry Guy, dude."
"Okay, Katie. Let me know when you hear more."

I knew before I hung up the phone. I'd known my entire life. I was a coward, and when it came down to it, I would avoid, lie, or manipulate rather than face the truth. There was no way I'd be going to that funeral.

George looked at me dispassionately.

"What happened?"

"My friend killed himself."

"How'd he do it?"

"Hanging."

"Oh, he was just looking for attention."

George chuckled after delivering the coldest words I had ever heard. I looked at him and tried to hide the wound.

"Oh, it's no big deal. I'm just really callous about death. I mean, come on, it's just better to let it roll off," George added, mockingly.

I looked away so I wouldn't start crying. That was George's moment—his defining moment. I was hurt and scared and facing the mounting avalanche of my crumbling life, and he could have done something. I needed something, anything, a word, a hug, a look of empathy, a hand on my shoulder, something to let me know that I wasn't alone. Instead, all he gave me was a contrived distance, a hollow, a pompous man putting on what he considered to be the correct performance of someone who did not fear death. But we all fear the end, and George's act was no better than the rest of ours. If ever you are looking for those who are truly callous toward death, look for those who remain silent. The rest are liars.

George kept rambling on about god knows what, and soon he was on to a tangential story about himself and his covert espionage missions. Yes, espionage. George claimed to have worked for an unnamed branch of the government and said he still kept in touch with the boys over at Lantern 6, as he referred to it.

There was something I'd known all along, but I hadn't wanted to admit. Something deep within me knew, and at that very moment, it was all over. George was a liar and a cheat and our whole thing was falling apart. But the challenge was not in identifying the truth; every human being has a built-in compass that points true north. The challenge was in knowing the truth and accepting it with grace and humility. I didn't. I fought. I fought and I fought with all my energy to try and force the outcome toward my desire. But truth does not give us what we want; only what we need.

The truth was I had known George to be a degenerate conman for quite some time; I just wouldn't accept it. From the very beginning, I started catching obscene moments of delusion, but each time I would excuse it for the sake of my desperate heart. Not him. I needed someone to be my redeemer, and I couldn't face collapse in that situation.

In the beginning, before I tried meth with George for the first time, when I was still a freshly retired pot trafficker, I used to carry around a pocket-sized notebook everywhere I went. Throughout my tenure as a dealer, the book was not only a fluid to-do list, it was my ledger of choice for all outstanding debts. Anything I considered important would go into that book, and I was often combing through to see which checkbox I could tackle next. When George was first recruiting me, he would spend hours talking about his wild past and his immense professional network. This was important in the art of swindle because one must constantly reconfirm affinity with the mark by relating stories of similar taste. You deal drugs? I dealt drugs when I was younger, too, then I graduated to larger venues. That was the next part, always pointing toward the grand tomorrow. George would talk about how much money he had tied up in investment A, the FTSE stock exchange; investment B, import/export business with a partner who lived abroad; investment C, a multitude of properties which were all his from San Diego to Los Angeles to the high desert of Apple Valley; plus a myriad of other lucrative, albeit non-confirmable, wealth. All this was designed to get the mark salivating. It worked. I wanted in.

Being the studious young apprentice that I was, I would jot down business ideas in my notebook—ideas George had thrown out as easy, no problem, cash-cows—and follow up in the weeks to come to see when I could begin my franchise as drug dealer gone legit. For one reason or another, the ideas never panned out. The partner was tied up in another venture he had with yet another unnamed black-market delegate, or the season wasn't right, or we had to wait until the next large injection of cash from the mortgage company so we could buy into the big boys' room, which demanded half a million at least. One day I sat down in George's office and pulled out my notebook, wanting to review some of the pending business ideas he had mentioned, and George was not pleased.

"Oh come on! Not today with that shit," he chided me, and his look was one of annoyance.

"It'll be ready when it's ready," he assured me. The palaver was the first give away. The stall was the second.

One day we were driving, and I asked George about the almond business his friend was part of and supposedly would have no problem taking my cash as a silent investor.

"Any word from your friend with the nuts?"

George tensed his eyebrows and let out a perturbed sigh.

"Let's just give him a call now," he suggested with lassitude and guile in his tone.

George took out his cell phone, pressed some buttons, and put it to his ear.

"Hey, Benny, it's George."

I was driving, and George was sitting shotgun with his right hand holding the phone to his right ear.

"Ha. Yeah, I know what you mean. Hey listen, sorry to hound you on this, but I got the kid with me here, and he's all puffy about the buy-in and wants to know when you guys will be ready for him."

George chuckled the way an adult reacts to a child.

"Yeah. You remember I told you about Anto? He's new to our thing and eager to start playing. I told him to sit tight, but you know how these young hotshots can be."

George laughed again, allowing me the courtesy of looking over at me this time to really soak it in.

"Yeah, so listen. Maybe you guys can . . ."

Suddenly the phone rang. The phone that George had to his ear and was talking and laughing into began to ring with the volume and audacity of a phone going off during the Lord's Prayer in a Catholic church. I turned my entire head to fixate on George's face and watched the instant rise of a new color, like a chameleon settling on a new branch. I beamed at his face and watched as the color went from pale flesh to a shade belonging to aging alcoholics and white men caught in a lie. Somewhere between pink and red is a shade reserved for the devil, and only in his natural environment does the sun shine through the hologram. Once hidden, veins on George's nose and cheeks illuminated their blue-green trails, and the pores opened up as large as craters. Everything was ugly and exposed and forced to stand naked in the light for a moment.

George shifted his head a few degrees and peered at me from the corner of his eye. Our eyes met for a split second before he pulled back into character and all the colors instantly shifted back into form. He pressed a button on his phone and put it back up to his ear.

"Hey, Benny. Sorry, we must have gotten cut off. So, like I was saying . . ."

My attention faded out. I knew what had happened, and I didn't need to hear the rest. But what was I to do? How do you question a false prophet who swears the miracle you have been waiting for your entire life is just around the corner? Easy for the strong to answer, but let them have the same confidence with a broken heart. Oh, my gullible broken heart.

Like I knew that day in the truck, I knew now. George was rambling and most of what he spewed were lies. A friend of mine hanged himself, and George couldn't even muster a little sympathy. I crawled back into the cave and smoked meth by myself.

Steer manure, gypsum salt, garden soil, and me. Now that the wall was complete, and the cave's depth had been excavated to an acceptable level, it was time to finish the aesthetic facade of the cover project. The dirt that had come out of the cave, the dirt that I'd excavated by hand out of a fucking crawlspace—that dirt was not the best base to lay sod over. I needed to buy outside dirt to mix with my dirt so all the dirt could be happy and nice. Motherfucker. I went to Home Depot nearly every day and filled up my truck until the shocks rode low. Then I drove back to the house and took each bag off myself. Bag after bag, I spread the ingredients over the top layer of dirt then manually mixed it with a shovel. Bag after bag, I bought out of my own pocket because I believed I was investing in something. Next, I ordered a pallet of sod and began that tedious process.

It was a Saturday, and the house was busy. Yesenia had the kids that weekend, and she was knee deep in the trenches of house chores. I took a break around noon to go up to the house for lunch. George was in the kitchen watching Yesenia do the dishes.

"Hey Anto. You hungry?" she asked me with a kind smile on her face.

"Starving. Any chance you have anything?"

193

"Oh yeah. I made some enchiladas last night, and they're in the fridge. You just have to warm them up."

"Thank you, Yesenia."

"No problem. I just don't know how you work down there for so long. I mean, I'm exhausted from cleaning the house today, and you guys just never seem to stop or take breaks from whatever you're working on."

George's eyebrows lowered into a look of concentration and a small grin rose.

"Yeah. I'm pretty beat today, too, Anto. How about a little help with the fun bag for us?" George gleamed a big smile at me.

I hated when George asked to smoke my meth. I hated when George didn't pay. I hated when George reminded me of all the time and money I was wasting without so much as a thank you or a little help in return. And now, George was asking to smoke my meth with Yesenia, who, up until that point, I assumed was not aware that George and I were meth addicts. I looked at him with a questioning glare.

"What's a fun bag?" she asked.

"Oh, it's fun," he answered. "You know how when we take ecstasy we go out all night and dance and you have plenty of energy? Well this is the energy part by itself without all the euphoria. It's nice on days like this when you need a little pick-me-up," George rambled on, then turned to me, "So, what do you say Anto? You mind sharing a little with us?"

And with that, he had me. More and more I purposely would not smoke around him because I was tired of not having a symbiotic meth relationship with George or ever receiving any help in the cave from him. But clever old George pulled another great sleight of hand as he evoked not only the gratitude I felt toward Yesenia and all the cooking and laundry she did for me, but also the embarrassment I felt at having my meth secret spoken about openly in front of a hard-working mother of four. I didn't feel I had a choice, and with that, Yesenia went downstairs to check on the boys and made sure they were all involved in an intense series of video games before we all went up to the third-story bedroom, locked the door, and smoked crystal methamphetamine together—one big, happy family.

What do you do with a space left vacant by fill-dirt meant to keep foundational piles from collapsing in on themselves? Many ideas were bounced around until George got tired of me asking questions and decided to point me in the simplest, yet most structurally ridiculous direction. Enter the world of concrete.

Every single speck of concrete, which came in either 50- or 80-pound bags, began its journey in Home Depot. From the aisles where it was stocked, I took each bag and loaded my cart. The process continued from the cart to the bed of my truck, from the truck to a loading spot just outside the crawlspace entrance, and from the outside to the inside of the cave. From that stack, each bag was manually fed into the little concrete mixer I had managed to squeeze through the opening, piece by piece, and assemble to full size only once inside the cave. The next step in the evolution was realizing Home Depot left pallets of ready-mix outside near the loading area, so I could just pull my truck up, load, and then pay inside. Naturally, I eventually abused that privilege and loaded up my truck at night, just before closing, and never bothered to go inside and pay. Tweak, tweak, tweak.

But the idea was not to pour an entire concrete retaining wall inside the cave. The idea was to build a hollow block wall around the perimeter where the sheared earth walls now lay exposed and shore up the pressure enough to get by. The same routine I followed with the bags of concrete was now repeated with cinderblocks. One by one I moved each block from stage to stage until I finally got a large enough stack down in the cave to start building.

Concrete is porous, taking in both moisture and radiant temperature from the surrounding environment. Handling hollow blocks for a living was rough business, not only because they require the tempered forearms of a silverback, but also because of the cracking one has to endure when first adjusting to the wicking action. I hadn't lifted a bucket of dirt in weeks, and now, finally, normal circulation was returning to my mistreated hands. I was afforded the pleasure of full sensation in my hands again only to immediately develop stonemason's hands. In the morning, when I awakened and began the first few movements of the day, the skin on my hands was so dry from constantly handling blocks that it split open and bled as if my hands were held together by a shabby stitch job from a horror story. My sheets were stained with drops of blood constantly.

The long San Diego summer was no more, and now, the short days of winter were a brisk reminder of death. Cold wind slithered by the door of the cave, and my delusions became more pronounced. The concrete mixer offered a soothing white noise as the slush went round and round. I sat on an upside-down bucket, resting for a moment, worrying about the pace of the project and reviewing all that still needed to be accomplished. I still didn't have enough power down there to run the full load of lights that would be required, and I hadn't figured out how I was going to tie into the wastewater line so I could have some sort of drainage. And what about . . . and what about?

I put my face in my hands, pressed firmly on my temples, and rocked back and forth slightly like an Israelite in prayer. A deep sense of impending doom had infected my mind. There was no way the project would ever get done. How long had I been working on it now? Six months? A year? I didn't know anymore. And I was just now starting on the actual structure of the room and not even close to bringing in the equipment needed to grow some weed. Fuck me. I'll never make it. It's impossible. I'll go crazy, or I'll kill myself, or the whole fucking house will come crashing down on my head.

Mutiny was in the air, and George was angry. He came down to the cave one day on a tirade. Turned out all the guys who worked for him decided to leave and start their own mortgage company. George was furious. He paced in circles and blew off steam while I faded out and thought back.

He had told me so many stories that I was now forced to look at every single one and consider it suspect. I remember the time my mother had been in town, a couple months after I'd first met George, and she was going through a tough time at work. My mother had never had issues with her job because she was simply a workhorse, and eventually, her confidence and determination always won out. But my parents were split again, and my mom was living in Southern California because she took a job with a new company. The company was rife with corruption, and the good old boys were having a tough time persuading my mom to get in line with the program. As such, the games and politics became heavy with tactics to force her exit. She mentioned this to George one day when she came to visit me.

"What was the name of the company again?" George asked my mother while we were all sitting in his office. I sat proudly by, waiting for George to offer some superior insight with which to impress my mother.

"Sylgenco. They sell testing instruments to all kinds of industries like laser manufactures and the department of defense," she replied.

"Sylgenco. Sylgenco? Hmmmm. I think I recognize that name from some of my earlier businesses. I used to be in the defense contractor world. Let me give my friend a call and see if he knows anything."

George picked up the phone, pressed some numbers, and gave us both a look of calm assurance.

"Hey, Harry, it's George. How you been?"

He kicked his feet up on the table, sank back into his chair, and put one arm around the back of his head.

"Yeah, so listen. I've got someone here who's involved with some of our old circle I think. The company is called Sylgenco. You remember them? Oh yeah, that's right. Balsenco was the original name, they just changed it and added something in the front but it's probably those same old snakes from before, huh? Yeah, yeah, I know, I'll tell her. Yeah, okay. Hey, thanks for the info, buddy. Okay. We'll talk later. Bye."

George chuckled slightly as he hung up the phone, then looked at my mom and offered a soft gaze.

"Yeah, so you're involved with some guys who run in a bad circle. Former black ops guys who retired then started a company to keep their hands in the stream of tax money pouring out of the DOD. I don't think it's worth your time to stick around. They're just going to squeeze you out if you won't play by their rules."

"Oh. Wow. Yeah, Yeah. I had a feeling something wasn't right with those guys." My mother had a tone, and a certain look in her eyes, when she got worked up by people who fed her bits of paranoia, and my mother always took the bait.

"So it's okay. No big deal. Just protect yourself and get out of there as soon as possible. But in the meantime, as you're looking for a job, have you thought about investing in some property or perhaps another avenue of passive income? We have a lot of options here, you know, for people like you who have sizable savings and are looking to invest instead of letting their money sit stagnant."

I faded back into the cave. George was still ranting about the guys who left his mortgage company. I felt it, but I didn't want to accept it. George was angry because someone called his bluff, and now, I was seeing the panic as the cracks began to burst. But if I was seeing the fragility and the lies now, what did that mean about everything he said before? What did that imply he was doing with my mom? If this, then that, and that means that I'm . . .

Couldn't do it. Not then. The last thing I needed was to ruminate on the truth. All I would allow into my mind was the goal, the end target. I had to finish the project and get those plants growing, just long enough to get my money back, then I could leave and build another cave, or look for another avenue, but there was no way I could swallow all the sunken cost and walk away with my tail between my legs. George's story may have been falling apart, but I was already deeply invested. Between the forty grand in cash I gave him to invest, the thirty I'd spent on the cave project so far, the time I'd poured in, and the leash of addiction to which I had become a slave, there was no way I was walking out now.

darkness and the hollow, part 5

Big Bear California: A serene little mountain town east of Los Angeles known for winter skiing and summer getaways. I knew it for a different reason. When I began using meth, it was never an issue to score dope. I didn't use that much, and one of the guys George was scheming with on a side business was always able to plug me with an eight ball or two when I needed it. Eventually, I graduated to his dealer, a true shadow type, with pupils always the size of pinheads and a downtown apartment full of rave kids, tweakers, and a harem of runaway girls sleeping on the couch. Things were good for a while as I would stop by downtown on my way back from picking up a pallet of retaining wall blocks from the stone yard in Chula Vista. I even bought some freshly stolen tools he sold from the wide network of tweakers he had scouting for him, many of whom worked at Home Depot and similar retailers.

The one thing you can always count on from meth connections is that they will eventually let you down. Sooner or later, usually sooner, the algorithm will spit out the predictable answer. A meth dealer will disappear on you one day, without warning, usually when you are fiending for dope the hardest. One day, my downtown connection was gone. No word, just a cell phone number that wasn't in service anymore. The first time you know you're a junkie is when your connection goes away, and you feel the panic submerge your head.

Fortunately for me, around the time of my first drought, George took me with him to run electrical wiring at his parents newly-built home in Apple Valley. Oh, Apple Valley, shit hole of shit holes, an oasis of white trash in the high desert of inland California, and the birthplace of my mentor, George Meggitt.

I had told George about the difficulties I'd faced scoring dope as of late, so he arranged for us to meet one of his friends from childhood. Enter Donny Stone. Donny was a grizzled looking man, mid-forties, with the skin consistency of a leather knapsack from the gold-rush era. He lived alone in his cabin up in Big Bear and made a living as a contractor/handy-man— the typical modus operandi of a functioning late-stage meth addict.

Donny was the first and only person I had ever met in the meth ecosystem who was kind and seemingly not out to fuck me. Donny hooked us up with a half-ounce, on credit, that first time. Then, I began seeing more and more of him as he became my only stable meth connection. I had driven up the I-15, through the Inland Empire, and up to Big Bear more times than I could count, more times than I cared to remember, on my way to see the dope man. Donny and I became friends, and we would talk for hours, while smoking meth, about everything from construction to what George was like in his early years.

Donny's house was located in a tranquil mountain setting. The road ran along a steep canyon and tucked up to the lip, with a steep hillside dropping below, were the homes of mountain people, those who chose to live away from the hustle and noise of the fast city. The landscape was dominated by giant trees as far as the eye could see: western juniper, Douglas fir, Jeffrey pine, and many others towered over the hillsides that once drew hordes of settlers with the fever of gold rush. If gold rush was anything similar to meth addiction, I can understand how an entire indigenous population would be wiped out in the process.

We always sat in his shop, a space that lead to the underbelly of the cabin, full of tools of every imaginable type, and talked for hours

202

while I combed Donny's mind for useful tips on construction and looked around for refurbished tools he'd be willing to sell.

"So what's the next step after you get the blocks laid?" he asked.

"Well, I want to build a floor above the high, rough surface of the concrete footings, so George said I should use some kind of Simpson tie that will anchor into the concrete I fill the hollow blocks with and allow me to run a support beam. On the other side, I can anchor a ledger board into the existing foundation then run my joists from those two points."

"Yeah. That makes sense. Make sure you connect all your ties to one board when setting them into the mud right off the bat. Don't try to level each one separately."

"Okay. I hope I get this right. Doesn't seem like I can have a second shot after I pour."

"You'll be fine. George is going to help you with the final setting, isn't he?"

Donny hit my heart with that question. I looked away and took another hit off the pipe. A gigantic cloud of smoke came out of my mouth and for a moment, I couldn't see Donny anymore.

"I doubt it. He never helps. He gives me advice once in a while, but he never comes down to the cave unless he wants some smoke."

"Yeah, George is like that, Anto. Don't get wrapped up in waiting for him to be your savior. George is only out for George."

"Was he always like that?"

"I've known him for over twenty years, and he is still the same. I mean, shit man, he still owes me for all kinds of stuff, including the money he used to start his company, but there are things I've just learned to let go of."

"What do you mean about the money for the company?"

"Well, before George took off to San Diego, while he was still living down in Apple Valley, we were both in on this play. An old lady was looking to remodel her home and refinance at the same time, and I was referred to her for the contracting part. Then I told George about it, and he somehow convinced her to give him all her savings, and then he took off to San Diego. That's how he got the money to start the mortgage company down there, but I figure he owes me because it was me who brought him into the thing in the firstplace."

I sat there with my jaw dropped.

"Wow."

Donny chuckled a bit and took another hit. As he was holding in the smoke, he squeaked out a question.

"Why, what did he tell you?"

"Certainly not that. From all the stories he told me, he's made it sound like he has plenty of money from all the different businesses and the mortgage company was just a cover he was using to have something legit on the books."

"Well, I don't know, I guess that may be true, but I know that George used that score to run out of here after he got out of prison and start over in San Diego."

"Well, what about all the time he spent working for the government and all the connections he made and that whole life?"

"I don't know about that. George may have done all of that, but all I know is he went inside for a while, and when he got out, he had

204

to start all over."

"Why did he get locked up?"

"Manslaughter."

"What happened?"

"George was running a chop shop back then and ripped some guy off and the guy came back one day to get even. George shot him and then got busted for the shop, dope, and manslaughter, and got sent up to Chino for seven years."

"He was locked up for seven years? And before that he was running the shop?"

"Well, yeah. He's been the dark prince of Apple Valley as long as I can remember."

My world was collapsing, and my savior was hollow. George was just an ex-con trying to climb back out of a hole. I was tweaked out of my skull, and the drive back to San Diego was a long one.

It must have been one of the winter holidays, I don't remember exactly which one, but I do remember George and Yesenia were out of town and they asked Veronica and me to watch their house. As soon as we got there, my mind was on the project. With so much to do, and so much truth to cover up inside myself, I just couldn't come close to the idea of having a quiet weekend with my girlfriend. My expectation was for her to join me. I thought she would embrace the nobility of my work, sense the urgency, and offer to help in any way she could.

I waited, and she waited. I was in the garage, and she was on the couch. I was waiting for the door to open and her to poke her head in and ask what I was doing. She was waiting for her lover to come embrace her and choose her over work.

A couple of hours passed and still there was no sign of Veronica. The sun was whispering its last goodbyes and a cold reminder numbed my nose. I walked into the house to find Veronica curled up on the couch watching South Park. I sat next to her and unfolded her legs, allowing her feet to rest on my lap.

"Are you almost done out there?" she asked without looking at me.

"Well, I mean, not really. I have so much work to do that I feel like I'll never finish. I was hoping you would come help."

"Anto, you work like a crazy man, and you barely take time off, and I was hoping this weekend would be for us, not for work."

I kept my attention focused forward on the TV while my heart sank with disappointment.

"Plus, I'm really tired today. I've already fallen asleep, and I just don't feel like doing anything," she added.

"Okay. Let's just watch TV," I said in a passive tone.

"I'm sorry. Last night just took a lot out of me and my head feels very slow and dull."

"Yeah. That's typical. Your dopamine isn't firing at full output. It happens after you take ecstasy."

"Oh. Wow. That doesn't sound good," she said with a hint of innocence.

"Babe. You know that when we take ecstasy, and go dancing all night, that it's not exactly doctor approved, right?"

"Yeah. I guess. I just never really thought about it that far. Anyways, all I know is I'm exhausted, and I feel like I could fall asleep any second."

"You want to try something that will wake you up?" I asked her.

"Uuhh, yeah, I mean, what is it?"

"You know how the ecstasy sometimes keeps you up all night?"

"Yeah, every time. You always pass out, and I'm left there staring at the ceiling all night."

"Really? I'm sorry. I had no idea."

"Yeah, I know. You seem to fall asleep with no problem, and I always wondered how you did it."

"Well, the stuff inside that keeps you up is usually some kind of speed. I use it from time to time to help me with work, so my body is probably used to it, and I can fall asleep easier."

"Oh. I didn't know you use speed."

"Well, I mean, I don't really do it a lot, but it does help me when I'm tired, so I smoke a little crystal when I need a pick me up."

"Crystal?"

"Yeah, it's just a better kind of speed. Same stuff but cleaner than what they put in E."

"Oh, okay. Well, what does it feel like?" she seemed interested.

"It just kind of wakes you up and gives you a little, uuhhh, well, it's like something that takes away your shitty feelings and gives you energy," I explained.

"Well, what do you think, should I try it?"

"I mean, it's your call. You don't have to. I just thought since you said you were tired and feeling shitty from last night that it might help you a bit."

"Okay. How do you do it?"

"I'll be right back."

I went to the garage, grabbed a butane torch and my meth kit, and came back to the couch. Veronica watched intently as I scooped some shards into the long, skinny neck of the pipe, then tilted it up and tapped the mouthpiece so the pile slid down into the bowl. Torch lit and held in my left hand, I passed the bowl of the pipe through the whistling fire a few times and watched as the crystal melted to liquid. With the brew ready, I inhaled on the pipe, taking in a massive hit, and set the running torch on the coffee table while holding in the smoke. Then I exhaled into her mouth as she breathed in. Veronica looked on with wide, attentive eyes, then let out her bit of smoke.

"I don't think I can do everything you just did and not drop something," she said.

"Okay. You want me to hold it for you?" I was nothing if not helpful.

"Yeah."

"Okay. I'll get it ready and hold it, and when I say go, you just inhale."

"Okay."

I picked up the torch and started swirling the bowl over the flame. Then I took a little puff to help the smoke pick up, and when it was ready, I held the pipe at a delicate angle in front of Veronica's face. She put her left hand over my fingers with a light touch, then inhaled far too quickly and with too much force. She pulled her head back in surprise and coughed once as a serving of smoke jumped out of her mouth, and I quickly interjected, "Try to hold it."

She put a hand over her mouth and nose and diligently tried to follow my instruction but lasted only a few seconds before she erupted in a coughing fit. As she coughed, I sucked on the remaining smoke pouring out of the pipe and put the torch back on the coffee table.

When her coughing subsided, I looked into her eyes and smiled.

"How do you feel?"

"Uhhhh. I'm definitely not tired anymore, but I don't really feel super different, like when I drink or take ecstasy."

"I know. I told you, it's not like that."

"Can I do another one?"

"Yeah, sure, let me get it ready for you. But let's only do two for you tonight because I don't want you up all night while I pass out again."

She laughed and flashed a big playful smile at me.

"Do you know how many times I've watched you fall asleep in five minutes and wondered how you always do it so quickly? It's like I'm dating your snoring more than I'm dating you."

We both chuckled a bit, and I leaned over and gave her a kiss.

"I'm sorry. I'm just so exhausted from work all the time that when I finally do lie down it's like my body just dives right into coma mode."

"Yeah. I know. I know, and I still love you. Okay, now let me get one more."

I got the pipe heaving again, and this time, she took in a veteran sized hit, held it in, and exhaled a steady cloud of fumes.

"Is it normal to have to go the bathroom? I really have to go right now," she asked.

"Yeah. Crystal is a natural laxative so it tends to clean you out."

"I don't like the name crystal. Can we call it something else?" she asked.

"Sure, babe. Whatever you want."

She looked at the TV, smiled, then looked back at me.

"How about Towelie? It sounds so much more fun."

I raise the pitch of my voice to an over-exaggerated squeal and gave my best impression of Towelie from South Park: "Oh yeah, you're right. It does sound more fun like this."

She laughed, then got up and walked down the hall.

"I gotta go to the bathroom. I'll be back."

As our laughter faded, I was left sitting on the couch, propane torch still running on the coffee table, pipe with congealed crystal meth coating the bowl in my hand, and an open sunglass case cradling a little baggie of dope. Directly in front of me were windows and glass across the entire front of the house and the view outside was calming. Mission Bay and downtown San Diego by way of lights reflecting in the darkness of space. Maybe this thing will work out? Maybe I can work harder? Maybe it's not destined to collapse? A mix of emotions ran through me, and I took another hit for good measure.

There were three levels to the cave now. The floor with a height of ten feet, the mid-level section at five feet, and the high storage area with only three feet of clearance. After finishing the hollow blocks, I filled them with concrete and set my Simpson ties into the top. At the opposite end, along the preexisting cinderblock foundation, I used a powder-actuated Hilti-shot to secure ledger boards all along the perimeter, then ran joists so I could lay OSB sheets on top and make a smooth subfloor. I even nailed studs along the exposed front face of the cave and built myself a tool wall from pegboard. Next, I jackhammered through the front foundation and connected a squirrel cage blower to the air duct that lead to the waterfall, which I had buried under the yard. Things were moving again, and I was starting to feel a little wind at my back.

One day, I realized money was running low. Now that the core infrastructure of the cave was coming into view, I needed to be thinking about the equipment that was required to run a grow room. Water pumps, ballasts, cooling tubes, growing medium and plant food—none of these things were found in Walmart, and my once healthy reserve of cash had somehow dwindled down dramatically over the past year.

As I was sharing my concerns with Veronica one night, she opened her heart and opened her doors and invited me to move into her home. That meant I would have an additional fifteen hundred a month to throw at meth and the cave. So it came to pass that I was living with my newly addicted girlfriend.

More dissension grew among the ranks of George's empire. One of the guys George had on speed dial was an escrow agent who ran with a fledgling crop of country club debutants towing their portly husbands around by the balls. Apparently, George had convinced this crowd to invest with him and, one day, one of the wives wanted to pull out. No can do, said George, and proceeded to lay a pile of shit in front of her so pungent that all the other fair maidens smelled it and demanded their husbands march right up to George and get their money back.

One day I was working in the yard, near the waterfall, when a man I recognized walked up the driveway. He had a lean build and moved without tension. His clothes were faded but not worn through and looked as if they'd all been purchased at a thrift store. He wore a shaggy Beatles haircut, large rectangular glasses in the style of Henry Kissinger, and a trimmed mustache.

"Hey, Anto. George around?"

"Hi Sam. Not today. Probably down at the office."

"Naah. I was just there, and his secretary said he hasn't been there all day."

"Huh. Well, I can tell you for sure he won't be coming here to help me, so this is definitely not the place to find him."

Sam offered a sympathetic nod, the same look everyone gave me who had known George for more than a few years. I didn't recall exactly how, but Sam and George knew each other from the old days, from the Apple Valley days, before George came to San Diego with a new vigor for life.

"Is George ducking you, too?" I asked while shoveling some rocks around the base of the waterfall.

Sam took a moment, waited for me to catch his line of sight, and pondered for a bit.

"Yeah, I haven't heard back from him in a while, and the mortgage hasn't been paid, so the bank is up my ass about it," Sam shared.

"Why would they be on you about George's mortgage?"

"Well, this house is in my name. I mean, you know, George can't put anything in his name, so he asked me to help him out with the paperwork, and I agreed. But back then, there was plenty of money

212

coming in from the mortgage business, and from the export business I had running, so it wasn't a big deal."

I didn't try to hide my disappointment. My jaw fell open.

"You're the export partner? And this house is in your name?" I asked, dumbfounded.

I leaned on the shovel handle and looked down at the rocks. My equilibrium was in a spin, and a sense of nausea gripped my stomach.

"Well, yeah. I've been running refurbished farm equipment down through Mexico, but my partner down there bailed on me. George had a little piece of it, but it was never anything big for him. Couple grand a month."

"And what about this house?"

"Well, you know George and his history, so nothing can be in his name. His dad signed the papers for the mortgage company, and when George came to me for help with the house, I agreed," Sam continued.

"He told me there was a guy in Australia who ran the exports with him and that it brought in a lot more than a couple grand a month," I could feel my emotions starting to rise.

"Who? Greg? He's the only one we know in Australia, and he was never anything more than an old . . ."

I cut Sam off and told him I needed to go finish something in the garage. I went to the bathroom and cried. I cried and I cried as I felt the expanse of the great void, the darkness and the hollow, in perfect unison, leaving a black hole that collapsed everything around it. Everything was nothing. I was nothing. It had all been a pack of lies.

What could I do? What could I possibly do? There was no point in confronting George. His character didn't allow for self-deprecation, and the only outcome would be further deception and more lies. My only options were to walk away from it all or keep trudging forward and hope the ship didn't sink before I got the plants blooming. I choose the latter.

A week later, I sat inside the cave on an upside-down five-gallon bucket, staring into the corners of my mind. It was mid-morning on a late winter's day in San Diego, and the temperature inside the cave was ten degrees cooler than outside. I could see my breath. I was bundled in an old sweatshirt with the hood pulled over my head, a dark sand-colored Carhartt jacket unzipped in the front, paint-stained jeans, and black Caterpillar steel-toe work boots on my feet. I leaned back against the cinderblock wall and stared toward the rear of the cave. Along the back wall, I'd spray painted a giant Batman symbol, in full detail, as I once fancied myself a superhero on a righteous crusade. I stared and smiled. The only part still missing from the raw infrastructure was the electrical sub-panel needed to handle the ten thousand watts of lighting I planned on running through that place. Everything else was ready. I had built my masterpiece, and now all I had to do was put together the finishing touches.

I heard footsteps shuffling near the entrance, then the grate being removed.

"Hey. Anto. You in there?"

George removed the grate, squatted at the entrance, and peered in. He couldn't see me because I was behind an angle of the hollow blocks that left me in the shadows. I thought for a moment about whether I should respond. More than likely, he was only there to smoke my dope, and I certainly didn't feel like sharing.

"Anto? Hello?"

What's the point? He knew I was there. My truck was parked on the street.

"Yeah," I responded with indifference.

"Oh, Hey. I couldn't see you."

George reached through the opening and grabbed the handle I'd secured just above the entrance. He slid in carefully, making sure not to sully the trousers and button-down shirt he was wearing. One step off the ledge, and he walked down onto the main floor, stood in the middle, and looked around.

"Wow. You've really got this place done nicely, huh?" George observed with a smirk on his face. George was never able to deliver a line with pure sincerity. Ever since the beginning, there was always a kind of grin on his face when he talked, but back then I thought it was inclusive. I thought the joke was on the rest of the people, the people who paid their taxes and worked a corporate job. I interpreted his grin as evidence of the bond between him and me, of the promise that we were going to put one over on them, that I had come to the right place, and that he knew and I knew that we were not like them.

But now, I looked at his grin and realized there was no him and me; there was nobody but George in George's world, and the grin was only a synthetic attempt at hiding the rotten soul that lay beneath. George looked at me in a playful way.

"Hey, uh, any chance you got some smoke?"

Anger. Hatred. I knew that was all he wanted, and there he was, giving another performance that was battering what was left of my eroded heart.

"No George. All out."

George looked straight into my eyes, and I panicked on the inside.

"Oh really? Huh. Well, no problem."

He knew I was lying. He knew my addiction was, and had been, at full maturity for months by then. I couldn't last the morning without a hit. One day without dope, and I was in a panic. Two days, and I was in withdrawal.

"So, uh . . . listen. We need to talk about something," George said as his eyebrows pressed together, and his tone jumped quickly to authoritative. I sat on my bucket and felt my stomach twist. Neurotic fear flooded every cell of my body. I said nothing, but nodded my head in affirmation.

"Yesenia and I were talking, and we think it's time she moves in permanently. Not just her, obviously, but the boys, too. So with the boys coming to live here, I just don't think this whole thing is going to work out. I know you've worked hard, but I think it's time we just cut our losses and move forward, you know?"

I sat on my bucket, and the world stopped spinning. Every noise was silenced, every voice in my head stopped talking all at once. A deep, focused awareness came over me. I was totally present in that moment. Nothing had existed previously; nothing would come to be. I felt a definition inside, I am one with this. I am one. I am.

Slowly, noise picked back up, and I was pulled away from that place of pure stillness. Then the hordes of savages in my head were all screaming, and I was left with a private mutiny. My mind ran through a list of safety checks and tried to regain control. I looked at George and launched the last safety net I could think of.

"What about the forty grand I gave you? I need that back now," I said.

Without batting an eyelash, George left me to sink.

"Oh, well, I told you that money along with two hundred of mine is all gone since the FTSE went to shit three months ago. I lost a lot of money right along with you."

"You never mentioned that, George."

"Yes, I did. You were just too tweaked out down here to hear me."

I said nothing more. Instead, I just looked back at the Batman sign and faded into the corner of my mind.

I spent the next few days taking as much as I could out of the cave and moving it to Veronica's garage. There wasn't much to take. Everything I'd done over the past year was nailed, screwed, grouted, or connected with rebar. I had a small collection of tools and a few pieces of grow equipment I could take with me, but I couldn't squeeze the blood back out of that dirt. That dirt was all I knew, and that cave had become my home. What the fuck was I supposed to do now?

One night, Veronica and I were watching TV, and she was asking me about George. She felt my broken heart and didn't press too hard as I explained what had happened. I shared the abbreviated version with her while leaving out the part where I trusted that man with every piece of my soul and now felt betrayed and ashamed. I didn't need to say it; she could feel it.

"Well, what do you think you want to do now?" she asked with gentle temperance.

"I'm not sure. Maybe get a job working construction or something."

"On the plus side, you have some of the equipment that you bought for the project and a whole lot of experience. I mean, how long would it take you to get that thing running somewhere else?"

"Yeah, I mean, I don't know. If I didn't have to dig another hole, I

217

could probably get it up in a month I guess."

"Well, why don't you do it here? In the garage?" she inquired.

I didn't grasp the magnitude right away, but soon a flood of exhilaration filled my chest.

"Are you serious? You would let me build it here?" my voice lifted.

"Yeah, of course, babe. I mean, if all you need is a month, then let's get that thing done finally and get you some money coming in."

Stop. Rewind all the way to the beginning, and play again. I had a glimmer of hope. I may pull this off after all, I thought. Perhaps I wasn't a failure; perhaps I would have my day in the sun.

"Thanks babe! Fuck yeah, we can get this done. "

My mind started racing a million miles per hour.

"You want to smoke some Towelie to celebrate?" I asked her, with the frenzy of a kid on a sugar high.

She laughed at my visible elation.

"Yeah, okay. Let's smoke."

the monster in the darkness

It is usually on the third day that delirium truly takes hold. They say after day five or six, the mind begins to recalibrate in order to find a functioning stasis, but I'd never made it that far.

There was a room in the back of a garage that sat under a house on a steep slope in a residential section of Pacific Beach, California. It had become my tomb. Across the street, at the junior high school, children scurried in playful frenzy. I had been working in my cavern for months, but each day seemed to fly by like a movie on fast-forward.

The room, 10'x15', smelled of sawdust and cement; cinderblock walls guarded three sides. The concrete floor was always unswept, and no visible light sneaked in from the outside world. A light bulb burned brightly in the middle of the room, shielded by a metal construction guard, connected to an extension cord, hanging from open ceiling joists. Exposed studs on the front wall were penetrated by electrical wires and concatenated by junction boxes; copper and ABS piping crisscrossed the bays. Something grand was being built here.

I held a sheet of plywood with one hand under the edge while the opposite knee pinned it against the open framing. The other hand quickly grabbed the power drill hooked to my tool belt. Two screws had been pre-started into the plywood. I hoped I had measured correctly. The plywood was heavy.

The screws hit their mark, and I was able to release the pressure of my supporting hand; a few more screws for reassurance. Directly below me was a three-foot deep sump of which to be mindful as I backed away from the wall. It was time for a small break before the next phase. My energy depleted quickly because I'd been awake for three consecutive days.

Outside the den, in the main garage, a moderate workshop consumed the space. Tools hung from pegboard, a workbench was covered in sawdust, and metal shelving overflowed with supplies and power tools. I dropped my tool belt to the ground with one swift tug to unbuckle the strap then fell heavily into the comfortable office chair that was noticeably out of place in this blue-collar oasis. I was a workingman, and this was a well-deserved break.

From behind a cabinet, I took out a bag of glass, four-inch test tubes lying next to a stack of instruction manuals and reference guides. A yellow MAPP plumber's torch was sitting on the workbench, unmoved from the last break, so I turned on the gas and lit the flame. The sound soothed me, as if I were a child in a crib listening to a lullaby. I let the scratchy whistle sing for a minute as I gazed attentively at the calming heat signature.

To make a new pipe, I first took the closed end of the test tube and swirled it in the tip of the flame until it glowed iridescent orange. Next, at just the right time, with gentle pressure, I blew into the open end of the tube, creating a small bubble in the malleable glass. Then, I pointed the flame on one spot of the bubble, blew out a bit, and popped a small hole. I had done this many times before, so the pipe came out flawless.

After filling the newly-blown oil burner with a scoop of opaque, shard-like morsels, I passed the utensil over the continuously running torch and heated the crystallized compound into liquid. The pipe swirled elegantly to spread the boiling goop more evenly, then I inhaled plumes of smoke emitted from the simmering brew. Synapses misfired and endorphins flooded what receptors might still have functioned. The world refocused in an instant. I felt my mind align back into a purpose like a fillet knife running across a wet stone. I expelled a large cloud of smoke from my lungs and admired.

I enjoyed reading while smoking meth because I firmly believed the brain to be more absorptive, and able to focus with greater attention, when aided by the drug. Modern ADD medicine is founded on the same principal and uses the same base chemical compound. That day's lesson was on high-intensity lighting; lumen output per foot ratios and acceptable ballast-to-bulb distances. I pondered the new information and considered revising part of my layout. My legs were kicked up on the low rack of the workbench as I leaned back into the chair, one hand holding the pipe where little slices of smoke made silent escapes. The other hand held open the reference manual. Fixated blue eyes glared intently at conversion charts.

Those moments of relative calm were always the most difficult. When I wasn't physically working on the project, when my mind was allowed to idle down even one revolution, that's when I felt the grip retighten around my neck. Paranoia and despair danced over the shallow grave of my buried heart. I tried to focus on the book, or let the meth sooth away my discomfort, but my thoughts had long been lost to the violent riptide of neurosis. How much longer could I go on like that? How long could I keep my addiction a secret? How long until the project was finished? How long until it all came crashing down? On the periphery of my strained vision, I noticed something moving in the shadows. I was scared to look, but I could glimpse it in my mind's eye—time was stalking me from the corner of the garage, staring, grinning, waiting.

There was no choice but to continue on; I had to prove them all wrong. The project's success would be my defining moment, my grand redemption. They would see. They would all be sorry. I was going to outmaneuver the whole system and end up on top. Until then, I had to willingly suffer and do whatever it took to finish that goddamned project. One more hit, then back to work.

The sound of school traffic permeated the garage door, so I knew it had to be either morning or afternoon. Otherwise, I had no idea what month it was. Every muscle in my body screamed as I rose from the chair. Three straight days without sleep led to heavy delirium and physical agony. The tool belt felt heavier each time I picked it up and buckled it back on. I tried to focus on the task at hand as I walked back into the project room.

I picked up my trusty four-inch Makita grinder that was lying on the ground. In order to work more quickly, I'd removed the guard and put on a slightly oversized cross-cut blade—the kind of blade used for wood. A high-pitch hum rose in octaves as the machine spun up to ten thousand revolutions per minute. I held the tool securely with two hands, stepped mindfully over the sump, delicately lowered the blade into the wood, and cut along the measurements. I executed with flawless precision. When finished, I switched the tool off while stepping back over the sump, but something caught my attention as I made the turn. Something drew my focus for a split second, and I forgot everything, including the still spinning blade.

It was as if someone had smacked my hand with a ruler. That's how it felt when the blade hit two fingers on my left hand. Serious injury always comes as such a surprise and leaves you dumbfounded, like a frozen batter staring at a nasty breaking ball. I raised my left hand to assess the situation. Something didn't look right, but I couldn't quite figure it out.

The subconscious registers traumatic events before any of the five senses. Panic flooded my nerves. My heartbeat doubled over one exhale. I dropped the tool from my right hand and put my left hand behind my back. My brain searched frantically for some kind of reset switch, but all I found was the solace of counting.

"One. Two. Three. Four." Each count separated by heavy, pleading breaths.

Something tapped the palm of my hidden hand, but the math didn't make any sense.

"Fuck."

There was no point in hiding from it any longer. I took my left hand from behind my back and put it up directly in front of my eyes, palm facing in.

"Motherfucker."

The pointer and middle finger were severed, hanging on by flaps of flesh, each dangling lifeless, limp, and silent. Fear flooded my heart and curse words of every sort filled the empty room. The worst part of an injury is not the pain, but the realization of the freedom that will be taken away. I couldn't afford the time to convalesce, not now, not after I'd sacrificed so much for the project. Time stood in my blindspot, laughing and shaking its head.

It was a moment as heavy and defining as I had ever come to embrace in life. It was the first time I truly considered the possibility of being insane. I hadn't seen my friends or family for well over a year. A secret addiction grew with exponential force inside me. Living like a hermit, up for days, high on crystal methamphetamine, and now I had accidentally cut off my fingers. How did I ever get so far from home?

I unbuckled the tool belt, allowing it to fall to the floor with a hearty thud as if in surrender. Sawdust danced up from the floor. Quickly, I wrapped up the injured hand into the bottom of my t-shirt and started stumbling into the garage, through the workshop, and toward the door I was mortified to open. The door to the outside world was a barrier that held back the truth. The door allowed me to shut out the dozen voices in my head that screamed for help, for sobriety, for sanity. Outside lay a world completely unsympathetic

223

to my cause and hostile toward my way of life.

With a few fingers of my right hand, I turned the doorknob while still gripping the edge of the rolled-up shirt, inside of which was cocooned a throbbing, bloody mess. Opening the door seemed like cruel amusement for the audience of gods sure to be watching the farce. I managed to get the door cracked open enough to wedge my foot in then swing it open with fumbling panic. Spears of sunlight hit my eyes in a full-frontal assault. I couldn't remember the last time I saw that pernicious orb in the sky.

Schoolchildren across the street had front-row seats. From an innocuous door in suburban America, a monster emerged, the front of his clothing soaked in blood. He was hunched over, pressing something important to his abdomen, catching his steps side-to-side like a drunk, mumbling, with a shade of midnight painted under his eyes. Surely the children would not soon forget what they had seen there that day.

In the driveway, I leaned against the hood of a red Chevy Blazer to catch my balance. Scenery was spinning. Clouds hung where concrete should have been. I could hear a familiar sound, a voice, but couldn't gain enough bearing to figure out where it was coming from. The hood felt like it turned completely vertical and sent me crashing to the concrete. I slid off with a hearty thud; half conscious, slow-motion vision. With this new vantage point, I could see clear under the car and out to the sidewalk. My girlfriend's feet were pacing back and forth.

Veronica was 34 years old; seven years my elder. She had auburn hair with a slight curl well past her shoulders, bangs, light complexion, and an hourglass figure. She wore a black pantsuit with a white collared shirt underneath, tailored well around the bust line. Veronica spoke with equal levels of business acumen and blue-collar know-how, topped off with a pinch of flirtatiousness, because she had played the game long enough. The game was corporate sales, and she was talking shop on her cell phone.

I struggled to my feet. A large bloodstain colored the concrete. Breaths were short with panic. As I came around the side of the car, Veronica broke off her conversation mid-sentence. Her eyes shot open and her mouth fell ajar. All I could manage to say was:

"Hospital. Now."

On the rear windshield of the Chevy Blazer was a "How's my driving?" sticker. The car was owned by Veronica's employer so when I urged her to run stop signs, she would not abide. At the end of my tucked-away hand, I felt my heartbeat pounding on war drums, pulsating rage, and spewing out blood. From the backseat, time leaned forward and whispered incendiary words into my ear.

I barked at Veronica with what vitriol I could muster, but most of the steam was merely overflowing fear. It felt as if my heart had moved down into my hand, the heartbeat declaring its presence with booming reminders of promise lost.

I leaned against the window and stared dispassionately at the passing scene. Beach community suburbia interwoven with upper-middle-class college kids and a sprinkling of homeless every couple blocks. Disinterested yoga pants walked first-world dogs while yammering on cell phones. Mexican nannies with white babies. Washboard abs almost always without a t-shirt. The great chase for an endless summer. How had I ended up on the outside?

Suddenly, I was exhausted in every cell of my body. I faded into darkness. It was quiet. It hadn't been that quiet in months. I cried, and I smiled at the same time. Veronica shouted at me. She forced me back into consciousness.

We pulled up next to a small neighborhood clinic, and I rumbled out of the car with the elegance of a wounded rhinoceros. Inside the clinic was an amalgamation of bland, but I recognized the place from my visit the year before. Sterile linoleum floors reflected cool white fluorescent lights; no color stood out on its own. They all blended lazily together to create a cacophony of silent screams. The waiting room guests all looked up from their magazines and cell phones as I burst on the scene. The receptionist tried talking to me, but I was responding in mumbles and grunts.

"I cut off my fucking fingers," I finally managed to blurt out loudly into the room.

Soon Veronica took over as official translator while I slowly lost focus behind her. The room started spinning. I reached for the water cooler to balance, but miscalculated. My face found the mark instead. Water was gurgling as I lay on the floor, my eyes turned in the direction of the audience. Most eyes were still fixed on me, although I managed to lose the attention of a couple sorority girls who typed feverishly on their cell phones.

When my eyes opened again, I was confused and sedated. Two EMTs stood above me and, judging by their volume and proximity to each other, they were discussing something enigmatic. How did one man require so much morphine? Blurs and streaks washed across my eyes as I tried to focus. The screen went black at times.

Shiny stainless steel everywhere and labels reading "gauze" and "syringes." Through a window, I could see a movie playing with scenery of some kind. I was in the back of an ambulance traveling down the freeway.

I woke up in a room full of gurneys and commotion. People wearing scrubs and holding clipboards moved feverishly around the hive. One of them spotted me and walked directly toward me.

"Hi. Do you know where you are? You're in a hospital. You have a serious injury and need surgery."

I nodded my head languidly.

"We have to give you a shot, and it's not going to feel good. Can you help us out and try to stay calm, please?"

Slow floating nod; morphine and meth, pain and barbiturates, fear and stimulants.

A man walked around the side of the bed and placed a glass syringe with a stainless-steel casing on the tray next to me. The needle was at least four inches long. I stared intently. I could tell he was speaking to me because his lips were moving, but everything sounded garbled. Slowly, he began peeling crusted gauze from my hand. Layer by layer, I was reminded of a life in collapse. Above his left breast pocket, I read the custom stitching: "Anesthesiologist."

My body reacted before my brain could register the pain. When the sensation finally came into focus, I felt something hot digging into my flesh around the bone of the stub of my severed left pointer finger. The pain was so vile that I couldn't muster a response. I almost vomited. I turned my head to look at my hand. This cannot be real, I thought. A hand covered in dried blood, two fingers facing the wrong direction, raw flesh, and exposed bone. My stomach twisted again. The man stabbed and swirled the needle through the meat while injecting some kind of foreign substance. I felt tears rolling down my cheek.

When the feeling of molestation finally stopped, I looked at the man and begged with sad, fragile eyes.

"Please don't do that again."

"I'm sorry, but I have to inject the other finger. "

My heartbeat revved up as anticipation built. I was stone-cold sober at that moment. When the needle slid into the middle stub, I felt metal ping off bone. I never knew bone was so delicate and full of feeling. A hollow vacuum swept up my arm, through my chest, and down into my belly. What kind of ungodly awareness was this?

A thunderous war cry erupted in the emergency room as rage took over on instinct. With my right hand, I grabbed the perpetrator by the shirt, pulled him in close to my bloodshot eyes, then launched him back with a mighty thrust.

"Get the fuck off me!" Spit flew from my lips as I yelled with ferocity.

In an instant, the room went from beehive to wax museum. Everybody stopped dead in their tracks, silent, staring at me. The only movement in the room came from two large men, dressed in white scrubs, walking toward me with purpose. They held me down, one arm each, and demanded my calm and cooperation. After a minute of resistance, I finally relinquished, allowing the foul man his sadistic toil.

Traces of consciousness faded in and out of vision. I was alone in a room with white tile walls, shiny trays full of torture devices, alien machines lurking overhead, and a submarine somewhere finding its way with sonar. A nurse, then a doctor, said something to me nonchalantly in what seemed like blurry, slow motion dreams.

I woke up in a corner of a room with a wraparound curtain drawn over any vantage point to the outside world. The veil was somewhat translucent, decorated by a light flower pattern, and behind it I could see a shadow moving. Something smelled putrid, hidden deep beneath layers of disinfectant. My hearing faded back in slowly, and I noticed the heart monitor: Beep. Beep. Beep. The shadow bumped the curtain, sending shivers up my spine. I chose to close my eyes and fade back into darkness.

When I woke again, the foul odor was pervasive. I tried to readjust in bed, but as I put slight pressure onto my arms, a throbbing began to erupt in my left hand. I looked, then I remembered. I raised the injured hand and held it directly in front of my face. Heavy gauze wrapped a gruesome surprise. A quick attempt at bending the suspect fingers exposed something rigid inside. Two small, shiny metal pins stuck out through the tips of my reattached fingers.

A pungent aroma of rancid meat wafted arrogantly by. Was this the collective smell of death I was up against, or could I really distinguish the reek of my own splayed flesh? I became convinced I could smell my own fingers, and the thought tightened my stomach.

The curtain pulled apart quickly, and an impatient nurse entered the cocoon. She was portly and looked to be purposely puffing out her cheeks as if holding her breath. A monologue of demands ensued.

"Do not get out of bed, don't touch anything near your left hand, and only in case of emergency can you press the button for my assistance. I'll be back in a bit with your discharge papers to sign and prescription information. Your clothes are in the closet and I'll help you get dressed when it's time. Please contact someone who can pick you up from the hospital. "

She pointed to a phone on the nightstand next to my gurney, then walked away. The curtain was left slightly ajar.

Reflections on life come at the most inopportune times for drug addicts; usually when we are out of dope. Although it hadn't even been a full day since I last smoked, and painkillers were festively saturated in my bloodstream, I still felt the early onset of withdrawal. A million ways to feel regret flooded my heart.

I called Veronica to let her know what the nurse said and to wait for my next call when it was time to be picked up. Hours went by, and the painkillers started to fade. Through the crack in the curtain, I could see families come in and out to visit recovering patients next to me. Hearing encouraging conversations between loved ones was a cruel reminder of my loneliness. The button for the nurse's assistance had been pressed a dozen times, but no response from the cavalry. I called Veronica.

"Pick me up in front of the main entrance in twenty minutes. "

The first steps out of bed were top heavy. Clumsily, I wobbled to the small closet where I hoped my clothes would be. Bingo. I slowly put on my shorts, which had a large crusted pool of dried blood down the front, and took a hospital-issued brown sweatshirt since my t-shirt was nowhere to be found. I winced in pain every time I involuntarily flinched the wounded fingers. I could feel the stitching holding them together.

There is an art to bypassing authority while in the throes of intoxication, and I was master of that craft. The pain, the drugs, and the withdrawal all combined for a noxious effect, but I walked out of the room, down the hall, and straight past the nurse's desk with nothing more than a casual demeanor. No one seemed to notice.

In the elevator, I stood behind a gaggle of nurses, listening to them gossip about a handsome doctor and his proclivity for newly-arrived staff. The group sighed in collective defeat.

Outside, the sun stung my eyes, so I kept my gaze fixed to the ground while walking. I found a bench and sat sluggishly. The main entrance was bustling with activity. Walkers scooted by one languid step at a time with senior citizens in tow. Skin sagged, protruded, bounced, and overhung in every imaginable direction. Families walking into the hospital held bright bouquets; those walking out held each other. A man paced furiously within a three-foot radius while desperately inhaling a cigarette.

Veronica pulled up, so I made my way toward the car. She was dressed for a business meeting, professional and well-presented. She asked many questions, but no answers were given by me. I just sank into the passenger seat and closed my eyes. The ride home was silent. I prayed to wake up and realize it had all been a dream but, in the dark confines of the hollow, I heard time humming a sinister tune.

When we got home, I fell on the bed and went to sleep for two days. The first person I saw when I woke up was Donny Stone, and he was kind enough to have brought me a fresh supply of meth.

old friends

When I opened the door, I saw him standing back five feet, respectfully distant, with his hands nervously held together, palm over knuckles. He looked at me with a careful glance, testing the air for hostility, and kept his stance meek and his eyes gentle. I didn't know what to say, so I stood there, silent and still.

"Hi, guy," he finally uttered with an apprehensive smile and the heavy accent I'd known my entire life. The way he said it—the words he used—that was from a thread of something we once had together. He was trying with all he had, and I didn't know what to do.

"Hey, Dad," I finally managed to say with a tiredness to my words.

I hadn't seen or spoken to him in well over a year. It seemed like a year; I wasn't sure, since I didn't know what year it was.

Every few years, the relationship between my mother and father went to shit. Every time it did, I was left with a river of animosity between my father and me. It was always him I blamed and, after the floodwaters receded, nothing was ever spoken about, nothing was ever resolved. Sometimes, we came back together through apathy. Other times, it was staged or coerced by my mother. But never did we deal with the fundamental angst between us. Instead, we kept building on top of a corroded foundation, and no one bothered to question our methods.

233

When I was 19, he took off. Tension was rising over financial control between my parents, and one day, my dad was gone. Word got back to us that he was in Europe, and mom started the divorce talks again, only to reconcile in the same ambiguous way as I had seen when I was younger.

At 22, I graduated from college. I hadn't had any real interaction with my father for years, and I wasn't keen on him attending the graduation ceremony. But, as my mother always did, she managed to corral the family back together.

I graduated in the spring of 2003 in La Jolla, California. By the time they called my name, I was drenched in sweat. The graduation robe was made of the most unforgiving polysynthetic blend, and happened to be midnight black, so it felt like I was an ant under a magnifying glass walking up to accept my faux diploma. After the ceremony, I searched for my family among the crowd and finally got a chance to remove the blistering gown. I didn't see my dad right away because he was standing off to the side. My mother was front and center with all her hugs, cheers, and pictures.

When I finally did see him, I couldn't help but smile. Oh, you silly immigrant, you. Everything about him was out of place for that vogue community, but there was such a sincere smile on his face that it broke right through the wall I had built around my heart. Around us I could hear the typical phrases of congratulations spoken with all the superficial intonations of Californian affluence. People were dressed in their Del Mar outfits with lavish ladies' hats bobbing over the crowd and oversized designer sunglasses covering everyone's eyes.

My father stood solemn, and his clothes were unadorned. He was wearing his formal outfit, which consisted of old khaki pants freshly ironed, a white collared shirt over ten years old, and a dark sports coat of decent wear. He had never worn sunglasses in his life. His simple, short hair, now about half gray, had never been subjected to any styling products. He dressed in the style of an old world, perhaps considered chic in Vienna during the sixties; not shabby, but certainly not in line with the La Jolla brunch crowd. Both his hands were gripping the lower lapels on his coat, just below his sternum, and between his hands, hanging from his neck, was a makeshift diploma only my father couldrender.

He had taken my sister's diploma and made a high-end color copy, then gone to work on it in a slow, methodical fashion for which only a man of his ilk could possibly have the patience. Using just the right amount of white-out and the skilled hand of a calligrapher, he augmented a few key portions so the diploma would appear to be for me. For my name, he used an old Bosnian nickname that would pull through a thread of Slavic pride that only a man who grew up under a communist regime could appreciate. To be educated in his time was not only a luxury, it was something that risked bringing unwanted attention from the authorities. He had the ersatz diploma laminated and, using frayed twine, he hung it around his neck for all to see. With generations of dignity and pride, and a big smile, he stood in front of me and put out his hand to shake. The only thing he said was, "A little hot today," but that was all I needed. We both laughed a little and let all the unspoken words between us drift away.

There were problems again a year later. I was back at home. My mother had moved to Southern California for a job, and my parents were on the outs again. My father and I were nasty toward each other, and the end result was me packing up and leaving the house I grew up in for the last time to move down with my mother. He didn't say anything of note; he didn't even look at me. One day, we were arguing in the kitchen while he was eating bread and jam over the sink looking out the window. It was the silence I remembered, and the malign inflection he so masterfully wielded that turned everything around him to ice. Without saying it, he told me to get the fuck out and not come back. So off I went, running to mama again.

A year later, my mother invited me to join her for Christmas Mass.

I was living in Pacific Beach, and she was up in San Juan Capistrano. When I arrived at her place, I found my father was there, much to my surprise and disappointment, and my mother was acting as if nothing were out of sorts. She always played dumb and pretended everything was fine. I managed to make it to Mass, but it was in the church that I found myself seething beyond control. A standard nativity scene decorated the chancel, and all the families were dressed in their Sunday finest. My father was to the right of my mother, and I on her left, and my view was such that as I looked down the row at them, I could see the priest off in the blurry distance to form an unholy trinity. What a lineup of frauds, I thought to myself. My mother prayed with deep reverence as she clutched a rosary in her hands. My father stared off impassively into the distance, obviously tuned out and grappling with his own moral compass. In the background, the priest mustered all the zeal one could realistically manage for a tale he had told far too many times. I wanted nothing to do with any of those people.

At the end of Mass, as the priest and his acolytes made their slow procession down the nave, I left without saying a word to my parents. I drove down the I-5 and cursed the beautiful scenery. It was sixty degrees in December; no clouds, just a perfectly-placed sun over the Pacific that made the horizon glimmer and dance, reminding me of something distant I once had known. The freeway was practically empty at noon, and I felt perfectly at home in that desolate landscape. Even Camp Pendleton looked deserted, like an abandoned mental asylum, and I wondered where all the crazies had gone. I spent the rest of Christmas alone, in my apartment, playing online poker, chain-smoking cigarettes, and drinking whiskey.

I didn't have much contact with my father after that. Pretty soon, I was back in the business of tax-free sales. Somewhere along the way, I met a man who offered me the world, and when it was over, I found myself staring at the same sun, the same ocean, with a horizon like the one I had seen the day I drove away from my family on Christmas.

Now, there was my father, standing at my front door, and I could see a mercy in his eyes that made me want to tell him everything. Less than a week earlier, I had cut off my fingers, and my parents were in Croatia at the time. When they heard the news, they flew back immediately, and when they landed, my dad got into his truck and drove the eight hours to San Diego from San Jose without skipping a beat.

I wanted to tell him so much. I had so much poison leaching through my body, so much angst flooding my heart, and my mind was all darkness those days. But how could I begin? If I started telling him pieces, I knew I would not be able to hold back; the whole thing would crumble, and I was not ready yet. I was not ready for that. I was not ready for the great purge. I was not ready for the revolution. I was not ready to drop all the masks, to give up all my angles, to stand and tell the truth.

I was so happy to see him that I wanted to cry, but we didn't hug or even shake hands. I just invited him inside, and we spent the evening talking about the accident, cautious and apprehensive, like old friends walking across an ancient, overgrown bridge together.

238

the teacher of pity

I was slouched in the passenger seat, staring out the window, letting the freeway lights parse my wretched existence into flashes of memory. In the distance were the lights of the Coronado bridge, indifferent to my saga like the eyes of a distant lover. The window was cracked open and air was screaming into the car; the sound was all-consuming. I desperately needed fresh air. I needed anything I could get at that point to keep from falling into a disabling withdrawal. The breeze across my forehead gave just enough relief to keep me semi-lucid.

Veronica was driving us down the I-5 south. It was ten in the evening on a Sunday night, and the San Diego freeway was empty. We hadn't said a word to each other since getting in the car. All I could hear was the sound of rushing air. I was curled in a ball with my arms wrapped around my stomach and facing as far away from her as I could manage. I didn't know which was worse: withdrawal or pent-up acrimony.

We had been out of meth for three days, and I was well into the sickness. My habit took me upwards of two grams per day, so dropping off the edge was a long fall, indeed. Veronica didn't use as heavily, so she was better able to manage, but I suspected she had been hiding a reserve stash.

The situation was beyond toxic. Veronica tried to end our relationship a month earlier, but I wouldn't leave. I lived at her house and wouldn't accept the truth. The tension, paranoia, and hatred were heavy in the air, but that night, we came together, united by our one dismal cause.

I had done those trips before, but never with her. Usually, when my supply was getting low, and I knew Donny Stone couldn't score, I would drive down to Tijuana alone and roll the dice. Sometimes, I would get ripped off, and sometimes, I would end up scoring some decent shit. Through my previous attempts, I'd managed to find a source who came as close to trustworthy as was realistically possible in the Tijuana drug racket. I had called Jose earlier that day and told him I was coming down.

I had never been out of dope that long since first indulging two years prior. I kept waiting for Donny to come through, but each day was another case of meth story fiasco: this person got arrested and that person went to sleep for the first time in weeks. I eventually found myself in bed, weak and nauseous, as the days became longer and felt more cruel. On the third smokeless day, I finally realized I was on my own, so I asked Veronica to drive me to the border.

When I told her I had done this before, she was surprised. I hadn't mentioned the capers I'd gotten up to, and botched, in search of dope when Donny Stone was out of pocket. All Veronica knew was the nice man we affectionately came to call Uncle Don, the guy who drove down from Big Bear every few weeks and made a normal event out of his drug deliveries, like family visiting from out of town. I never told her what happened when Don wasn't able to plug, and she never bothered to ask how it came to be that we always had a steady supply of meth.

I had scoured the greater San Diego area, going from one junkie referral to the next, ending up in decrepit, run-down houses, abandoned, full of squatters, or passed down from generation to generation of degenerates, reeking of piss and full of wide, contentious, predatory eyes looking for someone to rob, all in pursuit of the next fix. I think the only thing that kept me from being hijacked on those expeditions—from Escondido, to San Bernardino, to the back alleys of Tijuana—was my intimidating size. Time and time again, I saw the look of a tweaker sizing me up and reconsidering his method of swindle. In the end, my downfall was always trust. Separate me from my money in the guise of friendship—a tweaker could tell me he needed to go to the dealer's house and that dealer didn't trust anyone else coming along—I was desperate enough to believe the story and give him my money. Then, I would wait at a gas station for hours. Anticipation and hope followed by suspicion, panic, anger, defeat, and finally shame; time and time again, I wallowed in demoralizing shame as I realized I was a slave to crystal methamphetamine, and I had been cheated once again.

It was an odd way to bond, but the withdrawal brought Veronica and me closer together than we had been in months. Despise me as she did for not letting her have her house back, her life back, there was still a sense of compassion in her, and seeing me sick pulled heavy on her heart. She brought me water that day and cared for me while I lay ill in bed. That act alone held more compassion than any other kind deed had during our good times.

I waited for night to make the trip because I was more comfortable in the dark. Walking the crowded streets of Tijuana, on a sun-filled day, while dope-sick, was awful. The sun is not a sick junkie's friend. But as the moon rises, so does the level of danger. The streets of Tijuana at night were like a mining town of the gold rush era: loosely lawful and prone to violence. Every form of vice was available to satisfy the degenerate palate.

My weary eyes were fixed on the passing scenery. On the high banks of the highways edge, fence lines indicated a steadily decreasing property value. Finally, we reached our exit.

Camino de la Plaza
LAST USA EXIT

We passed the outlet shops and a few parking lots as Veronica pulled into the passenger-loading loop at the very end of Camino de la Plaza. Already there was a different level of action, and I hadn't even crossed the border. There's a compelling correlation seen around the world, i.e., as wealth increases, so does isolation. Rich neighborhoods are desolate and quiet. Conversely, the rougher the neighborhood, the more people tend to socialize, loiter, mingle, or just emanate a sense of unity that only the poor seem to grasp.

Through the commotion, I spotted the jackals strategically positioned among the grazing herd, their leering eyes always betraying predatory intentions. I counted three, but I was sure there were more. One stood with his back against a building, hands in pockets, scanning the crowds. Another was talking to a buddy and smoking a cigarette, but his stare never met his friend's face; decoys and shifty eyes. The third was next to the metal, one-way revolving gate, the mouth of the beast, the all-consuming inhaler of souls where gringos went to indulge and Mexican nationals came back from 12-hour workdays. All three men honed in on our car as we pulled up.

"Are you going to be okay?" Veronica asked me, feigned sympathy in her tone.

I couldn't look into her eyes. I looked down at my shoes and felt my eyes begin to swell.

"Please give me another chance." I whispered with my eyes closed.

"Anto. We've talked about this already, and I told you I'd see how things go. You asked me to give you a ride because you were sick. So can we just focus on getting you back here safely tonight?"

I stared at my shoes and absorbed the gravity of her deflection. It was over; all of it. I was just a chicken still dashing around the yard, not accepting the fact that my head had already been lopped off.

"Make sure your cell phone has a signal. I'll call you when I'm heading back," I instructed.

"Okay. Be safe."

I didn't look at her or say anything in response. I opened the door and struggled to my feet, leaning against the top of the door for balance. My knees were shaking and my legs felt withered and feeble. My stomach was twisted and angry, and my head was loose and hazy; a little like I was drunk, a little like someone punched me clean on the temple.

The air was thick with car exhaust. The border checkpoint on the freeway, visible through the chainlink fence, was loud and imposing. Bright lights beamed from every conceivable angle down onto the bottleneck. I walked slowly toward the revolving gate, needing extra effort to keep my balance, and I saw one of the vultures flick his cigarette and start moving briskly in my direction.

He caught a stride directly next to me but never looked at my face. When he spoke, he did so looking forward and using a muted tone.

"Hello my friend. You need help getting anything tonight?" the man inquired of me.

"No." I was curt.

"Are you sure? I can get coca, or girls, or maybe just some mota? Whatever you need my friend."

"No."

"Steroidas. Amphetamines. How about a donkey show?"

"No."

I adopted a firm but neutral tone, never saying more than I had to

243

at the risk of revealing weakness or giving him a reason to call his buddies over the border and have them mug me with impunity. My cell phone rang just before I reached the gate.

"Anto. Are you okay? You're walking like you're drunk. And why is that guy following you?" Veronica sounded nervous.

I swung through the gate and stepped into the neutral corridor between two worlds. The pedestrian border crossing going into Tijuana had the appearance of a prison yard with chain-link fence everywhere, razor-wire lattice, and a 50-yard strip of concrete between two gates that was the path of truth. Poverty has a way of demanding honesty from a city.

"I'll be fine. Stay on the phone with me," I assured her.

The vulture didn't pass through the gate, and I was walking through the show before the show. Makeshift stands sold a few basics like jeans and horchata, and little kids ran up to me tugging at my jeans and yelling

"Chicle! Chicle!"

I put one hand in the pocket with my wallet and kept the other high to my ear, holding my phone, so they couldn't dig or grab.

"Just stay on the phone with me until I get into the cab," I said to Veronica.

"Okay. Why? What's going on?"

"Makes it easier to look like I have somewhere to be instead of just a wandering junkie."

The truth was that I wanted her to stay on the phone so she could feel the full weight of guilt I was trying to lay on her. I wanted her to know just what I had to go through to keep us supplied with steady crystal. It was all I could think of at that point to keep her from leaving me. I had nowhere to go, and everything I had worked for over the past two years was built into the garage of her house. I couldn't bear losing it all, so I thought if she knew just how hard I had worked to keep her from going through withdrawal, maybe she would allow me a little more compassion and not boot me out of the last hope I had of achieving something in life.

I exited the high-gated corridor and entered the streets of Tijuana. Lights and sounds, smells and people, everywhere. It was 10:30 on a Sunday night, and there was no shortage of action in TJ. Visually, Tijuana looked like a group of children had over-decorated a place for the holidays. Plenty of colorful lights were everywhere, and the buildings were all painted in a playful mishmash of bright hues. The odors were stubborn in the air and did not pass by easily with a breeze. It smelled of diesel fumes and garbage and fornicating dogs. I walked toward the plaza where I told Jose to pick me up. All the food vendors had retired for the evening, so their kiosks waited in silent moratorium. Empty kitchenettes looked dreary in the shadows, like circus grounds at night.

I kept walking and pulled out a cigarette to hang from my lips. Young women walked by dressed in alluring outfits, as if they were going to a nightclub, but it was standard attire for a single lady out on the town. A man in a cowboy outfit was standing with one foot perched on a step, offering wild Mexican love stories to one of the beautiful young ladies. She smiled and gestured animatedly as she rolled her eyes in that irresistible Latin style, causing the gentleman caller to put a hand on her arm and assure her of his genuine interest.

The streets were dirty and the garbage cans all had reached capacity hours ago. Dogs roamed the streets without reservation. People stood, people walked, people lingered and chatted. People were everywhere. I spotted my taxi waiting in the usual spot, just past the bus stops.

"Okay. I found my taxi. I'll call you later," I told Veronica.

I hung up the phone and climbed in the passenger seat.

"Hello my friend. Que pasa?" Jose asked with a wide smile on his face.

"Not much Jose. Don't feel good tonight."

He looked at my face and his smile receded a few degrees.

"No problem my friend. I already called my guy, and he is waiting for us."

"Thanks, Jose. You mind if I smoke in here?"

"No problem."

I lit my cigarette, and he started the car. Perception shifted from first person to third as I watched the scene playing outside the car like a movie. We left the hustle of the border plaza and hit the freeway. Two minutes since getting in Jose's car and already I had lost my bearings. Tijuana freeways were not like American ones. They did not shield you from the face of poverty. The night was dark, but not dark enough. The bleak reality of shantytowns announced itself quickly, and I was left to reflect on what real struggle looked like.

A few minutes later, we pulled off the freeway and drove into a quiet neighborhood. We pulled into a parking spot directly in front of an empty basketball court in a semi-empty park. The park was dark, but the court was brightly illuminated by stadium-style lighting. Around the caged perimeter, there were shadows watching me, the glow of cigarettes revealing their positions. Jose asked for my money and told me to wait in the car.

Surrounding the basketball court were trees with wide overhangs and thin, ghoulish branches that danced in the night's breeze. The lighting was morbid. For everyone except me, the trees provided cover from the bright lights that beamed from high above. I was left blatantly visible, exposed, while monsters lurked in the shadows.

Jose had walked down the block, and I lost sight of him. A couple strolled by on the sidewalk, hand in hand, and they both stared at the out-of-place gringo sitting alone in the taxi. A man emerged from the shadows, stood for a few moments staring at me, then stepped back into darkness and leaned against the chain-link fence. He watched me and remained still.

I knew I was in danger, but I did not care. What was the point of trying to fight it at this point? Anyway, my thoughts were elsewhere, away from Tijuana and back across the border where Veronica sat waiting for me to return. She was going to leave me, and the thought was boring a hole in my head. Deep anxiety coupled with the pulp of withdrawal left me alone in a car, on a street I did not recognize, far away from home, ruminating as I realized the insanity of my own internal bluster.

A darkness inside me rose, and the monster awakened; something clicked, a gear found teeth, and a long brooding anger saturated my blood. The game I played was a mixture of narcissism and manipulation. I was a child crying for his toy. I was a boy lying to his mother. I was scared and angry, so I turned my focus on the woman who was waiting for me across the border. She wanted to end things, to leave me or, more accurately, have me leave her. She knew the cards she was holding. That garage was all I had left, my last chance at redemption, and I had sacrificed far too much to walk away. And there I sat, in that miserable fucking city, sick and trying to score meth, while she waited across the border safely, probably smoking a little right then, because I knew she kept something for herself, that miserable fucking cunt. I called her, and she answered on the first ring.

247

"Hey. Are you done?" she wanted to know.

"No. I'm waiting. I don't know where I am. My guy left me waiting in his car, and I'm in a bad place."

"Oh my God, Anto, what are you going to do? What can I do? Can you just come back?"

"No. Too far, and I don't know how to get back. I'm just going to wait and hope these guys don't rob me."

"What guys? Oh my God. Are you okay?"

"I'm in front of a park, and there are people watching me from the shadows. They haven't approached the car yet, but I don't know how long they'll leave me alone."

"Oh, Anto. What do you want me to do?"

"Just stay on the phone with me. I feel better hearing your voice."

"Okay. I'm here. I'm here."

I took a few moments' repose and lit a cigarette as the silence calmed me down.

"I know I fucked up babe. I know I've been spending way too much time down in the garage, but I swear I can change. I can fix things, Veronica. Please give me another chance. Please stay with me."

"Anto, please. Not now. Not like this. We've already talked about this, and this is not the time to go over it again. "

"Why would you leave me when I'm almost there? Why would you kick me out when you know I have nowhere else to go? When you know that everything I have I've put into that garage?"

248

"Maybe that's the problem, Anto. You're obsessed with that garage, and that's the thing you're really scared of losing more than me."

"But I've been working for us. I'm doing all this for us so we can have a nice steady stream of income, so we can finally get some cushion, some time, so we can both get off meth, and get back to what we used to be. Normal people. We just need to make it over this last hill. We can't give up now. And what about me sitting here in Tijuana? Do you think this is all for me, too?"

"I appreciate you doing this, but I never asked for any of it. I just don't know, Anto. I never said I made up my mind about anything, but I needed to share with you how I felt."

"I know what's coming Veronica. I know you're going to leave me. You don't have to play it off like you're still thinking about anything."

"Anto, I really don't want to have this conversation again right now. Can we please talk about it later?"

As my anger faded into acceptance, a great wave of despondency washed over me. I'd lost her, and I knew it. I could hear it in her voice. Begging didn't work; neither did the guilt trip. What other forms of manipulation could I possibly use? It was teetering there before me, but I would not accept it, the great revelation of failure. Was this how it all came crashing down for me? Was this where it ended?

I was leaning off to the side of the passenger seat, huddled in a ball against the door, holding the silent phone to my ear, with slow tears steeping on my face. The driver's door opened suddenly, and I flinched with fright.

"Sorry my friend. Nobody has any crystal around here. Only coca. You want coca instead?" Jose asked with eager eyes.

"No, Jose. I need crystal. Can you get it anywhere else?

"Sure. Sure. No problem. We'll go to my friend's work."

"Okay. Lets go."

I put the phone back to my ear and told Veronica I would call her back.

"Okay. Be safe, please," she pleaded with me, and I shook my head as I disconnected the call.

I lashed out at her in my mind: Be safe, please? You want me to be safe while scoring dope in Tijuana? And what the fuck do you care at this point? You're willing to kick me out at the lowest point of my life, and you want me to be safe in the meantime?

A long-winded argument ensued in my head as Jose drove back onto the freeway. I played back Veronica's words and thought of different foul responses to use when I saw her again.

Be safe. Be fucking safe. What a joke. What a hollow lie. That miserable fucking . . . I never should have . . .

And on and on it went that way inside the mind of the demented. I was back to anger. Always back to anger. I lived inside my head, running through "what if" and "I should have said this" scenarios. But I was only talking to myself, having conversations with the voices in my head, and the audience was growing restless.

Jose had a mini DVD player set up on the middle console of his cab. He opened it up and pressed play as he drove. The MGM lion gave his dispassionate, surly roar, and I recognized the pipes of Chris Cornell begin the introduction of James Bond, Casino Royale. Mexican bootleg movies—perfect.

A few minutes later, we pulled in front of a large nightclub that looked like a remodeled warehouse. A long line of boisterous and well-dressed youths snaked around the building. Men wore collared shirts unbuttoned far past appropriate, with heavy metal shining from their exposed necks. Every haircut was flawlessly faded and had been retouched that day. And the women—oh my, the women. Dresses clung to Latin curves like Saran Wrap. Every dress was minuscule, and every heel a tower. Black and white were the colors of choice. Dark brown thighs stood at perfect angles to accentuate fertile childbearing hips. Oversized hoops dangled from earlobes under beautiful, flowing manes of black hair. The lionesses stood close to their mates, stroking, cooing, and primping.

We pulled into a parking spot marked "reserved," about a hundred feet from the front door, and received a nod from a bouncer holding a clipboard.

"Wait here my friend," Jose ordered.

As if I had a choice. Jose left me in the cab, and I didn't bother to watch where he went. Instead, I focused my attention on the movie and tuned Tijuana out. Tuned out, tuned out my life, tuned out the sorrow and the loneliness. Distracted myself from facing the truth. God, I needed more meth so I could tune out everything else, hurry up and finish the room, and save my relationship.

It felt relieving to lie to myself: She'll come around, I know it, as soon as she sees what I'm able to make in that garage. It'll be a fucking cash machine, money growing on little trees. Just gotta get one more bag. I'll make this one last, cut my smoke in half. I'll start tapering off the shit, and I'll finish the room, and I'll make her love me again, and then I'll get clean and then . . .

Shadows moved in my periphery. Commotion. Shouting. I looked up from the small screen and saw men dressed in combat fatigues, pointing AR-16's, storming the warehouse. They moved in small groups to different entry points of the building, always in a phalanx assembly. Their heads were covered with black helmets, and they wore large ski goggles across the eyes. The pods moved with symmetry and fluidity as if all part of one organism.

The line of people waiting to get into the club was now a panicked fire drill. All the bouncers were face-down on the concrete with a soldier standing over them and a gun aimed at center mass. Men ran away from the frenzy at full sprint. Women scampered away in small, awkward, stiletto shuffles and held their dresses up at the bust line. One woman fell to the concrete as her heel snapped, and she was trampled by the crowd multiple times before she could get back up. I noticed she was not wearing any undergarments.

After a few minutes, the commotion settled, and it was apparent the soldiers now had control of the structure. A handful of men were lined up against the corrugated metal siding as soldiers patted them down. One suspect turned back and said something to the soldiers, who responded with the butt of an AR-16 square across his jaw. His face hit the wall with a bounce and left a Jackson Pollack in midnight red spattered on the canvas before he hit the ground.

A soldier crept up from my blindspot, and the first thing I saw was the wandering barrel of an assault rifle. When I turned to look, I saw him standing at my most vulnerable angle, pointing his gun at my face, and shaking his head with cold, calculated dominance, as if to tell me not to move a muscle. I felt my balls immediately tuck and hide, and all I could do was look away and turn my attention back to the little screen on the center console. The soldier slid into the shadows, and I kept my eyes fixed on the movie. I was just a guy watching a flick, hoping they didn't decide to pull me out of the car. I was so scared that I didn't dare take my eyes of the screen for the next 15 minutes.

The driver-side door opened abruptly, the cabin light came on, and my intestines nearly spilled everything as my rectum held the dam closed for dear life. Jose plopped in and quickly shut the door.

"You okay my friend?" he asked nonchalantly, as if discussing last night's dinner.

I turned my gaze to meet his eyes, and he cracked a playful grin when he saw the terror on my face.

"Don't worry. It's no problem."

"What the fuck was that Jose? Did you know that was going to happen?" I asked in a panic.

"No. No. No problem mi amigo. I didn't know, but I got your shit, so everything is bueno."

I looked around and saw nothing. Everyone was gone, as if nothing ever happened.

"What the fuck was that Jose?"

"Is no problem. They come for some narcos who party at the club."

"They looked like soldiers. Holy shit Jose. Was that a raid?"

"They're like your DEA my friend. But they no send everyone to jail. Maybe narcos pay, maybe narcos no come home again. But is no problem for you."

Jose handed me a cigarette pack, inside of which was something other than cigarettes wrapped in multiple layers of plastic. He told me not to pull it out, just to put it in my pocket. He gave me a serious look, in case I forgot there was a police raid nearby not more than 15 minutes ago. I did as I was told.

We drove away, and the movie was still playing on the mini screen. On the freeway, I took the bag out of the cigarette pack and hid it in my underwear, tucking it snuggly under my balls. Soon we were back at the border plaza, and Jose let me out close to the pedestrian bridge on the Mexican side.

"Thanks, Jose. I'll call you and let you know when I'm coming down again."

"Okay my friend."

Everything felt better already; Pavlovian anticipation. Now that I had an eight ball hidden in my underwear, the battle was more than halfway won. My brain connected missing links and I felt a pre-rush as serotonin and dopamine receptors blossomed in anticipation of being pollinated.

Even Mexico felt lighter now that I was almost home. My armor receded, and I no longer kept my eyes on constant rotation to scout for predators. Stray dogs became less hostile, and as I walked through a small park, I caught the eye of a rose in bloom. She looked at me with effortless grace, pink and white voluptuous petals flaunting her femininity, standing on a tall, slim stem, and unafraid to show her thick, exposed roots as a declaration of years of dedication to a proud culture. I marveled at the simplicity. How could I have forgotten? How long had it been since I'd seen the world? How long had I been living in the myopic darkness of my own mind?

As I approached the entrance to the walking border checkpoint, a group of children ran up to me and started gesticulating playfully.

"Chicle! Chicle!" They all shouted, dancing at the same time. One little girl, no older than five, didn't know yet; didn't know what she was doing, didn't know the burden of the poor; didn't know what the gringo in front of her represented. All she knew to do was mimic the older kids, so she jumped up and down and waved her arms, and smiled and laughed, as if it were all just a game.

What a smile! What a beautiful, radiant, innocent smile. The older kids pushed the box into my chest, and some tried to sneak a hand in my pocket. But that one little girl just stayed in the background and danced as though she were on a playground, a true child of God.

To calm the feral pack, I took out my wallet and handed over one American dollar to the alpha. He snatched it out of my hand like a lizard catching flies. I shooed them away, and the leader accepted my gesture as he ran off with the box of gum. His herd followed. The little girl was slow, so before she finally took off, I managed to slip a five into the front pocket of her overalls and pointed her toward the fleeing pack. She trotted off in clumsy little steps, and I watched her with shame. What a shame that she didn't yet know to pity herself. What a shame that I was there to teach her.

Thankfully, the walking line was short at that hour of night. I called Veronica as I made my way toward the immigration checkpoint and let her know all was well and to wait for me outside the building.

The officer who called me up to his station was about as typical as they come. Fade, high and tight. Mustache, thick and trimmed. Stare, ominous and distrustful. I did my best to play the role I needed to play: Gringo partying in TJ, booze and whores, friends left earlier because they couldn't find me, and I woke up in a brothel and didn't know how I got there. You can say a lot with just a look and intention. I handed him my ID and felt my heart palpitating uncomfortably in my chest. My sphincter tightened. I needed to take a shit.

"Purpose of your trip to Mexico?" he asked.

"Fun weekend," I tried my best to look him in the eye, but quickly retreated, as I was certain my entire life was written on my forehead and equally certain he could read it all.

"How long were you in Mexico?"

"Came over Friday night."

"Alone?"

"No. There was a group of us," I lied.

"What happened to your buddies?" he pressed.

"Got split up. I think they came back yesterday."

He stared a hole into my soul, and I stood there wilting. Seconds felt like years, and my entire life was distilled into that one passing judgment.

"All right. Be careful next time. You don't want to be down here alone."

"Thank you," I managed to squeak out in a high, cracking voice as I forced an uncomfortable meeting of the eyes with this man who had allowed me to continue my own delusion.

He handed back my ID, and I scuttled off. I could feel the sweat soaking my armpits and trickling down the small of my back, but I made it; I was safe, back over the border, and I had what I came for.

Veronica was waiting for me just outside the station, and I quickly climbed into her car.

"Get me the fuck out of here," I practically shouted as I flopped into the passenger seat.

"Are you okay? Oh my God, I was so scared."

"I'm fine. I don't want to talk about it. Can we just go home, please?"

"Yeah. Okay. No problem."

As we drove, I reached into my underwear and pulled out the bag.

"How is it? Did you try it?" she wanted to know.

"Don't know. Didn't have a chance with all the shit going on."

As we pulled onto the freeway, I reached into her purse and pulled out the sunglass case in which she kept her pipe. I was fumbling with the bag and pipe, trying to scoop some shards into the neck of the oil burner, and my mind was exploding with anxiety and anticipation. Finally, I managed to get everything where it needed to be, flicked my lighter, and began melting the crystals and twisting the pipe.

We were on the I-5 north, and not another car was visible for miles. The freeway lights created a distorted projection of time as I stared down at the pipe, waiting for the right temperature, and seeing life in flashing segments of orange and black. The car was quiet, and my brain was fully focused. A little smoke built in the bubble, and my eyes grew wide as I put the stem to my lips, continuing the rotation and heat pattern, and came face to face with my maker. Glaring junkie eyes and flickering shadows on my face. The moon stared down at her poor, sick boy and wept as she looked on in silence.

I inhaled deeply, filling my lungs to capacity with the simmering narcotic, but something didn't feel right. I began coughing and let the smoke come back out sloppily. That taste. I knew that taste.

"Goddamn mother fuckers!" I mumbled between coughs and gasps of air.

"What's wrong?"

I put my pointer finger over the exhaust hole of the pipe and blew out. Instantly, it turned white.

"Fucking pieces of shit. This is almost all MSM. It's all cut." I was livid.

I stared at the tip of my finger, now powdered white, and felt the free fall of my gut as my brain computed the math.

"What do you want to do?" Veronica asked with gentle sympathy.

"What can we do? Nothing." I stared at the pipe in my hand.

Then I put the pipe back to my lips and began reheating the compound.

"Why are you smoking more? I thought it was no good?" she wondered.

"What else am I supposed to do? Hopefully there's a little bit of real shit in here, and if there is, I'm not wasting it."

"What if it's all cut?" she asked while looking over at me.

"What if? What if Veronica? So many what ifs."

She turned away because she knew what was coming. I looked down and kept smoking with spurn.

gone all night

Dark were the days when she wasn't home; bleak was the darkness when she was gone all night. All night—she'd been gone all night, and I had been watching the clock the entire time.

Why would she hurt me like this? Why would she be so cruel?

She knew I loved her, and she knew I needed her, so why would she deliberately choose to torment me?

That evil, malignant, fucking cunt. Fuck her. Fuck her and her cold heart. She knew.

She knew exactly what she was doing to me, and she chose to do it anyway. Or maybe not?

Maybe it was just a mistake, a misunderstanding?

I was overreacting. Fuck, man. I was so far gone that I didn't know what to think. But I couldn't stop thinking. That was all I could do. Sit there and think. Ruminate. Brood. Lament.

I didn't even want to get high anymore. It made my mind spin too fast. I wanted all the voices to stop. It was too loud. It was too crowded in my head, and I had no control. No control.

No control of my mind. No control of my life. All I could do was sit there and bear witness to the absolute wreckage that was my wasted life. I was fully aware, and fully conscious, yet willfully apathetic in all regards except the continued destruction of self.

Fuck it. May as well smoke a bit more and try to get some work done.

Just a couple hits.

Not too much.

The night began normally enough. I was down in the garage, working on the room, and she was up in the house, practicing with her band. Sound carried easily down the hall, and through the floor, as it rained down upon me a storm of resentment and spite. She was singing about me now, and her words buckled my knees and cut out my heart.

When we first got together, she often spoke about her songs and the cathartic quality they carried for her. She was singing about her ex-husband then, while they were going through the early stages of a divorce, and she let lethal words fly without hesitation. There were no parables, no attempts to disguise the meaning; she simply opened her heart and unleashed her truth. It felt reaffirming to listen to her then, when the barrel was pointed at someone else, and I was the knight waiting heroically for my opportunity to rescue the poor, neglected princess.

How disenchanting it was to listen to those songs from the other side, upwind from the hunter's barrel, while I lived like an ostracized leper in the garage. I tried to block out the sound, but it was no use. The music drowned my thoughts. She hated me, and she was singing about it at the top of her lungs. The bassist couldn't keep tempo after the second verse, just before the chorus, so they practiced the line over and over again.

". . . and I just need to be free from you, free from you, from yoooouuuuu . . ."

One more time from the top.

Fuck it. I couldn't work with that shit in the background.

I thought to myself, she wants to air this in front of her friends, humiliate me like this, then I'll get high and get my head right. I'll get high because she's cold, and I deserve reprieve. I'll get high because it's a Thursday. I'll get high because . . .

My bag was getting low. Fuck. I'd been smoking like crazy that week. Just got an ounce a few days ago and already I'd put a noticeable dent in it. It was her fault. I was smoking more because I knew I was losing her. I knew she didn't believe in us anymore, and she was distant. Her eyes always shifted quickly away from my gaze when we crossed paths. I was nervous, and alone, and felt like the world was about to fall on my head at any moment. So I smoked.

I smoked for comfort. I smoked for purpose. I smoked for one more run.

I kept thinking, God just let me finish this last part of the room so I can turn these fucking lights on. Then she couldn't get rid of me. She couldn't kick me out if the garage was humming with 8,000 watts of high-pressure sodium and metal halide. No way.

If she didn't believe in me anymore, then she didn't deserve all the effort I put into keeping us away from withdrawal. She could hate me all she wanted, but there was no getting around the fact that we were both addicts at that point. She wanted me out of there, but I wondered how she'd fare going through detox?

At the very least, she didn't deserve an even split on the bag. I mean, come on, just on a physical basis I deserved more than her because I was bigger, so I needed to compensate. Now she was up there, singing her icy heart out about the monster that lived in her

261

garage. I would show her a monster.

During the day, while she worked in her office, she kept her stash right next to her in the desk drawer. In the evenings, she usually didn't stray too far from it, and I never had much opportunity to look around. But that night, as with other nights she practiced with the band, she put the bag in the master bathroom, tucked inside a tampon box. I figured it out one night because that's what tweakers do; we scour like cockroaches in the dark.

So, once a week, I had an opening. She left her bag vulnerable to attack, and I usually took a pinch. Not too much, but just enough to make me feel like I'd won something back. After all, she was threatening to take everything away from me. I decided to take more than usual that evening. That time, I wanted to steal a sizable chunk because she was singing a new song—a song about how much she hated me. I hate you, too, bitch.

I skulked along the pathway from the garage, keeping to the side least visible from the living room. I had the advantage because they were in the light, and I slithered in the shadows. At the front door, I stood and waited, listening for the right time to open the door, needing to synchronize with their music so they couldn't hear the squeaky hinges. Bass drum, high-hat cymbals, guitar— then I quickly turned the knob, oozed in, and closed the door with a surgeon's glide. They were still jamming when I made my way down the hallway unnoticed.

No sense risking detection by turning on a light, so I worked like a prowler in the dark room. I found the bag and pinched a hefty piece, probably three grams, then began heading out, but my heart suddenly skipped. The music stopped and someone was walking down the hardwood hallway.

Steps of death.

Paranoia and meth.

The steps cut short and went into the bathroom in the hallway. It wasn't her. It was Greg, the bassist, and I could hear him lift up the toilet seat and start pissing a long overdue, multiple-beers stream as I crouched in the other bathroom, separated by thin sheetrock and thick fear.

"Let's do another shot of tequila!" Veronica called out from the living room.

Greg rumbled his assent from the adjacent bathroom, and the group concurred. Now I was stuck in her bathroom until I got cover sound to move again. Mirth resonated from the kitchen, and I decided to take a couple of hits off her pipe while I listened to the hoopla in the dark. Smoking crystal in the dark made me keenly aware of the level of dope fiend I had become. The flame became a beacon in a storm, and I stared into the glass hollow with wide junkie eyes while listening to the festive banter coming from the kitchen.

Finally, the music kicked up again, and I made my tiptoeing escape out of the house. That would teach her. Singing songs about how horrible a person I was when we got into the whole mess together.

Point the finger all you want, you poor little victim. You still have the thirst like I do, and we'll see how well you keep your tune when you're going through withdrawal.

I was working in the garage, high as fuck, tweaking out on how I was going to keep the smell down and manage the heat exhaust so a DEA plane doing basic reconnaissance wouldn't be able to pick up a heat signature with infrared cameras.

I've got it, I thought. I'll have all the A/C units exhausting into a separate room where I'll cut into the main four-inch plumbing line, tie in a y-connector, and attach a fan so all my hot, pungent, marijuana smelling air would be shot down into the main sewer line. Who's going to be able to pick up that trail? Every other air access point will be run through a triple filter of my own design: activated carbon charcoal, baking soda, and cat litter.

Genius. I was pleased.

I didn't hear Veronica come in because I was in the back room staring at the main plumbing tree where all the pipes converged. Better not fuck this up or I'll have shit everywhere, I warned myself.

She was staring at me, and I may as well have been staring off into space, tweaked out of my head, studying with fervor.

"Hey. What are you doing?" she asked.

Tunnel vision expanded to full awareness, and I plummeted back to earth.

"Oh hey. Nothing. Just thinking about how to tie in."

"Be careful. That could get messy."

We both laughed, and for a moment, I forgot that I hated her. She was dressed up like she used to be when we first started dating—dark blue, skin-tight jeans and a white top with spaghetti straps cut low to make her breasts pop out.

"Can I borrow your car?" she asked. "I want to go out and get some drinks with the guys."

"Yeah, sure. No problem. Keys are on the workbench by the Skilsaw," I replied.

She offered the tiniest of smiles, which I took as a faint whisper of hope between us, and walked out the door.

Hours passed as I tinkered away in the garage. Where does the mind go when possessed by the all-consuming tweak? Every aspect, every detail of utter uselessness so vitally important to the fate of the entire human race- then you realize you're only thinking about water pressure or tensile strength.

If only I had applied this level of fortitude to other aspects of life; I may well have cured cancer. But, as it stood that day, I paced frantically in a garage as the night chased the other monkeys into bed and the moon kept a watchful eye over her deranged son.

At precisely 1:36 in the morning, paranoia hit me like a heavyweight rib shot. She wasn't home yet. There was no controlling a mind on meth, and dementia is not solely reserved for the elderly. She wasn't home yet. My mind ran through possible scenarios like an FBI database. Where could she be? Was she in trouble? I checked my phone and saw a text from two hours earlier: "Ha ha. I hear surfers can go all night and still get up to catch the morning swell."

Oh, dear God, no. A spark landed on my gasoline-soaked heart.

I texted her back: "What the fuck is this text?"

Three minutes later, I texted again: "Did you send this on purpose, or did you mean to text someone else?"

Two minutes later: "You fucking whore!"

One minute later: "You've got some nerve borrowing my truck to go fuck other guys."

Blind rage consumed me. I pulled the hammer from my tool belt and started swinging violently. The workshop began to fall like a once mighty empire under barbarian invasion. What was made of wood splintered and broke. What was metal bent and leaned. The sounds were repulsive. Metal has a high-pitched scream when battered. The hammer made wood sound like bones being broken. I swung with every ounce of fury I'd collected over a lifetime of self-hatred. My breathing was strained and frantic. Spit flew and drool leaked as I mumbled obscenities. There was no more self, no more consciousness. I was as primitive as it gets—fully rabid.

My heart pumped indignantly, and my mind was lost to a dark cinema. Scenes flashed across the screen of my imagination. Veronica with someone else. The way she smiled when she wanted to be fucked, the lust in her eyes. She liked it when I played with her nipples while going down on her. She would bury her face in a pillow when I was doing her from behind because she wanted it hard and she was embarrassed at how loud she got.

And now, there was someone else touching her. Now, she was looking into someone else's eyes, holding his ass tight, pulling him into her, and telling him was okay to come inside her. I could see it. I could feel it. She was fucking him right then.

I regained consciousness in the big office chair, the misplaced throne of an excommunicated king now in exile. I tasted snot on my upper lip and my eyes were crusty when I blinked. My hands were pulsating with pain, swollen, and the knuckles were torn up and bloodied. I was alone. Alone in that fucking garage and alone on this miserable planet.

I didn't want to feel anymore. I wanted to die. God, I just wanted it to be over. I stumbled back up the walkway, into the house, and went straight for the pantry. The happiest, most loving dog on the planet, Betsy Ann, rushed over to greet me with her kind eyes and perpetual smile. But even she, that innocent creature of joy, was put off by the level of hate exuding from my soul. She quickly retreated to her bed and watched me cautiously from a safe distance.

I grabbed a handle of Jack Daniels, economy size, and sat at the kitchen table facing the living room, which was full of musical instruments. I took large, drowning gulps from the bottle and

266

swallowed with rage as I stared at the scene. That was where she sang about the monster. That was where we used to snuggle on the couch together, watching our favorite shows, and laughing endlessly until desire took over, and we found ourselves naked in each other's arms.

The house was eerily silent now as Betsy Ann watched me drown in booze, but my anger consumed the space with fierce aggression. I could hear my heart beating angrily, and I could not turn off the voices in my head. Conspiracy theories, victim narratives, and "fuck you" speeches ran through my mind, and I couldn't stop any of it. When I couldn't stand it in the house anymore I went back down to the garage where I belonged.

It was 3:39 in the morning and I was wide-awake, staring at the clock on my cell phone, waiting for a sound, drinking whiskey— and I was at total defeat. The rage had passed. All that was left now was despair. I sat, leaning forward in the chair with my forehead resting on my palms, and stared down at the sawdust on the concrete floor. The tears came slowly at first, then poured down like a storm. I was silent and weeping. My abdominals convulsed in spasms, forcing me to catch breaths as I cried. Oh, dear God, what had I done.

Tears fell below me to the floor and I watched as the sawdust absorbed and expanded--holding my misery in silence. Then the silence was broken by the sound of my wailing. I fell to the floor, curled up in a ball, leaned against the leg of my workbench, and rocked back and forth as I wept. I wailed like an abandoned child—scared to death and desperately needing his mother. Wailing turned to quiet sobs as I realized no one was coming for me. Snot was caked over my upper lip. Breaths were short and gasping. The tears wouldn't stop.

Dark were the days when she wasn't home; bleak was the darkness when she was gone all night. All night—she'd been gone all night, and I was whimpering in the garage, hoping she returned. Wide is the difference between knowing the truth and feeling the truth. I was broken and alone, and I felt it in the core of my spirit and the hollow of my bones.

hulky

The cat glared with a long, accusatory stare, and I was seething while secretly plotting his death. I was told the cat was in his declining years. As such, I imagined myself being kind, and quick to forgive any transgressions. That sounded nice and all, but that little shit was napping right on my pillow, never mind up on the bed where I had strictly forbidden the animals to congregate.

Hulky was old and crabby and had been with Veronica from the beginning. When she was young and struggling to make rent, Hulky was the one consistent figure in her life. Hulky had seen it all: the apartments and the houses, the boyfriends and the husband, the dinner parties, and the nights she cried all alone. Through it all, Hulky neither abandoned nor judged; he just stayed and listened.

Now he was an old sourpuss in his teenage years whose white coat was frazzled and bushy, the feline equivalent of an unkempt Afro. His face was frozen in an unpleasant expression, the way some old men can't help but scowl all the time. His hair seemed to shed by the metric ton, and his dander was particularly bothersome; or maybe it just seemed that way when I was looking to instigate a fight with a cat. I was not pleased by the fact Veronica let the animals sleep on the bed. I found it quite disgusting, actually, and soon after I moved in, I required some changes to be made.

Did my nose do well with animal dander? No. Was it at a level that demanded hospital-grade sterilization? No. But I played that card as pretext for banning the animals from the bed. Once I had set that precedent, I pushed for stricter measures and banished them from the bedroom altogether. The dog now slept just past the door frame and often stared at us with sad eyes. The cat, the old prickly bastard I'd come to despise, simply found a new place to rest in the evenings.

I came up from the garage one day to use the restroom, and as I walked into the bedroom, who did I see? Hulky Fucking Meow Meow, my arch nemesis, snoozing off the afternoon directly atop my pillow. I stared for a minute and waited, using only an unregistered awareness from the laser of hate I was beaming in his direction. He opened his eyes and looked at me with indifference. Oh, how I hated indifference.

I marched toward the offender, who was somehow pompous and stoic at the same time. Only his head moved to keep me in focus while the rest of him was as still as a monk in deep meditation. I grabbed a generous handful of loose nape, then tossed him across the room. Hulky plumbed himself in mid-flight, landed with all fours on the slick hardwood floor, which in turn allowed him a stage performer's exit as he slid to a stop. His back was to me then, so he turned his head and acknowledged me with spurn. He then elegantly lifted his tail to shine me his butthole, meowed once, and strutted off down the hallway.

A month went by, and Hulky was upping his game. He began pissing in the house. Veronica claimed it to be a symptom of old age, but I saw it as nothing less than a declaration of war. Every time I found a new puddle, I hunted him down. If he happened to be off wandering outside, I left the puddle to stagnate so I could take the cat and rub his face in his own urine once he returned.

Time rushed past me like a surging river after the first storms of the season. What was supposed to take me a month to complete had now veered way off course. Stubborn and myopic, I ventured deeper into the hollow.

In the meantime, I was fighting a continual side-war with the cunningly taciturn cat that now stood as chief bane of the household. Was it possible to pinpoint the exact moment madness took full control? I made a strong argument for that the day Veronica asked me to cat-proof the backyard. The paranoia began because Hulky would venture off through the neighborhood, only to be left unable, or unwilling, to clear the last few obstacles en route back to the house, thus leaving him to meow incessantly at midnight, just past the rear neighbor's fence. So Veronica, in a delirium of maternal fever, decided Hulky would be a target for large predatory birds, who would spot the white, marooned cat from on high and swoop down to claw the poor, senile old feline as if he were a small rodent. The bottom line was this: Hulky was too old to go wandering out beyond the safety of the backyard. Now I was pitted in a fierce battle of wits to see if I could contain a cat within a rather irregular space.

The house sat tucked into an excavated hillside where the original slope was close to 60 degrees. The majority of the backyard was a steep hill with a three-foot chain-link fence around the perimeter. On the north-side property line the neighbors—a bedridden grandmother and her two middle-aged sons, retired mathematics professors who chose to live in straw huts in the backyard—had built a standard wood fence long ago but let it fall victim to wild ivy and decay. Now, the fence was in such poor repair that Veronica's dog, a 60-pound Australian shepherd, could squeeze out from time to time and end up running amok in the streets. That was the perimeter I had to secure for the safety of an agile, stubborn, and rather salty, old cat.

I began by blocking off the entire north side and the fence that bordered our shoe-averse neighbors. I built a makeshift border of stakes, runner boards, and orange plastic construction fencing. The pitch was unwelcoming, and the dirt hard and brittle, so I cursed with every stake I drove and every board I tried to nail. When I finally finished, I sat in the kitchen, eating a sandwich, and stared out into the backyard. From a covert hiding spot, Hulky emerged

271

and immediately went to inspect the new fence. Beginning at the bottom of the hill, he walked up gingerly until he reached the top. There, he found a gap and easily cleared the obstacle. Seething in the kitchen, an idea hit me, and I realized I could turn the cat's sovereign disposition to my advantage.

I repaired the gap on the northeast corner and ran a new line of plastic lattice along the chain-link, pitched back at a 45-degree angle, so I could leverage gravity in the service of my cause. With the new security measures in place, I found Hulky napping in one of his nooks and snatched him from his slumber. As we walked toward the rear of the house, I felt him tense and squirm in my hands, but I kept my grip firm so he would know who was in control. We stepped into the backyard, and I placed him on the ground while still holding his neck firmly. Then I gave him an aggressive smack on the ass, sending him sprinting away from me in fear.

The cat ran up the hill and started to hop the fence, but my new perimeter forced him back down in panic. He then found one of his secret routes, a tunnel under the fence, and squeezed his way through to freedom. Hulky had escaped yet again, but not without betraying another angle, one I would promptly close behind him. That process of backyard battleship ensued for weeks as I continued to cover escape routes and Hulky continued to impress me with his vast knowledge of secret paths.

I came up from the garage for lunch one day and through the sliding patio door, I saw the white bandit making his way slowly up the hillside, walking close to the fence line, the way a convict walks a prison yard. From the front door of the house to living room, there were five steps, fairly steep, one had to climb to go between. As I spotted Hulky outside, I ducked down, sat on the bottom step, and peeped over the top. I watched carefully in nervous silence.

Hulky reached the top southeast corner and inspected cautiously. Yes, my friend, I, too, happened to have noticed a possible weakness in the overlap of the corner, but will you be brave enough to risk the consequences? He sat in contemplation for a moment, then turned his head directly down toward me, a good fifty feet away, as if he knew I was watching him the whole time. Like a craven peeping Tom, I ducked down out of sight quickly and held my breath, hoping he wasn't able to spot me.

When I finally mustered enough courage to peek over the steps, I found him already up in the fencing, the loose plastic part that angled back over him, and he was trying to get through an overlapping gap out to freedom. But I could see that my trap was, nonetheless, effective. The plastic was slack and replete with holes that were just the right size for a cat's paws to slip through. As Hulky tried to navigate the uneven material, he couldn't keep his balance. He ended up on his side, unable to move on the treacherous surface, not unlike a beached whale on the shore. He began to groan and wail in that wretched, desperate cat pitch. I waited a while and watched, relishing my victory for a few minutes, and seeing whether he could manage to get himself out of the mess. After five minutes, I considered the event a success and went to rescue Hulky.

Weeks, months, I had no fucking idea what year it was; my neurosis was nothing short of asylum grade. Somewhere along the way, I cut off two fingers while working on the project. Within a week, I was back down in the garage trying to work on the room with those two salvaged fingers in a splint. Perhaps that would've been a good time to reconsider my options. Maybe get a job for a while, Veronica had suggested. When was the thing going to be done?

I got a call one day from Veronica's friend who told me not to be angry, and that he had bad news. Veronica had been fired. They were taking the company car, and the cell phone was already gone. She was driving with her former manager to the house right that moment so they could take her computer.

"Don't be mad, and please don't cause a scene when they get there," the friend pleaded.

I waited in her office like death waits for time. When she got home, I met them at the front door, beamed a death stare at the manager, and told him to wait outside while Veronica gathered her things. She was in the office, scrolling through files on her computer, and Hulky was by her side, on the table, watching attentively.

"You need any help? What can I do?" I asked as I walked into the room.

The space was brightly lit, mainly from the influx of sunlight that poured in through the two large bay windows facing the street. Her desk was in front of the windows, and on the adjacent wall was a bookshelf with miscellaneous clutter, reference manuals, and old blueprints from jobs on which she had bid. On the opposite side was a closet that spanned the length of the room with three separate sections of folding doors. A couple of doors were slightly open, and clothing of all types spilled from the seams.

"Do you know how to erase everything on here? I mean besides just the browsing history? I don't want them to have any of my files," she was panicked and spoke with excess breath over the tops of her words.

"I'm not sure, but I can fry the whole thing if you want," I replied.

"Yeah. Okay. Can you, please?"

I ran down the hallway, out the front door, passed the waiting corporate Bob in his casual Friday jeans and polo shirt, and down into the garage. In my shop, I quickly found what I was looking for: an extension cord that I'd cut on one end and frayed so as to leave exposed copper leads for both positive and neutral sides. Then I ran back up into the house. The manager tried to say something as I scooted by him, but I only offered a disparaging retort, "Shut the fuck up."

Inside the house, we put the laptop on the floor near an outlet. I

274

stuck the leads on opposite sides of the computer into identical USB slots then plugged the male end into the socket. The computer offered a few popping sounds, and the outlet produced a barely visible blue arc, before a click was heard from the main electrical panel nearby indicating the breaker was triggered. The screen was black, and the power button didn't seem to do anything when pressed.

"I think we're done here," I told her.

I waited in the office as Veronica went outside to deal with the embarrassing end to a job in which she had taken great pride. Hulky looked at me with fear, for he knew what typically followed such vitriol. But I did not react as I normally would have.

Veronica came back into the room, sat in the middle of the floor, and began venting. I followed along as best I could, nodding occasionally and only asking minimal questions. Why would they fire her when she was one of the top reps? A slew of conspiracy theories were generated in response, but something ominous, deep in my viscera, shifted around and revealed the answer without words: This was only the beginning.

As she continued her voluble purge, the words began to get chopped at the ends. Her eyes welled up. Slowly, she turned her attention toward the floor before she choked up and nothing remained audible. I rose from the chair and walked toward her as she buried her face in her hands and wept. I lowered into a sitting position on her right side and placed my arms around her shoulders. She leaned into me and cried with her nose on my heart. Deep convulsing sobs came out of her, forcing her to gasp for air. I put one hand around the back of her head and held the crown of her skull. She grabbed the sides of my t-shirt and pulled tightly. I adjusted my legs, unfolding the limbs into large tentacles that I wrapped around her midsection, and pulled her into the center of all that I was. She cried and she cried, and I held on to my lover for dear life.

"What are we going to do Anto? We're fucked." She squeezed out the words between spasms from her diaphragm.

"It's okay baby. We'll be okay. I love you," I whispered softly.

Hulky watched from the table as Veronica melted into my arms. The sun was a hand's width above the horizon, and the light managed a straight shot in through the window. Outside, the large pine trees swayed slightly in the wind. The cat, the sun, and the trees all held their breath as they watched the heartbreaking saga take another turn for the worse.

More eddies of time surreptitiously whisked by in the great river of void, silent and brooding. I felt there was a great calamity happening just below the surface, but I was not able to see it through my own reflection. Tension was building in the house, Veronica and I were growing further apart, and the garage was nowhere close to completion.

Veronica found another job. I began to sell scrap copper and aluminum I had lying around. I routinely ventured into the dilapidated industrial zones of Chula Vista and National City, learning what it was to be part of the scrap yard community. I barely came out of the garage anymore, as I'd cut into the main waste line so I could piss into a funnel lodged in a Y connector. I'd mounted a camera on the side of the house and watched with incessant paranoia the TV I had broadcasting the show that was now the outside world. George still stopped by occasionally and broke my heart all over again each time he avoided the elephant and acted like we were old buddies. I went deep into electrical theorem and practiced by replacing the entire main panel for the house, then running a sub-panel down to the garage, then figuring out how to transfer loads of different voltages using relays, timers, and sensors. Normally open, normally closed, number of contact points, line amps, load amps, and so on. Meanwhile, Veronica went on with her life.

One day, I found Hulky pissing in the middle of the kitchen, so I snatched him up, took him into the backyard, grabbed a ladder, and placed him up on an inescapably high branch in a tree. I took my time eating lunch and listening to his agony before finally getting him down.

Veronica and I only seemed to know each other as passing figures in a moribund play. We were rarely in the same room together, our eye contact was elusive, and when we did manage to converse, each of us was obviously spinning some angle of a story so as to keep the other at an emotional distance. One day, a conversation began in the bedroom.

"How's your finger rehab going?" she inquired.

"It's okay. I don't make it all the time."

"Why not?"

"Because I'm busy with work Veronica. I need to get those lights on."

"Anto. Maybe you should focus on your fingers and let the garage wait. I mean, do you really think you're going to get it done now?"

"Veronica, I don't have any other choice. Everything I have left I put into that garage."

"Well, maybe it's time to start thinking about something else?"

A terrible fear began to rise in me as she paused and looked into my eyes, with a long steady gaze, for the first time in months.

"What do you mean?" I asked.

"Anto, I mean this thing was supposed to, I mean . . . What are we even doing here?"

"We're trying our best to make it through this thing Veronica, that's what we're doing. We're two people who chose to lean on each other and now we're going through some tough times but all we have to do is keep working, and we'll make it. The money will start to come in and then we'll deal with the Towelie thing, and we'll be okay."

"Anto, we haven't been okay in a long time. I wanted to talk to you before, but then you had your accident, and I thought maybe that would change you a little, but you just went right back to your old ways and even worse. I mean, I just don't know anymore."

"You just don't know? What do you mean you just don't know? What the fuck do you mean!?" I was getting angry.

"Anto, please don't yell at me. This thing between us is not working out, and we need to start thinking about going our separate ways."

I thought to myself, it's happening again. Oh, dear God, you evil motherfucker you. My life is crumbling around me again, and the person I'd come to depend on was telling me I was not welcome anymore.

My mainframe was overloaded, and I could not tell which emotions I was feeling; everything was being released all at once. I looked into her eyes and finally saw what I'd been avoiding for months. She was already gone, and her heart was crusted over with a sheet of ice. She stared with indifference, and a wide canyon had opened between us. I began to cry as I felt the wind whip over me from the dark void below.

"Please, Veronica. Please don't do this," I pleaded.

"I'm sorry, Anto, but I just can't keep doing this. I'm not saying you need to leave right away, but let's start thinking about what we can do. Alright?"

Tears were streaming and my vision became blurred. I had no

energy left, and my stomach felt frail. I put my palms on the corners of my forehead, where my horns would be, and sat down on the floor in a clumsy fashion. I bent over so my face was close to my feet, and my hands squeezed the sides of my head firmly; panic, terror, complete hollow.

I cried, and I cried, and I drooled, and mucus bubbled from my nose. I rocked back and forth while squeezing my head harder and harder; complete delirium.

"Please, Veronica. Please give me another chance." I was desperate.

"Anto. I'm sorry, but we passed that point a long time ago."

Sobbing. Completely alone. Lost. Abandoned. Insane. I drifted in the cold, dark hollow, and I was about to stop resisting.

"Please don't leave me, Veronica . . . please. Not like this."

But my begging was barely audible through the spasms of sobbing. Even if she heard, she did not listen. I fell on my side into the fetal position and cried. I cried for Veronica, I cried for George, and I cried for my father. It was as if I was releasing an ancient prisoner, a rumor of a man who once tried to topple a king and long ago was thrown into the deepest dungeon and whose name was since forbidden to be spoken. My head rested on the hardwood floor, and I could feel Veronica's footsteps veer carefully around me as she walked out of the room.

When I opened my eyes, I was looking straight at the folding closet doors on the near side of the room, a few of which were left ajar. Within the closet, I could see the outline of something familiar. I wiped the muck from my eyes and allowed my pupils to focus. Then I saw him staring at me with deep equanimity. No revenge, no animosity; Hulky was stationed in solemn poise then politely excused himself from the room and left me be.

279

Months went by, and I did not leave. I forced myself on Veronica's life by way of apathy and disregard. I didn't leave because the only place I had to go was back home to mom and dad, and that would require a level of humility completely unacceptable to me. So I stayed in defiance of her wishes. Now, I let every minor project fall to the wayside in favor of focusing on one thing: getting those lights on. I knew I had her in a corner already with the nearly completed illegal grow room in her garage. If I managed to get those plants growing, then what possible recourse would she have? Yes, this was me. Yes, I did this. The levels of toxicity and vitriol in the house were at nuclear levels and somehow, I justified it, or avoided it, or just swallowed it with my eyes closed and forced it down into the hollow.

After the initial shock wore off, we came to some kind of strange homeostasis in the house. During this time, the lights finally came on in the grow room, and a sense of calm slowly settled over me. I spent day and night in the room making sure the timers were working properly, checking the pH of the nutrient supply, monitoring CO_2 levels, and so on. In a room full of marijuana plants, there was a noticeable presence, one that I felt out of a peripheral emotional sense. It carried with it the grace of an old grandmother slowly walking with her granddaughters as they play and run circles around her, and the old woman smiles.

I passed Veronica one day as I walked out of the garage and made my way up the walkway toward the house. She had both arms around a bouquet of clothing with hangers poking out of the tops.

"Hey. You want to come see the plants? They're getting really big," I asked with childish pep.

"Oh, not today but thank you. I want to make it to the store before they close. I have so much crap in those closets that I thought I would take some of the clothes I don't wear anymore and try to sell them at Goodwill."

"That's a pretty good idea. You want any help?" I asked.

"No, I'm okay. Thanks. You have plenty to work on, I'm sure."

I went to the kitchen for a snack, and Veronica continued with her task. When I came back down, she was loading the last of her stuff and her back seat was filled to the brim with clothes and miscellaneous junk. I went into the garage and continued to work.

At nine in the evening, I became worried.

At midnight, I was petrified.

At three in the morning, I finally accepted it. I smoked every morsel of crystal I had left.

Her phone went straight to voicemail, and none of my texts were being returned. I knew. I knew it was finally over, and she was gone. She had left me; or, rather, I had chased her out of her own home. It was a feeling unlike any I'd experienced during the span of my life. The syntax doesn't yet exist to accurately capture the essence of the hollow.

I didn't sleep that night. Instead, I sat in her chair, in the office that looked out onto the street, and thought about the day I held her on the floor, when she grieved the loss of her dignity, and I realized what she was really crying about.

The house was ominously quiet, like standing on a freeway at four in the morning. Then I heard the ethereal whisper of something coming toward me. I looked back toward the spot on the floor where Veronica had wept, and in the distance, I saw a little white, furry head slowly peek around the corner of the doorframe. One dejected chuckle escaped my lips, and I smiled at the only friend I had left—Hulky.

I moped around the next day like a beggar on the streets of Calcutta;

not much else to do but lament over the perversions of God. I lay down on Veronica's bed and put my face into the only pillow she had not taken with her. What is it about the smell of someone's hair that captures their beauty so completely? I took in the olfactory eminence of a soul that once loved me and now ran from me.

The day after Veronica left me was the most poignant day of my life. Everything was collapsing, but I had one last bit of hope. I was eagerly expecting a package to be delivered that day, my resupply of meth, so at least I had that going for myself. The doorbell rang, and I rushed to answer. When I looked outside, all I saw was a cardboard box on the porch.

I took the box, opened it, and pulled out the teddy bear that was inside. The stitching was torn where the butt would be, so I stuck my finger into the stuffing and felt around. I swirled and I dug, but I didn't feel anything. I took the bear to the kitchen, grabbed a filet knife, and split the bear in two; nothing but stuffing inside. I looked at the box again and noticed a second layer of packing tape across the seam. I sighed, then I laughed. I laughed in honest defeat. I laughed alone, and the sounds echoed down the hallway. What a feeling of immense proportion. Now I've done it. Now I know exactly what I've done in life.

In the evening, I sat at the kitchen table and ate cereal drearily. Hulky stared at me from inside his cathouse, and I noticed his water was out and food were running low. I filled up his bowls and took them, along with his sleeping pillow, down the hall and into the bedroom. He watched cautiously. I returned to the kitchen, grabbed his bag of treats, and began walking back toward the bedroom. He quickly followed me, and I sprinkled his cat food with savory bits of whatever was in the treat bag. I sat on the edge of the bed and watched him surgically pick out the tidbits. I listened to the obnoxious lip-smacking he produced, like a fat kid eating candy in a movie theater. What happens when irony becomes aware of itself?

The next morning, I woke up and was not well. I'd been there before, so I knew what to expect physically, but I'd never had to do it alone. I was alone and out of options. Everything had collapsed, and now I had to face my baptism by way of withdrawal.

I got out of bed with difficulty. My head was pounding, and all sense of equilibrium was tilted. My steps were short, and I dragged my feet as I used the wall for support along my trip to the kitchen. Strained breaths and weak knees. When I reached the kitchen, I forgot why I was there, so I just stared at the mess. The sink was overflowing with dishes, and the counters had bits of dried food everywhere. I sighed, then walked back to bed where I fell in as dead weight.

When I woke up, it was dark, and I was confused. The sheets were wet and my pillow was on the floor. I felt frozen down at the molecular level, and my teeth were chattering uncontrollably. Water. Need water. I stumbled into the bathroom and stuck my mouth under the faucet. I drank between gasping breaths of air. Oh shit. Too much. Then it all came out of me. My stomach pumped violently.

I woke up in bed, and it was light again. Hulky was staring at me from the dresser. I didn't blink, and neither did he. I was sweating and naked. Finally, I managed to rock myself to a sitting position. I sat with my elbows anchored on my knees and my head in my palms. My stomach was frightened. There was no hope. There was no God.

When I stood, up Hulky leapt out of the way to safety. He watched me carefully from the doorway. I stared straight down at my feet as I shuffled about because I could not lift my head. No energy. No reason to live. I made it to the bathroom and took little sips of water from the sink. The mirror was not friendly. Neither was my stomach. I was hungry. I was scared.

I made it to the kitchen and found cereal, but no milk. Cereal and water from a dirty reused bowl. I managed to keep it down.

Halfway through, I was exhausted and breathing heavily. My nose was stuffed, and I was breathing through my mouth and trying to not choke on cereal. Standing erect was too much effort. I leaned on the kitchen counter. Dizzy. Nauseous. Weak and feeble. Back to bed. I wanted to sleep forever.

Woke up. Bright lights. Dark outside. The clock on the dresser was flashing 12:00. The bed was wet again. The room smelled of something fowl. I rolled to the other side of the bed and closed my eyes.

Woke up on the floor. The floor was wet. Cat hair stuck to my cheek and lips. Sat up. Head felt terribly squeezed. Held my head and felt a bump. Tender. Swollen. Crawled into the bathroom. Sat on the toilet. Fire came out of my ass. My body ejected with anger. My head was buried in my palms. I stayed on the toilet for a long time.

Woke up in the bathtub. Cold. Shivering. Diarrhea in the tub. Diarrhea on my legs. Turned on the waterspout. Freezing. Turned on the water handle. Crying. Gasping for air. Cold. Washed myself. Back to bed.

Woke up and didn't feel like death. It was light outside, and I was hungry. Managed my way to the kitchen decently. Still weak and my steps were old man shuffles, but not death. I was not death.

I ate a granola bar then poured myself some whiskey. I even managed to smile a bit. Okay. I can do this. I went back to bed and turned on a movie while sipping my whiskey. Hulky stared at me from his pillow, and I looked down at him and pointed. Yes, my friend.

The next day, I woke up and decided it was time to venture out. Although I still felt feeble, I knew I had to secure some basic supplies. I went to Home Depot because I had a credit of $116 from a return, so I used all of it to buy whatever they had for food; Kit Kats, Red Bulls, peanut butter cups, Gatorade, and Snickers bars.

For the next two weeks, I lingered around the house and ate junk food. I checked on the garage, which was now full of marijuana plants, and spent as much time as I could tending the canopy. The rest of my time was spent trying to find Veronica. I sent her emails and spent hours staring at her Myspace page. Where could she be? Why didn't she come home?

Delusion was difficult to let go of. Loneliness is man's greatest threat. I spun myself in circles, running through different scenarios where I could convince Veronica to come back. Maybe if she knew I was clean now, she would give me another chance. Maybe I could help her get clean. I thought for hours at the kitchen table while drinking all the liquor she had left in her cabinets. One day, the electricity went out and never returned.

Finally, I received an email and some vague references about living in a hotel some nights and sleeping in her car at Balboa park other nights. I spent days scouring the park and the surrounding hotels, hoping to catch her. I was sure if she would just talk to me and see that I was off meth that we could work things out. More junk food. More booze.

Some days, she emailed me. Some days, I stared at my computer waiting for a response. I was hopeful, but maybe she needed a little motivation. I called her friends, all her old friends that she hid from and lied to since she met me, and told them I was looking for Veronica because I needed to get her clean. We were drug addicts, hooked on crystal meth, and I had gotten myself off it, so now I needed to help her do it, too. I went to her ex-husband's house and gave him a similar version. Everyone was shocked and disgusted. Regardless, I continued my assault on her reputation.

In three weeks, I had gained 38 pounds. I came home one day to find the locks changed, but I just kicked the door open and continued to squat. Another week went by, and the emails had stopped. My parents called to tell me they were coming over. Veronica had called them, and they needed to talk to me. I stood firm in my resolve and told them I had it all under control. Yes, I had been addicted to meth; but now, I was clean.

I've got this. I love her. And I am going to fix it.

My mother shook her head in embarrassment. Oh, my poor boy, she told me. Just come home with us. This is over.

"No, you don't understand," I insisted.

No contact. Not from Veronica, and not from my parents. I sat alone in the garage and looked around. I looked around at all the things I had built, and I reflected. I remembered each piece and all the struggles involved. Nothing worked right away. Everything had a learning curve. And everything had a story behind it. But now, I was alone, and there was no one to appreciate what I'd done. Just me, and Hulky, and a garage full of memories. Fine. I gave up.

I began taking apart the grow room. One by one, I took the plants that were all still alive, even without light, and cut them at the stalk or ripped out the small ones by the roots. It had taken me two years to get to that point, and in four hours, I had it all torn down. In the end, I had 14 industrial-size garbage bags full of cannabis plants. I drove around town to find isolated dumpsters in which to disperse them.

I was sitting in the garage one day getting all my tools together. I'd rented a storage locker and had begun transferring my belongings there. As I took my tool board apart, two police officers walked in through the open door.

"Are you Anto Ljoljic?"

My breath was weak as I replied.

"Yes."

"Anto Ljoljic, you are formally issued this restraining order. You are to vacate the domicile and stay away from a Ms. Veronica Hillesum at a minimum of 300 feet until the court date listed. You are allowed to take one bag of possessions with you today, and we will monitor and escort you during the process to ensure all possessions are basic essentials."

I stared at the officer in shock. She did it. She finally called my bluff. One of the officers went into the back room and looked around. When he came back out, he asked me:

"What were you growing in the room?"

"Tomatoes," I answered.

The officer smiled aggressively and held his hand over his baton.

"Tomatoes? Right. Let's go upstairs so you can get your belongings and then get you the fuck off this woman's property tomato man."

I said nothing and looked away from his instigative stare. As I packed my belongings, I held in the tears. The officers watched carefully and reminded me of the time allotment frequently. How embarrassing. How utterly humiliating. Everyone had left me, and they all thought I was insane. In the corner of the room, Hulky watched my every move while lying on his pillow.

Before I left, I asked the officers if I could feed the cat. They allowed it. I took his bowls and topped them off, then set them down next to him in the bedroom. He looked at me and meowed. I scratched him on the head and smiled.

"I'm sorry, my friend," I said softly. Then I walked out, never to see Hulky again.

288

the color of water
and the meaning of life

Driving long distances alone was similar to being incarcerated. If a man was able to transcend the discomfort, he could use the opportunity isolation affords to journey inward, to meditate, to face the darkness, and be one with his true self. Conversely, a man can allow the monkey-mind to take control—filling gaps of boredom with anger, rehearsing plots of revenge, and avoiding long-repressed demons buried in the sarcophagus of a battered heart.

I left work around two in the afternoon. As I saw it, the world owed me. Still recovering from a completely imploded life less than two years prior, at thirty years old, I considered myself a repressed talent, a star diffused to the complacency of mundane life. I worked the counter at an electrical supply warehouse, which meant I took shit in the form of predictable blue-collar punch lines on a daily basis. Electricians tend to fire off zingers with the same commitment and intellectual capacity as children asking circular questions. I found myself willingly participating in the art of dick jokes and one-upping on a daily basis.

When you think you're better than your job, it's easy to excuse laziness and corner-cutting. I left work early because I thought I was entitled to do so. After all, hardworking warehouse manager, Gary, left early every Friday in order to beat traffic going home to his house 100 miles away, so why shouldn't I be afforded the same courtesy when visiting my girlfriend in LA?

I shaved a corner by leaving early and hit the 101 heading south. The journey began on the plus side of my imaginary tally board. I was always keeping score of something, and everyone I met caused an instant assessment of "better than" or "less than" inside my head. From San Carlos through Sunnyvale, I either passed, or was intuitively aware of, all the market-leading companies of which I was not a part: Facebook, Google, Apple, Lockheed Martin, NASA, and Yahoo. I had friends at each one, and every connection was a brisk reminder of my marginal status in the beehive of Silicon Valley. Negative tally marks made their way to my scoresheet.

Speeding down the freeway, I was trying to win back a piece of whatever it was they stole from me. I didn't know who "they" were, but they made me angry. Downtown San Jose was pocked with graffiti, and I cursed the deviants still enthralled in the pseudo prestige of street mentality. Why couldn't they grow up like I did? Fucking idiots. They should all face the soul-crushing blow of betrayal then see if they still stood for their righteous ethos.

Gilroy set me climbing over the Santa Cruz Mountains by injecting all five senses with garlic. Farmland to either side as far as the eye could see, and signs along the road declaring fresh fruit and vegetables for sale. The two-lane road would be serene if I could have passed the pretentious 18-wheeler doing 35 in a 60. Thirteen cars crawling behind him, and still he didn't use the opportunity to pull over and let us pass. Fucking asshole.

Anger is easy to find when life is a constant game of who got the best of whom. My radio began to cut out, fading away the voice of the sports-talk personality du jour. I shifted allegiance between meatballs frequently. Now I couldn't even practice the mental riffs I would certainly conceive on the fly, if only I'd been lucky enough to get the effortless position of professional loser-wrangler.

In my mind, I scoffed at the masses of complacent, fat Americans who vested all their emotional stock in the outcome of a game played by men who bore no affiliation to the fans, except to have achieved their own personal destiny within the relative proximity of where they, the jiggly comatose herd, had decided to stake their claim onto a thirty-year commitment to marginal failure delineated only by relative levels of acquiescence. They gave up on their dreams. Meaningless jobs became acceptable, and wives grew fat as whales, so they found self-worth by attaching purpose to the outcome of sports. How long before I was one of them?

It had been less than two hours in the car, and already I had danced through multiple layers of neurosis. Strong pace.

Where does the mind go when left unclogged by the checklist of daily activities, drive for instant gratification, or other distractions from the present moment? Like most western neurotics, I oscillated between nostalgia and anticipation. I put in a CD and relived glory days of old: Hello John Fogerty.

The music sent me back to a time I considered my pinnacle. I reminisced about driving loads of weed up and down the coast. Hours spent alone on the road thinking about how clever I was for constantly getting over on the system and not having to participate in the malaise of corporate life. The rush was impressive, and highly addictive, when walking into a crowded gas station or restaurant along I-5 while twenty pounds of weed was concealed in my trunk.

Families en route to their vacation would disgust me as I watched them stuff their mouths with In-N-Out burgers, defeated sweatpants hiding mounds of gelatinous capitulation. I always brought food from home or chose a relatively healthy option, thinking, once again, that I was one-upping the herd in a non-defined game tallied on a non-existent scoreboard. A drug dealer judging the overweight. Pride judging gluttony, thinking they should focus more on vanity. Brilliant.

And so, as the same CD played songs from the height of my now crumbled empire, I waded through faded memories of a life once worth mentioning. I was someone important once, but it all came crashing down in magnificent fashion when I met the man who played me like I thought I was playing everyone else.

I'd made it through Pacheco Pass and was headed down the endless straightaway that is I-5 south. My black Frontier zipped down the highway at 100 miles per hour. Memories and distractions eventually ran their course, then my mind was left to float in a void.

Signs for Coalinga County reminded me to seal the car from outside air in preparation for the coming effluvium. I could tell the wind was blowing north because the rank odor of manure assaulted me well before I could see the endless fields. As far as the eye could see, and as vast as the mind would wander, tens of thousands of cows wallowed on what looked like barren dirt but was probably their own feces. They waited patiently for their time on the slaughter block, and I sped by in a hurry on my way to a life slipping by. Harris Ranch cattle lot proudly claimed the title of largest on the west coast. Indeed, it was the largest pile of shit I had ever seen.

The killing fields didn't faze me. Instead, I reminded myself of the bright glow of love I was driving toward in Los Angeles. I had met Genevieve three months earlier while attending DUI classes in Hollywood. In a room full of people waiting for an opportunity to talk about themselves, she usually sat quietly with grace and impeccable posture.

At 28 years young, I returned home from San Diego a defeated man. Still stumbling from a ruthless combination of heartbreak, addiction, and betrayal, I managed to slowly crawl my way back into the routine of a normal life. A longtime friend got me a job with the electrical supply company his stepfather owned, so I was given an opportunity to work my way up a fast track toward a coveted management position. I began as a delivery driver.

During the day, I would rumble around the Bay Area in a twenty-foot flatbed, delivering conduit and wire to construction sites. After work, I would hit the gym to regain the confidence of my youth. On weekends, I would get piss drunk and often supplement the booze with cocaine. I felt the universe owed me a hall pass to act a fool, given the abhorrent hand I had been dealt in San Diego. By kicking meth, I believed I had earned my seat at the bar. That routine provided great comfort.

Eventually, the odds caught up with me. One night, one fateful Thanksgiving, while on another rock-star caliber binge, I made an illegal u-turn after leaving a bar in my hometown. The job wasn't progressing as fast as my ego expected, and the DUI added another layer of resentment, so I asked to be transferred to the Los Angeles branch of the business in order to settle into a culture I was certain would be more fitting for a man of my ilk. It was there, while living in the epicenter of all that was shallow and self-absorbed, that I found Genevieve hidden among the wolves. By the time I had worked up the nerve to ask her out, six months in Los Angeles had left me lonely and with even less purpose than before, so arrangements had been made to transfer me back to the Bay Area for work. Long distance relationships were difficult for a man like me.

Genevieve was stunning, a real-life version of Jessica Rabbit with a shy smile that made me scream inside every time I saw it sneak out. Radiant earth stones always accentuated her flawlessly sculpted face, and an ultra chic pixie cut crowned her exquisitely. She was the perfect mix of LA fashion and lost hippie soul. Five years my elder, and twenty years more mature, Genevieve had a poise about her that I had never witnessed before.

She was a recovering alcoholic, 18 months sober, and still serving out a mandatory two-year commitment to DUI classes after having wrecked her car, under the influence, and busted for the second time. She wasn't just sober now, she had something that flowed from her soul, some kind of spiritual thirst, that made me want to be around her all the time. Every other weekend, I made the miserable drive down the corridor of haunted memories to be with my waiting angel in a city deceptively claiming to be full of

293

them.

I was driving on a restricted license, but I never concerned myself with the idea of hedging against consequences in life. I hit the Grapevine in Southern California well shy of four hours on the road. Consequences, however, were what this particular trip down to LA was all about.

I reached the heart of Los Angeles at twenty minutes before seven. Gen wasn't due to be off of work for another hour, so I passed the time appropriately by having a few beers at a nearby restaurant. I was sitting alone at a high bar table, pressed against the window, looking out onto West Third Street in Beverly Grove. Large gulps made for quick refills. Outside, a young couple engaged in conversation, dressed in postmodern rocker chic outfits, walked by a homeless man who was sitting on the sidewalk, leaning against a light post, hunched over to one side, drooling and mumbling. The Ray-Ban wayfarers didn't give the slightest indication of concern as they both gingerly veered around the human obstacle.

Inside the restaurant, a loud buzz filled the air. Everyone seemed to be bred from amazingly attractive genes. My tally board filled with negative marks as I absorbed the hustle of Los Angeles. People looked important and appeared to be discussing important things. I felt grossly unimportant because no one had offered me a chance to be recognized; recognized for what, I did not care. Genevieve sent a text announcing her departure from work, so I picked up the pace on my last two beers.

She was even more beautiful than I remembered. When she asked why I didn't come pick up the key and let myself into her apartment, I shook it off and mentioned having a couple beers at the restaurant instead. I drank five. She smiled and gracefully flashed her emerald eyes at me to absorb my words, then casually looked away to hide the fact that she knew I was drunk.

We had sushi for dinner then headed home for an early night.

As we brushed our teeth together in the bathroom, I purposely swiped my pelvis by her butt. She smiled at me through the reflection in the vanity mirror and shook her head "no" in a way that only made me want her more.

"You know, I already took the first pill. No booty for you tonight, mister. You and your friend down there have already done quite enough.'

I grabbed a hand full of her rump, sighed, and gave my best puppy-dog look. Genevieve offered one sarcastic chuckle in response.

The next morning, I woke up arid and groggy. As I stood in front of the sink, sipping coffee and staring out the window, Genevieve walked up quietly behind me, put her arms around my waist, and rested her head on the top crease of my spine.

"Hey, lover," she mumbled in a groggy morning voice.

"Good morning sunshine. How you feeling?"

"Nervous. I took the second pill a few minutes ago."

"How long do we have?"

"A couple hours."

"What will happen, and what do you want me to do?"

"I'm going to get sick, with bad cramps, and sit in the bathtub the whole time. You just hang out, and if I need anything, I'll let you know. "

"K."

It was casual then, in the same way it had been casual when she told me. Two months into our relationship, Genevieve mentioned she was pregnant. Immediately, I had a great sense of calm, a surrender to fate. I never told her, but inside I felt willing to take on the responsibility of raising a child with her. Instead, the conversation went immediately to the topic of abortion, both of us drifting into it without much resistance. I had never discussed such a heavy topic before and was amazed by how mundane it felt. Two weeks later, we stood hugging in the kitchen.

When the time came, she quietly excused herself and walked into the bathroom. I stay curled up on the couch with a book in hand—Smokescreen, by Robert Sabbag. The walls were thin. Sound carried through effortlessly. Shower knobs squeaked, then water began to run. For thirty minutes, nothing seemed awry. I sat on the couch, consumed by my novel.

A soft moan was heard through the wall. I looked up and stared at nothing while perking up my ears. Water was still running. A few more moans, then a faint whimpering sound. I sat on the coach and listened. My mind raced to find a way to help but couldn't come up with any viable solutions.

Why hadn't I told her when we were talking on the phone that day? My heart felt that question, but my mind quickly charged in with a slew of pretext. We'd only been dating for a couple months. How could I tell a woman to consider having a child if I hadn't even told her I loved her? Did I even know how to love anymore? Would she think I was desperate and vulnerable? Besides, had my heart healed from the demolition I'd suffered in San Diego? Was this all nonsense? On paper, the abortion made sense. We barely knew each other, and I still lived in my mother's house. How could any reasonable person reach any other conclusion beside an abortion? I agreed with all the logic, but my heart was sobbing as I listened to her wallow in pain.

I stood up and began pacing around the living room. The moans became louder. Peeking down the hallway like a nervous child, I saw the bathroom door slightly ajar. Four times I tried to make it near the door, and four times I retreated in fear. Finally, on the fifth attempt, with my eyes looking straight down at the floor, I managed to venture close enough to the door to be able to say something to her. I leaned against the doorjamb, fumbling for words, listening to the sound of a woman grieving in a bathtub.

"Hey, Gen . . . Is there anything I can do to help?" I asked shyly.

"No. Please go away."

Feeble words, under heavy breaths and panting, were stirring in the bathroom. I returned to the couch, defeated. For the next hour, I lay in the fetal position with a blanket covering everything except one ear, left exposed to listen in case a distress call was sent. Moments like that had the ability to run a flip book of memories through my mind. My thoughts meandered through the vault of hidden monsters. If only I had done this and not that, a million times over.

A scared voice cried out from the bathroom.

"Hey, Anto. Can you come here, please?" Gen asked with pain in her timbre.

I sprang to my feet and darted into the bathroom. The space was dark, cramped for my large frame, and decorated with a woman's touch. Shadows danced on the walls as candles of different sizes burned on every available horizontal surface. Elegant wicker rack shelving, with cast-iron framing sprayed gunmetal grey, stood above the toilet. The top shelf was lined with various bottles of perfume, creams, and lotions. The two shelves below were dedicated solely to jewelry, and Gen's taste was that of a Navajo princess. Earth stones soldered into large, forged-metal earrings and necklaces dangled on display; turquoise, amber, copper, and bronze dominated the scene.

A twenty-year-old built-in wall heater was glowing red on one side of the warm room. A small window above the back of the tub let in a single beam of sunlight. An iPod, perched on a docking speaker, sitting on the edge of the sink, was playing a soft, Buddhist meditation chant. The monks worked diligently to calm the room.

The shower curtain was pulled back. Genevieve was sitting in the bathtub, knees curled up, arms lassoed around her shins, and forehead resting on her knees. Her eyes were closed. A painful grimace tightened her face. She was naked and rocking slightly back and forth. No water was running.

"Hey, sunshine. What can I do?" I asked shyly.

"Sit with me and hold me, please."

I got undressed, throwing my clothes haphazardly in the corner behind the door, then carefully stepped behind Genevieve into the tub. The white acrylic lining was cold to the touch. Slowly, I slid down behind her using both arms as cranes to assist with the maneuver. My knees moved under her arms and outside her thighs, along the sides of the tub. I leaned back against the beveled edge and put my arms along the top lip, creating a pocket for her.

Genevieve reclined into the tender embrace of her lover and cried. I wrapped my right arm over her shoulder and down across the middle of her chest. My left arm went down low, around her waist, then up her centerline, between her breasts, to form a seatbelt connection over her sternum. Through the back of her ribcage, I could feel her heartbeat against my abdomen. With my whole body, I gave her a soft squeeze, then kissed the back of her head. We both closed our eyes and listened to the sound of chanting monks.

Despite all my regrets, despite all the sorrow in my heart, even the deep sadness I normally felt was destitute in the face of that innocent moment. I felt her soul close to mine and fell blissfully into her heart. For the first time in years, I had no racing thoughts barraging my mind. I was simply there, in that beautiful space. Past the words and the gazes, the touch or the smell of a lover's hair, there is an undefined method for connection between two souls. There are moments hidden between pain and sorrow that create a bend in space, an event horizon, and, in that space between emotions, the meaning of life can be felt but never understood.

Cramps lunged Genevieve forward, and she reached for shower knobs. Thundering water overtook the tranquil monks. Water poured from the spout and filled a shallow pool of warmth for our feet and bums. She sat forward, huddled over bent knees, and breathed deeply through her nose. I placed a hand on her shoulder.

"Would you like me to massage you?" I asked.

She took a slow, deep breath and followed with an anguished response.

"Sure."

I rubbed her neck softly, then trapezius and shoulders. Genevieve was struggling with pain in her uterus, and I was helpless to stop it. I cursed God for the cruel sentence on my lover. She sat whimpering in the bathtub, and my only repercussion was to watch her suffer.

The water in the tub turned a faint hue of red. Genevieve was at the angry phase of pain now, clenching her jaw and gritting her teeth, looking the devil straight in the eye. She mumbled tough nonsense and tensed her body. I had my ear on her upper spine and my hands on her shoulders. She screamed with her mouth closed. I looked up and saw the color around the drain darkening toward violent red. From the same angle, I could see a tear rolling down Genevieve's cheek. When she breathed in deeply, I breathed with her in unison.

Her body and her mouth let out one collective sigh, then she fell back into my arms again. I let her nuzzle into a little ball then

299

wrapped my big bear paws around her. I hummed a soft tune and let her fade into sleep.

By the time she woke up, the running water had turned cold. Genevieve stood up, stepped out of the tub, and began drying herself with a towel. I sat there for a while, in the cold water, just watching her. The room was dark now. Some of the candles had burned out, but the remaining flames keeping vigil created a divine glow behind Genevieve.

"How are you feeling, Gen?" I asked while looking up in awe at the most beautiful woman in the world.

"Better. Thank you."

A sliver of a smile creased her lips for half a second, and that sent my heart racing to the moon. I was madly in love with her.

back to corporate

They made north of thirty billion dollars per year, so they must have been important. Accordingly, if I could enter that exclusive club, I, too, would be able to absorb the current of dominion like the confluence of any river with the mighty Amazon.

I was interviewing for my first sales job at a big technology company in Silicon Valley. The buildings stood like modern idols to a sparkling demigod. The silver hue of the all-glass fronts blended with the sky above as if to demand questions of divine order. In front of the prim display was an artificial lagoon with a spout in the middle that shot water thirty feet in the air.

I was going to nail this thing. I was important. I deserved to be there. I parked at the far end of the car lot, farthest away from the main entrance. I was told to imagine they were watching me through the glass building as soon as I stepped out of my car. Exude confidence and don't pick your nose had been the admonition.

I got out of my car and put on the suit jacket hanging in the back seat. Dark-blue suit, crisp white collared shirt, and a matte sports-car-red tie in a half Windsor. I looked in the reflection of my side window, inhaled deeply, and practiced the look with which I would attempt to sell myself. I wondered whether prostitutes paused in similar moments.

I was a circus bear made to perform in front of four separate audiences. Each time a new person entered the room, I rewound the tape, feigned interest, and began the carefully rehearsed monologue that was my life and qualifications to work for the evil empire of Silicon Valley. I even had a nice story around my gap in corporate employment. No matter that I had no software sales experience, I brought the intangible qualities for which I believed they were looking.

Watching someone's eyes when they heard something that validated their existence was captivating, even if what was said was vapid and contrived. I told the people what they wanted to hear because such was the game of affluent, white America. We began with an assumption: One person was greater than the other. The greater would ask questions of the lesser to invoke a dialogue that was meant to prove that the lesser had amply prepared for the interview. The response should allude to, but not flagrantly boast about, the greatness of the greater. Sometimes, even pandering was considered an appropriate display of respect. So the lesser began vomiting all sorts of lies and rehearsed narratives, usually those he had heard others spew, in an attempt to make the greater feel important.

Once the greater caught a whiff of the elixir, he would then serve a gentle volley toward the lesser to allow him to state his case for stepping up to a higher rung of the false hierarchy. The greater would nod with a confident brow, then the two would perhaps reach the free-flowing portion of the insular mating ritual: I'll keep lying to you to make you feel important as long as you keep lying to me and telling me what I want to hear.

Why did it come so naturally to me, that foxtrot of deception? And why was it that no one since my father, while I was still in my teenage years, had felt compelled to call me on the farce? I played a fickle role in a life not my own. Everything was done for a pseudo audience.

Oh, I see you went to UCSD, my alma mater. Yes, yes, a tremendous institution and one set so serenely on the beautiful cliffs of La Jolla. I really enjoyed my time there. Blah, Blah, Blah...

There were two points of value I gained by attending the University of California at San Diego. First, I was able to continually reference the fact that I did, indeed, graduate from an above-average university and use it as a line item on my resume; box checked. Second, and of far greater use, was the grooming it gave me for corporate America. I did well in college because I excelled in a particular game. The game was to tell people what they wanted to hear, but not make it sound like you were merely a parrot. I attended class every day, listening intently and taking copious notes, then regurgitated the professor's material while placing a skosh of Anto rind on top, more for style than actual flavor, like a garnish at a fancy restaurant.

I'd been out of the scene for a while, but I remembered how to do it. What else do you people value? Mortgage games, yes please. Stock picks, why not? How about a little vacation home comparison just for kicks? Tahoe seemed to be a popular place or, if you were feeling a little naughty and really needed a break from your agonizing life, how about a bit of Napa wine tasting? Mmmhhmmm, I could disguise my voice and mimic the CliffsNotes of others and talk about all those topics as if I actually gave a shit about their manufactured and banal existence.

When life fell apart and I was left broken and alone, it was only then that I was able to see the machine for what it was. I had lied to myself over and over again by refusing to admit that nothing, not one single concept, thought, goal, or pursuit in my entire life had been of my own volition. Everything had been a set of rules or guidelines either forced upon me or, more than likely, those I had adopted through pride or apathy. I had seen the adoration of a crowd exalting around an achiever and had always been envious of the attention. It was not the hard work and sacrifice I saw; only the end result of fanfare and pride. I see the way you look with your shiny objects, and I see how others crowd around you, so I, too, wish to play this game.

My first day of work was poignant. I was left waiting in the lobby for three hours, then given a cubicle with no computer, and told to find something to do until they could set me up with the proper credentials and equipment. This lasted for four days and during that time, I found myself slowly adjusting to the frequency. I spent my time listening, watching, and mimicking until finally the pseudo-medication began working, and I accepted the collective despondence as natural. I'd been there before. I remembered.

Within that modern sanitarium scampered a wonderfully hilarious cast, and a script that could only have been assembled for the amusement of the gods. We worked for one of the most recognizable names in technology, and that was the inside sales building. Technology sales in Silicon Valley offered the same base elements of character as the financial industry in New York City; different commodity, same platitudes.

Regardless of the challenges, I still felt accomplished because I did get an increase in base salary by going to that new company, I had the potential to make some nice coin in commission if I ever sold anything, and it would be a valuable learning opportunity and a great résumé builder. Four years earlier, I was digging a hole under a man's house.

sunday

I was in my living room, comatose on the couch, trying to watch football but nothing registered. My cognitive output had flatlined, so I couldn't absorb anything. I was watching something on TV as a distraction like an overly medicated patient in a 51/50 psych ward. Two friends from high school, Henry and Baker, were scattered about the living room in similar states of clarity. Baker was rolling a joint on the coffee table, the fifth of the morning, and Henry was sprawled out on the carpet below me with a pillow jammed under his neck to give his head a viewing angle of the TV.

The room was a poignant display of the level of vested interest I had in the quality of my life. There was nothing hanging on the walls; no pictures, paintings, decorations, or other signs of permanence. The couch was 20 years old and the carpet hadn't been vacuumed in months. The kitchen table and chairs were from Goodwill and showed their age without shame. The TV was a hand-me-down. I saw myself as better than that place and didn't want to settle in because it would reveal my mediocrity. Something was coming; I was about to skyrocket to fame, and I was ready to leave at any moment.

The coffee table had some empty beer bottles on top, along with all kinds of junk food, and a few abandoned lines of cocaine from the night before. Nobody could stomach any more blow or booze. We all sat in silence, inert, with pot smoke lingering in the air.

"Where's Lefty?" I asked of no one in particular.

"Went home this morning," was the answer.

"What a dirtbag."

The room chuckled twice, using all the available energy reserves, then went silent again. I closed my eyes and tried to fade off, but the voices in my head got louder when I tried to sneak away. I peeked out through squinted eyes at the TV and offered a dedicated point of distraction.

I couldn't remember where the weekend had begun, but it was certainly at some happy hour somewhere. By the time Friday rolled around, I was always aggressive and salivating for booze. I began texting and emailing my friends well before noon to see who wanted to join me for cocktails, but everyone knew what the hidden implication was. Sometimes, my pompous attitude got to be too much, and I was left to drink alone. But sometimes, my friends would join me and indulge in the shit show that had become my life every weekend.

I worked in inside sales for a large technology company, and that year, I was crushing it at work. My life was a modern version of Jekyll and Hyde, only the monster didn't hunt for victims. Instead, I focused on slowly and steadily killing myself.

Excelling in my sales role was not a matter of sales acumen; it was solely based on timing and my ability to navigate bureaucratic red tape with cunning gamesmanship. It was amusing to see the similarities between my days of illegal enterprise and the game of software sales. Would there ever be a stage in my life when I stopped trying to get over on people?

My company had an interesting business model. We were so big and so aggressive that we really didn't care if we pissed off our customers. I sold business intelligence software that provided a way to bring multiple data sources together for a single source of information, thus allowing the customer to view, parse, and analyze otherwise disparate sources of data in order to spots trends, gain actionable insights, and make informed business decisions from a macro perspective.

The truth was it didn't work that easily, a soft science at best, and often times the project didn't even get off the runway for a slew of reasons. But that wasn't important. What was important was that we sold licenses and made our quotas.

My company sold a surfeit of products, so when new territories were given out the prevailing ideology favored finding which of our products my new accounts owned; then, giving them a call and leveraging the preexisting relationships and trying to get them to bite on the new crap I was peddling. From a distance, it seemed to be a viable approach, but there was a big catch: most companies, including our largest customers, despised us and wished us ill will. How could that have been?

In the world of perpetual software licensing, we entered into a never-ending cycle of cat and mouse games that always soured professional relationships. To begin with, there was the concept of an audit. If we, the big fortune 500 company, suspected a customer of not being honest about their license count, or if the particular sales rep was clawing for a few more dollars toward his quota, we could initiate an audit. Basically, we would force a legal standoff and demand that the customer verify license counts so we could assure compliance by forcing them to buy more if need be. Large companies lose track of internal software licenses all the time. Sometimes our affronts were warranted, and sometimes they were not; in either case, it was a means of generating revenue.

Another lovely axiom in software land was maintenance/support fees. In addition to paying for the face value of the software and ponying up a sizable chunk of coin for implementation services, the customer was on the hook for support dues, paid annually and in perpetuity. The logic was that we, the noble and good-hearted software company, spent resources on releasing upgrades throughout the year to fix the bugs in the software that needed fixing. Now, how many resources did we really put into fixing old mediocre software? Not as much as an honest effort. We then required a whole circus act around upgrades, all the while forcing the customers to continue their frustrating journey to use our software. The point being, we didn't make it easy.

Ah, but wait, there was more. What if customers reached a point where they wanted to terminate the relationship? What if they'd had enough and did not wish to continue doing business with the evil empire? Might they graciously shake hands and walk away? No. They were still on the hook for support, which we ran at a modest 22 percent of license cost, even if they didn't use the software anymore or, better yet, even if they had never taken the time to install it. We called it shelf-ware in the business, and customers were still on the hook for support. And if they didn't like it, we had plenty of lawyers on retainer standing by to take their calls.

Combing existing customers wasn't exactly like panning for gold; it was more like noodling in piranha-infested waters. But such was the dance in which we all agreed to participate, and in the end, people got paychecks. That was all that mattered, right? People had families to feed and the real world demanded bills to be paid. What else are human beings supposed to consider when making decisions?

After spending a year selling our worst application and listening to the row next to mine sell one of our best, I learned a few things. First, I had to get on the good team, and sell the good shit, or I was going to drown. Fate interceded one day at our annual sales kick off when, at the bar after the event, I happened to strike up a conversation with a manager from the good team. Shit-faced as we both were, one of us made an off-color comment about cocaine, and we both smiled. Immediately, we knew we were kindred spirits. I happened to be able to score at a sushi joint not more than 15 minutes away, so a few of us piled into my car and thus I established the foundation of a relationship that would eventually allow my transfer to the A-team.

The second thing I learned was that nobody in inside sales actually sold anything, in the traditional sense of the term, but they established a tight relationship with their field counterparts, the outside salespeople who were out on the streets, and took care of all their tedious regulatory and procedural backend requirements in order to leave a clear runway for the big leaguers to land their jumbo jets. In the process, the outside salespeople would catch wind of some smaller deals and toss them over the fence for the inside team to close. Sometimes the deals were fully baked; other times, the inside person needed to go through parts or all of a sales cycle. Either way, it was always by staying within the general orbit of the big fish that the guppies got enough to feed on.

How much work could there possibly be when clearing a runway? That was where you could really see the insignificance of human life up close—when you got into the backend methodology of corporate operating procedure. When dealing with a corporation of this size, the business must have a procedure and defined role for every piece of the process. Need a contract? We have a team in Costa Rica for that. Have a question about functionality? Different team for that. How about getting approvals for any type of concession in a deal: discount, support caps, language amendment, or just a simple change in the purchasing entities name? All of it had to be run through the approvals team, the case stated as diligently as a lawyer petitioning for a motion. Enter the executive summary.

The executive summary was a formal document put together by the sales team in order to state their justification for any concessions being requested as part of a deal. It was supposed to act as an audit trail, should the need arise, to be able to prove pricing was granted in an unbiased manner and not in collusion between the two companies. The pillars for a business case were discount precedence, competitive landscape, future revenue potential, and logo recognition. The ideal summary would state that the sales team was trying to penetrate a new account, a net-new logo who was recognized as a leader in its space, and was engaged in a vicious head-to-head sales cycle involving one of our most hated competitors, and the success of the project would act as a beachhead into the account and serve to open up a multitude of future opportunities as we landed and expanded into different departments or divisions.

Scenario number two would be an existing customer who was looking to grow their user base but now may be considering ripping us out and going with a certain unnamed competitor. If a flagship account was under attack, even with a generous discount history, we would need to step it up in order to keep the competition at bay.

Every executive summary was a combination of pieces of each previously mentioned scenario, and each one was 90 percent lies. Nobody ever came out and said it directly, but the best synthesis I got was from one of the best executive summary writers on the A team when I came over. He looked at me with a grin and said, "Wizards and warlocks, dude," and I knew what I had to do going forward. Comb the archives for summaries written by the preceding sales team, pick up on the general points they used and the competitor most active in the account, then amalgamate, concatenate, stretch, and use a form of alchemy long since robbed of spirit but still useful for sleight of hand. Presto; 73 percent discount approved.

There was an entire lexicon associated with the satire of enterprise software sales that was almost completely foreign to an outsider, not unlike the way military syntax sounds to a civilian. Taken one word or phrase at a time, bystanders would be able to follow along. But when you strung a whole paragraph of those together and listened from an adjacent cubicle, the essence became useless and vague. Sometimes I imagined myself as the star of my own comic strip; at other times, I heard myself spewing out the same nonsense I had mocked. The palaver reached such egregious levels that two whiteboards had been dedicated to documenting the buffoonery.

GAME TIME   TIE   REAL DOLLARS   GET IN FRONT OF THIS
OFF   THE NET OF IT
HEAD TO HEAD
IT IS WHAT IT IS   CHAMPIONSHIP ROUNDS
TEAM SPORT
NET/NET   COVER OFF
SYNC UP
FOURTH QUARTER MENTALITY   CIRCLE BACK   ORGANIC
STICKING NECKS OUT
IS THIS A DEAL BREAKER FOR YOU? LONG STORY SHORT
TEST THE WATER   VISIBILITY
TOUCH BASE
TEAM ALIGNMENT   KICKING TIRES
GO TO BAT FOR   PING ME
CARVE OUT   HONESTLY   ECOSYSTEM
DUCKS IN A ROW
LEVERAGE   SHARPENING PENCILS
SLAM DUNK
WIGGLE ROOM   XYZ LBS GORILLA/ELEPHANT IN THE ROOM
TOMORROW   HOTBED
WRAP MY HEAD AROUND THIS   ON THE BOARD
TRACTION   CIRCLE AROUND

ON THE TABLE   ON THE RADAR   30,000 FT VIEW
VALUE SHORT GAME
REACH OUT   CADENCE
DROP A LINE
ABOVE & BEYOND
AT THE END OF THE DAY   STRATEGIC PARTNERSHIP
IN THE LOOP   LOW HANGING FRUIT
TOE TO TOE   FIRE DRILL
READ SOMEONE THE RIOT ACT HEADWAY SPINNING WHEELS
WATCH WATER BOIL
FULLY BAKED   FAILURE ANALYSIS
THE ECONOMICS OF THIS THING   SPEARHEAD
DRAWING BOARD PENCIL IN   DISRUPT   PULL THE TRIGGER
BEACHHEAD   BEHIND ENEMY LINES
SHOOT AN EMAIL
GIVE YOU A BUZZ   THIS THING HAS LEGS
BOIL THE OCEAN
BUDGET FLUSH   LONG GAME BOTTOM LINE
DO HOMEWORK
BROACH THE SUBJECT   RUFFLING FEATHERS
A CERTAIN UNNAMED COMPETITOR   PULL RESOURCES

311

I lived two lives. During the week, I woke up at four in the morning to get a workout in before hitting the office early. I worked hard—in a corporate sales kind of a way, not by pick-and-shovel standards—and I not only played the role I was expected to play, I found myself settling into it quite comfortably.

But beginning late every Friday afternoon, at the first crack of happy hour, I was always the first to leave the office. I began pouring the potion down my gullet at a hearty pace, and that continued until sometime early on Sunday mornings when my body finally collapsed and all systems had come to a grinding halt.

So where had we started the current weekend? I couldn't recall. But I did remember ending up in downtown Los Gatos that night, downtown at the corner of trendy and vain, and I was rapaciously trying to cram blow up my nose because I was sloppy, having wandered too far away from the balance of pseudo-lucidity via cocaine and alcohol juggling. Somehow, we had made it home, and I immediately fell on my bed unconscious.

The next morning, I was up bright and early to venture into the kitchen and straight for the fridge to crack my first cold Modelo at half past eight. My house was a mess and the guys were still sleeping as I put down my first beer with long, easy gulps. By the time they woke up, I had the beginnings of a decent buzz settling in.

This was my favorite time of the weekend, Saturday morning, because I knew I had a wide-open window and no responsibilities. The guys were slow to rise, but I was eager to get the party started again. I was not quiet as I waited impatiently for them to awaken. They were hungover, groggy, and unenthusiastic when I started pitching the idea of breakfast at my favorite place. Eventually they capitulated.

Bill's Café was a convivial restaurant with a heavy-handed bartender. On weekends, it was typically packed with youthful scenery. I learned about the place from an ex-girlfriend who took me

312

there for the first time and introduced me to a vice I had not yet experienced: Morning drinking. And not just your standard Bloody Marys and Mimosas, but how about a shot of tequila before nine in the morning? Yes, please.

The scene was loud, and the waiting list had already filled up, so we lingered around for half an hour as I scanned the patrons while putting down a double mimosa. That was where I loved to be, in the middle of a medium-sized commotion, combing the scene to see if any women had noticed me. I didn't need much, but I'd take a peeking set of eyes behind a coffee cup or a double-take from a girl eating with her boyfriend. It didn't matter what the quality of contact was, as long as there were attractive women around me, and I had a drink in my hand and a grin on my face; then, my ego was free to frolic.

We got a table on the patio, and immediately I ordered four shots. Baker was passively quiet, as usual, and Henry sighed in frustration. Lefty chimed in with a cavalier "Fuck it, I'm in," which made us all laugh together and commiserate over the arrogant bully that was Anto on a bender. Twenty minutes later, we were on round two.

When the liquor settled in and pushed out any leftover hesitation of the responsible mind, there came a point of total freedom that was rarely felt in civilized society. It's difficult to fully let go because most of the time we're still wearing some kind of costume, trying to shoot some angle somewhere, so the depth of laughter rarely reaches full pandemonium. But there are certain moments, among the right friends, where full debauchery can ensue unimpeded.

So it was with us on that day. We spent the rest of the morning hitting it hard, and the laughter was of the gut-writhing variety. I didn't stop laughing for three straight hours. The topics of conversation usually centered on one of the group being shitted on by the rest and punch lines always included some embarrassing moment that had been sworn to secrecy but came bellowing out once the

313

momentum of the circus came through. We laughed about each other's speech impediments and physical appearances, about our broken hearts, professional failures, courting styles, lonely nights, and everything else that tended to remain off-limits for casual conversations. When the bill came, we laughed about that, too, but made sure to leave a generous tip on our three-hundred-dollar breakfast tab.

We saw no sense in stopping, as it was barely past noon. It was far more acceptable to continue drinking on Saturday at that hour. Off we went around the corner to a Mexican joint and kept the party going. At one in the afternoon, I made the call. Thirty minutes later, we had two eight balls of blow to add to the bedlam. It turned on a dime, right there, and the atmosphere changed without warning like a downpour in the jungle.

It always sounded like a great idea, but thirty minutes after doing my first line, I felt the energy get diseased and baneful, and the conversation became retarded to the point of null. Thirty minutes earlier, we were laughing so hard walking down the street that people stopped to laugh with us. Now our eyes were strained into unnatural diligence as we scanned the environment nervously, looking like a pack of tarsiers.

We called a taxi then headed off to a different part of town. We ended up at a bar where no one was consuming alcohol quickly enough for me. I grew impatient. Another taxi, and we were back to my car, but I hadn't sobered up a bit since I left it. Then we ended up at a strip club that didn't have enough flesh for me. What was I looking for? I always felt there was something just beyond my reach, and that I would find it at the next place I was in a hurry to get to. But every time we arrived, I was disappointed and could only console myself with more whiskey and cocaine.

We decided to take the party back to my house and mellow out for a bit. We stocked up on plenty of beer and cigarettes and returned to the safety of drawn shades. With the repetitions I had under my belt for bender weekends, certain things didn't register as alarming anymore. Sometimes, when I did enough cocaine for a consistent amount of time, my anus became so raw from constantly having to relieve myself and wiping far more than was healthy for such a sensitive area, that I would experience rectal bleeding. Yes, I bled out of my ass and didn't pay too much attention to it, choosing instead to clean it up and hoping it didn't happen again next time.

Another compulsive occurrence that had become commonplace was the eventuality of calling a prostitute when I did cocaine. I didn't bother to ask the group; I just flipped open my computer and started scanning the classified ads on Backpage, then called through to start haggling on pricing with escorts. It was stunning how little resistance I had given when paying for everything from low quality cocaine to imported designer suits, but when it came to paying for a call girl, I tried to weasel and bargain every time.

Hours went by and no escort was procured. I was in the weeds by then, hyper-focused on getting just the right look for just the right price and ingesting substances at a voracious rate. By the time we finally got a girl over, it was well past midnight, and not one ounce of pleasure remained among the group. Just a house full of dreary, predatory young men all insecure in their own depravity but forging ahead with strained conviction. We took turns with the young woman, each retreating to a corner of the house for flaccid fornication, more symbolic than effective, but somehow, through sheer carnal fortitude, we each managed to accomplish what we had been craving. Then I went to bed with a furious heart and lay wide awake until the sun began to rise. The shadows on my blinds gave off just enough shame that I was able to collapse in on myself, like a dying star, and drift off into strained and troubled sleep.

This was not an uncommon weekend.

Oh, how I hated Sundays. They were the last buffer between my two lives, and my anxiety always swelled to ungodly proportions.

We sat in the living room all day and barely any words were spoken. Lefty had gone home already, but Baker and Henry were steeping in the darkness with me. I hated them, and I wished they would leave, leave me to brood in isolation, like any decent man would come to do. But they stayed, oblivious to the racket yammering in my head.

Somewhere between 8:00 and 8:15 in the evening, every Sunday, from mid-spring to early autumn, an insidious ice cream man drove through my neighborhood, blaring his gonzo music through blown speakers, so the seed of the rotten lullaby was bored into the minds of the poor townsfolk like a boll weevil colony on the march. God forbid he actually got a customer, for then he would stand idle and allow the vile harmony to continue its auditory pillage while I covered my head with pillows and curled up in a ball on my couch. That was it. Sunday evening and the ice cream man had passed. The reaper was there to remind me of my commitments, and tomorrow I had better be in my cubicle. Everybody out. I needed to be alone.

first world depression

When one was as far beyond miserable as I was, falling asleep was the easy part. Staying asleep was difficult. And waking up was cruel. It was three in the morning, and the comfort of dreams had been ripped away. I went to sleep hoping I would hibernate for the entire year but was disappointed when I came to realize only six hours had passed. I didn't want to wake up ever again. To be awake was to remember; to remember was to feel, and feeling was unbearable.

On nights like those, I woke up at odd hours and talked to God. I begged, actually. I spoke aloud so I could hear my own words and not just the echo of demented voices in my head.

"Please help me," I pleaded with God.

I shuddered as I begged. Whispers of words were all I could manage.

"Please . . . Please."

Lying there in the darkness, my heart raced, and as I shifted positions every ten minutes, the pain in my back became more acute. For 12 days, the majority of my time had been spent lying down. Often times, when in the throes of a dark spiral, I was too afraid to get out of bed to urinate. Getting up meant having to be present, even if only at the most minimal of levels. On top of that, the idea

317

of turning on the bathroom light, and possibly catching a glimpse of my reflection, was terrifying.

After an hour of trying to ignore my bladder, I finally gave in and rolled to the edge of the bed. I slid out from the covers with clumsy defeat. My head was drooped, and my eyes looked straight to the floor, like Charlie Brown, as I took a few steps toward the bathroom. Feeling for the light switch, I held my hand against the wall for a moment to catch my balance.

It was dark. I was disoriented, and I was breathing strenuously through my mouth. I stood on the cold bathroom floor, leaning against the wall and waiting for the next burst of motivation that might take me the next four steps to the toilet. The window was open, and a cold wind came snapping across my bare chest. I shivered then slowly focused back.

It's always baffling when you realize you've been lost in your mind, slave to a memory or the scars of a broken heart, then come crashing back down and wonder how long you've been standing there.

As I faded back in, I noticed a songbird steadily chirping somewhere near the open window.

"Fuck you and your fucking song."

The bird continued its arrogant sermon. I read somewhere once that faith is the songbird who sings in the darkness of night. A sense of despair flooded my heart when thinking about those beautiful words. That bird had the courage to sing before any sign of light peeked over the horizon. It was four in the morning, pitch black, the night was full of predators, and the sun still hadn't given us any indication it would rise today. Yet there she was, singing with all her soul, because she had more faith and more courage than I could ever hope to understand. The bird believed the sun would come up, and she was eager to start the day. I prayed it would stay dark forever so I could be excused from the burden of life.

After two minutes, I finally flipped on the light switch and quickly scurried past the evil mirror. I stood over the toilet and looked down reluctantly. Everything was a reminder of a better time. Looking down, I was saddened by the presence of my gelatinous paunch. I grabbed a large handful of the hairy roll, then squeezed repeatedly, like a child squeezing a half-filled balloon.

"Jesus. You sure are getting giggly, you fat fuck."

I released the fold of fat, let out a sigh of disgust, then moved my hand down to an obviously frightened penis. I leaned forward a bit to clear the sightline over my tallow, and got a good open look at my genitalia.

"And what about you? What the fuck are you doing?"

I shook it a few times, but no response was offered. There was a time I would stand over the toilet and smirk with satisfaction while looking down at the proud member. In my early twenties, I seemed to live in a permanent state of semi-erection. Often times I would be noticeably chaffed, which only added to the sense of hubris I felt while interacting with my manhood. There was usually someone waiting for me in bed, and I was usually waking her up when I returned from the restroom for another round of young adults in heat. There had been no one waiting for me in bed recently, and my penis hadn't been used in months.

My urine smelled conspicuously acidic, but I didn't bother to flush when I was done. Instead I struggled back to bed, smacking the light switch angrily and mumbling obscenities as I passed. A small sense of relief relaxed me as I hugged a pillow and tried to go back to sleep.

As soon as I thought my mind was allowing me a break from dejection, an overwhelming fear tightened my chest. It was all going to shit. My life was a mess. I was in my early thirties, and I had let pivotal years slip by to indifference and selfishness. How many times had I cut corners in order to indulge in instant gratification? How many lovers had I let fade away because of overanalyzed micro-flaws? I was wide awake, and my mind was racing through a catalog of rotten memories.

Veronica. God, whatever happened to Veronica? Did she make it out? And what about Hulky? Oh, Hulky, I fucking miss you. And Genevieve, Yesenia, Jolene, Alicia, Allison, Kristi, Kyle, Robbie, Haylee. Ohhhhh Haylee, I'm so sorry.

The only cure in that situation, the only focal point I had found soothing enough to take attention away from my failed life, was to fantasize about murdering the person who left me with the deepest scar. There was a man who came to me in the guise of a mentor when, in reality, he was nothing more than a conman working his next mark. He left me broke and addicted but, more importantly, took with him any faith in humanity I was struggling to believe in.

When I was paralyzed by anxiety and fear, when the malevolent creature sat with me and whispered into the back of my mind, when all the shameful memories came flooding back into focus, those were the times I allowed the dark beast out of its chains. Nothing seemed to be able to soothe my thoughts other than picturing the look of pain on the face of the man who broke my heart. Five years had passed since we last crossed paths, but nothing was lost to the fade of time. I fantasized about murder . . .

I am sitting on the patio of a restaurant in Pacific Beach, California. It's nine in the morning, and the street sweeper is making a noisy pass. The crisp smell of ocean is in the air. I've chosen the far corner table and sit patiently waiting for breakfast. The table affords a perfect angle on where I know George will sit. He is a predictable man, a man of routine. I am dressed in a well-tailored, brown, single-breasted suit with white dress-shirt, dark burgundy laced dress shoes, and a wide-stripe tie, pink and burgundy with faint Glagolitic writing in light grey stitch. I relish being well dressed in this

320

fantasy so I can show George what I've become in spite of what he did to me. My jacket is unbuttoned, and a pair of silver-rimmed, designer sunglasses on my face pick up the silver tie bar at my sternum nicely. The waitress brings food, and I offer a mute nod of gratitude while holding my posture erect, knees crossed, and hands folded across my lap. My beard is full, dark, and groomed perfectly. I sit and stare, expressionless.

From my left periphery, George enters the frame, walking down the sidewalk toward the entrance of the restaurant, but I do not turn to look. I allow George to walk into my line of sight and tune out every other auditory variable except George's voice. Seagulls fade away and the street sweeper goes mute. George is mid pitch as usual. He is walking with a young man in his mid-twenties, and they are discussing mortgage rates and back-end point structures. George is dressed in a teal, untucked, Tommy Bahama shirt, black slacks, and black dress shoes with a fake buckle. Excessive hair gel spikes his hair, and Maui Jim sunglasses hide his conniving eyes. His hands are active while he holds the attention of the young man with him who is listening attentively.

They walk into the restaurant, stand in line waiting to order their breakfast, and George is still spewing out some diatribe while the young man nods. I watch from my perch and simmer. I used to be that young man by George's side once upon a time, and I remember getting breakfast with him. George and the patsy walk on to the patio and toward the table I expected them to take. George's table is 15 feet away, on a slightly elevated portion of the deck, but in my direct eyeline. As George is about to sit, he looks up at the man in the corner who is noticeably over-dressed by beach town standards. I haven't moved since I sat down, and I stare in the direction of George. George takes a second look, a puzzled look, then continues his conversation as he takes the seat offering him a direct view of me. For the next twenty minutes,

321

I don't eat or move. I stare intently at George and listen.

George is recruiting the young man to leave his current employer and bring his book of business with him to George's small-time mortgage company. George shares stories of excitement and grandeur, and his laughs are forced and awkward. Periodically, George looks up to see me in the corner, still staring in his direction, but my sunglasses allow him to brush it off as a different focal point. After I have heard enough, I push my chair back, stand, and adjust my cuffs to offer a perfect reveal. I walk over to George's table and stand uncomfortably close to him.

"Hello George. Do you remember me?"

George looks up at me defiantly.

"Well hello, Anto."

George can hold the stare of a madman with the best of them. He glares at me without blinking. After staring silently at each other for three slow breaths, I turn my attention to the young man.

"Everything this man says is a lie. In the end, his scam will go belly up and he'll leave you floating in the wind."

The young man says nothing but looks back at George, who now has a large vein protruding from his forehead and one eye squinted lower than the other.

"Just because you couldn't handle it doesn't mean I fucked you over, Anto."

I study him intently, looking straight into his pupils, and let all other senses fade away.

"Fuck you George."

I take two steps back, pull out a massive Desert Eagle, matte black, fifty caliber, and explode George's head like a watermelon.

"Bet you never thought I had the balls, did you George?"
The restaurant erupts in panic, and the young man still sitting at the table is frozen in fear. Skull parts and brain matter are strewn about. The shot echoes four to five reverberations down the main street of that small beach town in San Diego. People are screaming and running as I stand there and look at the disfigured corpse, now lying on the ground, with half its head missing. I take a somber breath to absorb the moment.

I faded back to reality while replaying each moment of the fantasy over and over with great satisfaction. I almost managed to fall asleep again but kept missing the void by just a fraction of thought reminding me of the vapid truth. I was a fat coward who was letting life drift aimlessly by. Short gasping breaths were all I could manage as self-loathing washed over me. I finally fell asleep with tears streaming onto my pillow.

Depression was a beautiful woman who intentionally baited my love then left me one night, without notice or reason, to awaken alone and afraid. Mornings were her reminders of my misery; her abandoned pair of earrings I kept for months in hope of her return. Every time I faced the daunting task of beginning a day while crippled by depression, I was reminded of all that was broken in my world.

I woke around eight then wallowed in bed, hoping some miracle would bless me with a new start. The sun had managed to find an unguarded crack in the window shade through which to slither its way in. I slurred a litany of vulgarities, then took a pillow and threw it at the window. Upon impact, the blinds on the window bellowed with laughter, while recoiling, and allowed larger slashes of light to crash upon my squinted eyes.

I continued to lie in bed for the next hour, hoping I could trick my body into a few more moments of sleep. Beginning the day meant admitting defeat. Beginning the day meant facing my failures all over again. I was so defeated, so far buried by self-loathing, that trying to forget about my life seemed the only viable option.

It looked like part of a comic book—the last-ditch effort of a man desperate not to face the day by forcing fantasies into his head. Homicide or suicide seemed to be the only effective elixir. In the night, I envisioned killing the man who hustled me. In the morning, I imagined killing myself. In my mind's eye, I saw myself moving through the mock animation of death rituals. The detail I could produce with imagination alone was staggering.

Back to the dark fantasy:

> I am sitting on the couch looking at the black pistol and admiring it. The fantasies change, but the gun always stays the same: Desert Eagle f i fytcaliber. I put the gun to my temple, then adjust the angle to different degrees, while considering the possibility of botching the operation and not taking my head clean off. Is it straight or off angle?

> Better just to stick it in my mouth and go bottom up. I grit my teeth around the cold metal and pull the trigger. Brains go flying everywhere. The scene pauses in my mind, rewinds, then goes back to the muzzle-to-temple scenario.

> Maybe I should have just stuck with the original idea?

> Pull, click, boom. From an observer's perspective, I view

my decapitation. Then I zoom in and become first person, feeling the light switch off. Pull, click, dark . . . Silence . . . Golden eternal silence. Oh, it feels so divine. Play, pause, rewind. First person, second person, first person again. On the couch, in my car, on the lawn in my backyard. Quiet. Bliss.

But I couldn't do it. I lacked fortitude in far more trivial matters and was far too shallow to allow the whispers of sympathy at my funeral. Committing suicide would be leaps ahead of where my constitution presently resided. And what of the awful mess left behind? How could I leave my mutilated body for someone else to dispose of? Not just any someone, but particularly the person who'd been there to clean up after me my entire life? How could I force the ocean of shame surely to swallow my mother whole if her baby boy would end his own life? I'd already caused enough damage to my family. Suicide would be unspeakably cruel.

The shame from thinking about suicide added to the rot already bubbling in my gut. It made for such intense anxiety that I threw the blankets off and sat up on the edge of the bed. I was breathing heavily, and my shoulders were slouched so far forward that my chest hurt from the basic effort of living. I stayed in that position for a while before slowly raising my head and catching sight of myself in the bathroom mirror.

"Wow. You disgusting piece of shit."

I stood and walked toward the image, put my hand on the edge of the sink, and leaned in for a deep look. Bloodshot eyes made me look like a junkie in the rain. I stared deeper and deeper into the center of my pupil until all I saw was the blackness. The pupil constricted to the size of a pinhead, then exploded into a galaxy. I blinked. Tears were rolling off the tip of my nose, but I continued to stare into the void.

"What is wrong with you?"

The sound of my voice scared me back away from the mirror enough to see my nose and forehead were pressed against it. How long had I been standing there? I looked down the reflection in the mirror to my hairy chest and was disgusted to see what had become of a once proud physique. My pecs had become so tubby and portly that my nipples gave the appearance of a pubescent girl's developing breasts—pointy and puffy.

"Jesus Christ. You fat piece of shit."

I struggled to get dressed. I put on the same sweatpants and sweatshirt I had worn for the past two weeks. From the bedroom straight to the couch, I went from one corpse's position to the other. I turned my back toward the living room window which, even though the blinds were closed, allowed enough light through to remind me I shouldn't have been wasting the day agonizing over privileged first-world problems. I pulled the hood of my sweatshirt over my head and used the drawstring to close the opening as far as it would go. I made some minor adjustments to fully cocoon myself, then I buried my face into the crack of the couch cushions.

The house was hot and musty, and all the windows and doors were closed. I rose from the couch with the elegance of a broke-leg horse. I peeled the sweatshirt off with turmoil and threw it into the corner of the room. Staggering to the patio door, I passed the kitchen table and noticed a pack of cigarettes left open on top, which somehow indicated that now would be a good time to start drinking. I slid the patio door open, lit a cigarette, and made my way to the fridge.

The 24-pack of Corona purchased the night before was still half full, so I made quick use of the leftover supplies. As I drank the beer in large, three-gulp pulls, I scanned the open fridge for any signs of life. Some condiment containers were still displayed along the door, but those had been empty for weeks.

The bottom shelf was completely taken over by the community-sized box of beer, and the middle shelf was void of any tenants. On the top shelf sat a heavily bruised banana, yogurt cup, and an empty Tupperware container taking up space for no discernible reason. I took a drag off the cigarette, finished the beer, opened another, and continued hanging on the door with my free hand, looking inside, hoping something would change. I shoved the toes of my right foot under the crisper handle and pulled open the drawer roughly. A wilted stalk of celery lay next to a plastic produce bag. I stuck my head close to the open drawer and saw brown rotting lettuce inside the grocery bag. I stared for a minute, contemplating and drinking.

I put the beer down on the counter and secured the cigarette between my lips. The bag let out a pernicious odor when I lifted it from the drawer. I held it out in front of me, like a bachelor holding a dirty diaper, and made my way through the garage and out the side door to the refuse container. The garbage can was still sitting on the curb, where I had left it three days earlier to be emptied and hadn't had the motivation to put back since. I walked from the safety of shelter out into the open viewing arena of my driveway, and the sunlight nearly blinded me. There was no worse walk of shame than that of a depressive, alcoholic hermit breaching his safety bubble into direct sunlight. I dumped the bag into the plastic curbside container and hurried back into the darkness of the garage, leaving the garbage can where I had found it.

I returned to the kitchen where I quickly finished the half-full beer, dropped the cigarette into the empty bottle, and left it sitting on the counter next to the ten other empties. I grabbed a new beer and new cigarette before sitting on the couch and turning on the TV. Never has there been a more detrimental invention for depressive recluses than OnDemand cable television. I enjoyed passing as many hours as I could watching shows with clever writing and wildly alcoholic characters. Deadwood, Californication, The Sopranos, and The Wire became strange versions of replacement therapy, and finger pointing, which alleviated the pressure of pointing the finger at myself. Full conversations ensued between the television and me.

Two episodes and seven beers later, I was feeling somewhat rejuvenated. Watching those shows lit the tiniest of fires inside me, which lead to small bouts of laughter, and the notion that soon I would have to leave my shelter again and venture toward 7-Eleven for a beer run. I forgot about the fear while lost in the plot lines and imagined myself as one of the dysfunctional, yet good-hearted characters, prone to bouts of horrible judgment and immoral behavior. I clung to fiction TV because I knew nothing was random about where I had ended up in life.

As I pulled up to the convenience store, I remembered how much I feared being in public. I felt the swell of doom drop on my head. Through the window, I could see Medhi was working, yet again. And yet again, I would have to face the well-intended small talk of the devoted immigrant while doing my best not to crumble in tears. I sat in the car and tried to gather strength. I was drawn back to focus by the sound of over-amplified rap music pulling up beside me. I didn't want to look. I knew I hated them already.

The music, the latest awful three-chained misstep of hip hop counter-evolution, was allowed to blare a hideous chorus at top volume. A young thug, noticeably white, popped out of the vehicle and did his best pimp-limp toward the entrance. The costume could not have been more fitting. He sagged a pair of black skinny jeans to the point that they constricted his leg movement and gave him the appearance of a man needing to relieve his bowels. A flat-billed baseball hat sat perched off kilter to the plumb line of his posture, but he accounted for the imperfection by tilting his entire head as counter balance. A white tank top revealed that said gangster lifted weights. The tattoos covering his arms were many and predictable, but I always had high appreciation for the sign of Christ, inked boldly, as a declaration that this devotee had never bothered to read so much as one word of the Old Testament.

Left in the passenger seat of the car, and equally unnerving for me to witness, was the girlfriend of the tattooed thug. She was taking selfies with her lips pouted, eyes squinted, and head cocked to the side in such a way that one might think she suffered from cerebral palsy.

How? Why? Why did they get to live in ignorant bliss, and I was left to blunder in such self-actualized hatred?

I got out of the car and did my best to stand with every shred of manufactured confidence I could muster. I despised everything those two clowns stood for, but I still wanted her to find me attractive, and I wanted him to show the slightest hesitation of fear when walking by me.

As I entered the store, Mehdi looked up and offered a sympathetic smile. Try as he did to hide it, it was not difficult for Mehdi to see I had been spiraling out of control recently. How many days in a row had it been? In front of the counter was an obese woman whose shirt did not hang low enough to cover the sagging cuff of blubber reaching down to her pubic area.

Give me a couple years. I'm sure I can get there, I thought to myself.

Behind her in line was the tattooed goon holding a 24-pack of Corona with a scowl on his face. Jesus. We drank the same beer. How humiliating.

I made a quick left in order to avoid crossing paths with the stooge and took the long way to the beer section. I took my time perusing the alcohol, as if I hadn't purchased the same item 12 days in a row. Then I went back down the candy aisle to consider the evening's dinner.

"Why don't you set the box down on the counter then go back and get your snacks?" Mehdi suggested with helpful honesty and a heavy Indian accent.

Mehdi was never snide and always even in his delivery but, even with the softest of touch, I was still embarrassed about this convenience store clerk knowing my routine so well. I set the booze on the counter and went back for the rest. I would begin the evening with an appetizer of Kettle Chips to snack on during the drive home, which was a total of two blocks. Next, after drinking more beer, perhaps some pretzels would be appropriate. By that time, some sweets would be called for, so I threw in a Kit Kat and some Reese's Pieces. Everything to this point was king- or family-sized. The main course, as usual, would be chicken-flavored ramen, and no evening of gluttony was complete without a trusty pint of Ben and Jerry's. I decided to rely on my old ally, peanut butter cup, once again.

Mehdi dutifully rang up my ingredients for self-medication and did his best not to pry too far, but his mannerisms were always innocently awkward.

"Have you tried the new Kit Kat minis?" Mehdi asked while offering a raised eyebrow and lascivious grin to emphasize the question, almost as if he were asking about a supermodel who had just left the store.

"Not yet Mehdi. One day."

I never looked at the total when buying binge products. It wasn't until months later, while looking at my credit card statement online, that I was truly able to absorb just how much money I had thrown away. For now, there was no sense in adding to the shame.

I stuffed potato chips into my mouth as wide as I could manage on the ride home. There was an insatiable urge in me to consume. Once home, I flung the plastic grocery bag on the couch, dispassionately watching it bounce off the cushion and fall to the floor, then settled the beer bottles neatly in the fridge like toy figurines. Potato chips were on the carpet, having spilled out of the open bag when I tossed it carelessly, but I didn't bother collecting them.

Instead, I simply ate from the floor. The next round of beers, cigarettes, and television lasted three episodes, ten refills, and fourteen smokes.

When the food started being plunged down my throat, like a farmer stuffing foie gras, that was when I was at my loneliest. Binge eating was the lowest of the low, and I was well-versed in guilt-induced vice of all types. Gluttony is merely displaced loneliness. There was a hole in my heart, and I was too afraid to address it; so I filled my stomach to the point of nausea instead.

I went back and forth between salty and sweet with the diligence of a dog fetching tennis balls. In a seamless transition, I faded from alcohol buzz to junk-food high. The television was merely a focal point for my eyes by then because the process of consuming was in full swing. Since childhood, I had relied on food as a cure-all whenever emotions got the best of me. I began sneaking food from the pantry then moved up to stealing money from my parents' wallets in order to keep a secret stash of candy under my bed. When I got older, I found adult hedonism generally favored alcohol, drugs, and sex, but, given enough time and desperation, I always managed to find my way back to the original vice every few months.

Every part of the gluttonous process had its own dopamine receptor. It began with the simple task of doing something. Eating was an action that would occupy my mind's attention, albeit with paltry effect, in order to divert brooding from whatever I was running away from. Then, there was the oral stimulation. Surely there was a list of psychiatric explanations for it, but, regardless of the cause, there was no denying I enjoyed the oral fixation between smoking, eating, and drinking. Next, there were the taste buds to consider. I read somewhere that a study using lab rats showed sugar to be more addictive than cocaine. I would not disagree. When you pair sugar with opposing doses of salt, you effectively circumvent basic models of diminishing marginal utility and allow far more room to play with before saturation is reached. The last factor being the most burdensome, yet also part of the intoxication, I had learned to draw pleasure from the process of physically filling my stomach. My stomach could expand to three times its natural size to accommodate for marathon eating, all the while never sending a signal to my brain to warn of possible overload. All I knew was not-full or bursting.

All those parts added up to one giant monstrosity of an emotionally unstable man doing all he had come to rely on to make the pain go away. I finished the chips, chocolate, and three-quarters of the pretzels in just under an hour—again, all in king- and family-sized packages. When I finally came back into focus, I realized my stomach had been sending emergency signals for the last ten minutes. My stomach was full, and a sense of melancholy gripped me. I lay back on the couch, curled up in the fetal position, and closed my eyes. My breaths were shallow because my lungs had no room to expand from the bulging stomach.

I woke up to the sound of my cell phone ringing and shut it off without bothering to look at the caller ID. No conversation seemed doable at that point. I picked up the remote control and selected whatever episode was next on the list to watch passively. It didn't matter what I selected, I knew every episode by heart.

Cigarettes weren't as satisfying without a decent buzz, but beer would have been too filling at that point, and not an effective intoxicant due to the recent gorge. Whiskey would probably do the trick. A couple cubes of ice and a generous pour into a pint glass, then I was back on the couch stirring the cocktail with my pointer finger.

It must have been sometime past five o'clock because I heard the droves of families, and dog walkers, chatting happily as they passed by on the sidewalk for their evening strolls. My neighborhood was comprised mainly of Indian and Chinese immigrants who had moved to Silicon Valley for the well-paying tech jobs. They represented everything I was ashamed not to be; mainly hard working and determined, like my immigrant parents. I was slouched forward on the couch with elbows on knees. I took a long, slow drag of my cigarette, not bothering to lift my head, and let the smoke sting my eyes. Then I picked up the glass, leaned my head back farther than necessary, filled my mouth to capacity with cold whiskey, and swallowed effortlessly.

I looked toward the window.

"Fuck you and your happy dogs."

I looked at the TV and pointed with my cigarette.

"And fuck you, too, Tony Soprano. "

I slid my cigarette butt into one of the dozen empty beer bottles littering the coffee table; every single one had finished cigarettes fermenting in the shallow pool of backwash. The whiskey managed to do half its job and mildly rejuvenated my waning buzz. Another full glass of sauce and three cigarettes later, I was back to the nostalgic attachment of fictional television characters. One episode transpired before my attention withered, so I peeled myself from the couch and lumbered into the kitchen to drink another glass of whiskey while preparing ramen.

I prepared ramen with so much water that the only adequate serving dish was a salad bowl which gave the appearance of a horse feeding from a trough. Back on the couch, and another episode was queued up on the screen.

Finishing a half-gallon serving of ramen made my stomach queasy. Once again at capacity, I lay back on the couch and assumed the fetal position. I closed my eyes and let the darkness commandeer my thoughts; tumbling images and short clips rattled through my mind. Why did my memory torture me so? I couldn't stop thinking about all the awful moments. I was amazed by the level of detail with which I could remember events surrounding heartache:

the kitchen table, Veronica's shampoo, George's eyes. I fell asleep thinking about the day I cried on the cold hardwood floor and begged Veronica not to leave me.

It was dark outside when I woke up. My face was wet with tears. When the sun went down, I felt excused enough to call it a day. I glanced at the floor and noticed the pint of ice cream I had left in the plastic bag many hours earlier. The nap managed to ease the pressure of my bursting abdomen ever so slightly, so I opened the container and looked at the melted froth. I drank the congealed liquid like a glass of milk and left the container among the sea of empty beer bottles and candy wrappers covering the coffee table. Self-enmity that powerful was difficult to achieve, but I had managed, yet again, to set a new standard. I staggered to the bedroom and flopped on the bed, chest down. And so ended another day in depression.

the day has come

My routine was strong, and I was achieving. I was sober. I had a girlfriend. I was checking off the boxes I was supposed to in order to get the prizes that would make me happy. I'd lost 30 pounds. I earned more money the previous year, legally, than I ever had before. Life was good, and I was starting to believe.

I sold software for one of the big names in Silicon Valley, and I often handed out business cards when exchanging phone numbers in social situations. It felt fulfilling to give someone a confirmation of my achievements in one card. I got up at four in the morning to work out. I was strict about my diet, and I didn't eat carbs after noon. I wore shirts tailored with darts so my shoulder to waist ratio was not ambiguous. Walking through the financial district of San Francisco on business was a favorite activity of mine because it afforded me the opportunity to catch a glimpse of myself, dressed in a sharp suit, in the reflective glass of important buildings.

I was certain this time I had overcome it; this time would be different. I changed my diet even more; strict organic principles, low carb, heavy on antioxidants, power foods, gluten-free, sugar-free, kale shakes, fish oil, and 50 other things I had heard on self-improvement podcasts. I hadn't had a drink in three months. I recently muscled my way into a promotion in a cutthroat industry. This was it. This was my time.

I exercised like an NFL linebacker, but a stubborn pouch of lower abdominal fat always mocked me no matter how shredded I managed to get. I was almost there. Just a bit more and I'd reach that point, that pivotal moment of monumental change, so I could look at myself and declare victory. Two workouts per day during the week and three per day during the weekends were starting to test my resolve.

I was dating then and had been for a few months. I was always dating and always for a few months. She was kind, and beautiful, and had a sincere heart—and I was amazed that she was attracted to me. She hadn't seen the monster. She didn't know about the things I had done. Even if she did know, she probably would have accepted me anyway because she was a salt-of-the-earth type. How did I always end up with these angels? The relationship had been going well for a few months. Everything had been going well for a few months. I had finally made it out of the darkness. No more depression. I was successful and handsome, but that belly fat was really bothering me. If I just got rid of it, that would be enough to push me over the top. Then I could live contentedly forever. Just one last piece to the puzzle.

It was 3:35 in the morning, 25 minutes before my alarm, but I was already awake. At that level of ketosis, sleep was almost non-existent. I stared at the red numbers on the clock. My brain was already off and running. That day was cardio in the morning. I hated cardio in the morning, but I had to do it. What was I going to wear to the gym? What else was on the schedule that day? Team call at eight.

When my brain was that foggy, I couldn't tell whether I was physically tired or not. I could feel my body eating itself because of the lack of calories, but I didn't know much beyond that. It was okay. That was what I signed up for. Get up. Do something. May as well do something. The cold ambient air stung my body when I threw off the blankets. I sprang from bed and slapped at the light switch.

Did I need caffeine, or didn't I? No sense risking it. Took it for good measure. I had gone through every form of over-the-counter stimulant over the years and seemed to have had built up quite a tolerance. Perhaps I'd just suck on jet fuel next. Stir, drink—bing, wide awake. Ketosis fog with a caffeine pep on top. I wondered how my nervous system felt about all this? Fuck it. I'd deal with it later when I noticed it becoming a serious problem. Until then, I'd keep charging forward.

Nothing moved on the roads at four in the morning. The only signs of life were the traffic lights, all dancing together in harmony like dominoes falling in succession. At the same bus stop was the same mound of abandoned humanity as the day before and the day before that. A homeless woman buried herself under a sleeping bag and leaned against her shopping cart. Her breath let out steam in the cold night to make her look like a smoking teepee. Someday soon, I would offer her some food; someday soon, but not that day.

There were two types of people at the gym that early: weirdos and the obsessed. Not sure which one I was. I started the treadmill at a brisk uphill walking pace, let some blood get moving for a few minutes, then picked it up to a light jog. Ten minutes in and I was running at full speed, but my lungs were failing me. Or maybe it was my mind? Why couldn't I catch that buzz? Why couldn't I get that runner's high like I had last time? Strange. Just didn't seem to have pep that day. Something was weighing on me. Couldn't run anymore. Severe exhaustion followed by self-loathing for not being able to work through it. What was happening to me? I found myself standing behind the treadmill, watching the belt zipping by at top speed, listening to the motor sing, feeling my shoulders slouch, and fighting the first considerations of the dark return.

It couldn't be. I had probably just overtrained. That was my body telling me I needed a day off. No problem. Nothing to get panicked over. By the time I was back in my car, I already knew the truth, but refused to accept it. I could feel it in my soul. I told myself lies, hoping to avoid the monster. But I heard its sniffing nose and felt the hot breath on the back of my neck. It had found me yet again.

The rest of the day was spent reaching out in desperation for something to grab onto. I was falling, and I was scared. Energy was completely drained from me, and I felt like a weak, abandoned child left to float alone in a dark sea of misery. Bleak. Despondent. Hollow. Yet again, I toppled with minimal resistance to my cunning arch-foe: depression.

By three in the afternoon, I gave up and headed to the liquor store for anesthesia. Son of a bitch, I was back at square one. I drank the pain away in my living room and watched the shadows slowly creep along the floor all day to blend with the design on my carpet. The next day, I met with my girlfriend for lunch because I wanted to tell her. I wanted to tell her how scared I was, and that I needed help. I wanted her to hold me while I told her all my secrets. There was so much pain stuffed down inside, and I needed to get the darkness out of me.

Surely I am sick, I thought to myself. What other possible conclusion could I have reached after years of this repeating cycle? Years and years of this same exact cycle; only the magnitude changed, and always for the worse. This used to happen once a year with much milder effects when I was in college. Now it seemed to strike every couple of months, and the severity of the downturn was alarming. I didn't just hope for passive suicide any longer; now I planned the event. I had to do something. I needed help.

We met at a coffee shop, and she walked in with style. Long, crisp, black business pants and a stride that made men peek. She was a dancer, so even her walk had a grace about it. She smiled when she saw me. She always smiled when she was around me, and she always made me feel warm. I could really make a life with her, I often reflected. She'd be a terrific mother, and she'd stick with me through the tough times. You can tell right away with certain people.

"Hey, Anto," she said while sitting down at the table.

I put on my best smile and tried to keep eye contact while we started the conversation with some small talk. Inside, I was growing more nervous, and it became difficult to follow her words. Eventually, she noticed enough discomfort to ask me about it.

"So what's going on? You seem distant."

What does one say? How did I tell someone I was broken? It felt so foreign, so impossible. People don't talk about this kind of stuff, especially not this soon in a relationship. She looked at me patiently, and I tried to find something to say. Nothing. I had nothing. Then I said the only thing I knew how to say in this situation.

"I don't know if this is working out."

She inspected my eyes quickly, then looked down at the table.

"Oh," she said, then looked back into my eyes. "Can you tell me why you feel that way?"

"I just don't think I'm in a space where I'm ready for a relationship. I don't know. Something just doesn't feel right."

"Okay. Is there anything I can do to help you?"

"No. I think I just need some space for a while. I'm sorry."

"That's alright. You don't have to apologize for the way you feel. I understand. You have a path to walk alone right now, and I get it."

We hugged goodbye, then I walked down the block straight into the nearest bar where I got good and drunk. I stayed there for five hours thinking about what she had said. I didn't think she knew. I thought I was giving a believable performance. What did she mean when she said I had a path to walk alone? Did everyone know but me? Could they all see through my mask? Beer and whiskey. Beer and whiskey. I stared at the TV in the corner as it replayed the

339

same sports highlights on an endless loop. I went back to the same bar every day for a week before giving in to drinking alone on my couch again. I drank for 19 days straight.

What if everything was broken? What if everything needed to be thrown out? What other possible conclusions could I draw? I was out of ideas, and angles, and juice cleanses. I began researching my symptoms online and quickly came to a striking conclusion. Not only was I obviously depressive, but what I considered to be my productive periods were most likely manic episodes. When you added in the alcohol and drug abuse, you got a fairly easy one to identify: dual diagnosis bipolar disorder.

If there was one thing I didn't want to be, or didn't want to accept, it was the possibility of being like the rest of them. Ever since I was a child, I'd always clung to the outsider persona because it validated the feelings of fear and insecurity lurking inside me. I found a home among the throwaways, then proceeded to numb myself from the truth for the next twenty years. Now what? Now I was faced with the possibility of crawling back to the normal people with my tail between my legs and admitting that not only did my way of doing it not work, but I needed their therapy and their drugs to take the pain away. Had I become another weak American, unable to make it on my own, and now I'd depend on a pharmacological ripcord to bail out on the difficulties of life? At least the booze was on my terms. I didn't want to be another medicated first-world failure.

I stopped working and stopped doing much of anything. I wallowed in my own misery and hid from the world. The only reason I wasn't fired immediately was because I worked from home so no one could physically see how little I was doing. When the time came to put on a show, I played it with passion. I met with my manager once every month or two and put on the right degree of showmanship. I said all the right things to avoid the elephant in the room, having sold absolutely nothing all year, and blamed it on a slew of factors outside my control. The truth was, I quit doing any kind of work except coming up with passable presentations for my business reviews. My long-practiced skills of deception and corner-cutting came in handy because I managed to keep my job while searching for the root of my madness and giving zero effort toward corporate sales. I justified my behavior by thinking I needed to keep the job for health insurance so I could get help for my broken head. Deep down, I felt entitled to my salary. Fuck them. Fuck everyone.

I began looking for help from anybody willing to listen. Parents, friends, and psychologists all gave me their best efforts, but nothing hit home. Something was always missing. There were always new lows to be experienced. Telling people I thought I was crazy, bipolar, and alcoholic then getting a slew of predictable responses made me think there was no hope. I didn't need any more of their isms. I needed to look in someone's eyes and feel the energy of genuine understanding. Months went by as I floated in the void. I gained thirty pounds. Some days were manageable; some days, I didn't get out of bed. One day I got to the gym, and another day I bought $32 of candy bars from 7-Eleven. I wasted time watching endless television, hoping I would wake up dead.

One random day, I got dressed and decided to do some work. I had my quarterly review coming up, and I needed to practice the lies, so I went to a coffee shop in my hometown with the intention of plunking down in a chair for a few hours and putting my PowerPoint deck together.

I drove my new Lexus and thought of the absurdity of my fraud. I got the new car because of the promotion and expectation of driving customers to dinner, but I had yet to have one single contact, in any of my accounts, get past a first meeting, never mind getting in my car. When I drove over speed bumps, I could feel my ballooning gut jiggle. I walked into the coffee shop with my shoulders slouched, stood in line, and stared down at the ground, too afraid to look up. This coffee shop was near one of the large, happy companies of Silicon Valley—the kind where everyone talked about cutting edge technology, and they all dressed like hipster clones. Being around chipper people made me feel more alone. I continued to stare at the ground.

I don't know why I looked up, but I did. I don't know why I looked straight in his direction, but there he was, sitting at a table alone, with a beaming, radiant, honest smile across his face that grabbed my attention like the first rays of the sun on a cold winter morning. I knew him from my teenage years, when both of us hung around Coffee Society. I knew he used to work for a music company but had recently gone back to working at a coffee shop because of an update I saw on social media. He must have been approaching his late thirties by then, and there he was, working at a coffee shop, back in his hometown, just like when I knew him twenty years ago. How embarrassing. I looked away because I didn't want to risk having a conversation and getting into our mutually failed lives. Why the fuck was he smiling so much?

The line for coffee was long, and the universe was more patient than I could ever have imagined. Eventually, he saw me, and I could feel him waiting for me to look over and make eye contact. Damn it.

"Hey, Anto. What's up man?" he finally said when I got close enough.

"Oh, hey, Adam. How you doing man?" I replied with a tone of manufactured surprise.

"Aahhh. Man. I'm great. Amazing. Outstanding actually."

Are you kidding me? How could he be doing great when he was here, doing this? My ego exploded inside my head and ran wild with doubt and mockery as I smiled and nodded and played the polite role on the outside. But there was something I could not deny. He had something, something not tangible but certainly present and overwhelming. When he spoke, he looked directly into my eyes, but with a soft gaze and a kind smile, and I could feel the truth pouring out of him like a blind man can feel the position of the sun. Most of us take the light for granted every day because we see it so often that it becomes mundane. But to those of us who have been living in the dark, there is a visceral experience when we sense hope again. I picked up my cup of coffee and immediately returned to sit and talk with my old friend.

The job had nothing to do with it. Meaningless. Trivial. The crux of the matter lay elsewhere. As Adam told me his story, I felt a dim light turn on deep inside of me in a place I buried my secrets long ago and assumed they would stay hidden for the rest of my life. His eyes shined, and his soul glowed. That was it. That was what I was after. How do I get me some of that?

In the past year, Adam had three friends die within the same month. Darkness filled his heart, and the solution he found was heavy drinking and eruptive anger. He was toxic to himself and to those around him, and nothing seemed to take the pain away. A friend of his suggested something she herself had gone through, so Adam found his way into a non-standard counseling course that helped deal with the pain. What he learned through this process was that the pain was not all due to the immediate loss he had suffered. Rather, it brought up with it a tangle of emotions he had been avoiding for years related to loved ones over his life, especially going back to his mom and his childhood. He said he wrote some letters, read them aloud to the group, and finally purged all the pain he had been too afraid to talk about. He spoke of his experience in a way that had me glued to every word. He finally got to deal with his broken childhood, and the catharsis enabled him to live freely today. Yes, please. I'll take two of those.

What struck me first about the woman to whom I was referred was how normal and average she was. She wasn't a therapist with a fancy office and diplomas on her wall. She didn't speak to me with a professional undertone, thus passively establishing a doctor/patient hierarchy. She was a middle-aged housewife who ran counseling sessions out of her home, and there was nothing about her ethos that separated us with bylines of social structure.

She asked me what I was dealing with, and I told her about the depression and the dark cinema that played on a continuous loop in my head. Then she did what no one else ever had.

Not only could she relate, but she went into detail about the stories she had kept hidden over the years, the haunting sources of shame, which boiled in her mind and had pushed her into a ball of tears. She spared no detail and liberally divulged parts of her past that people just don't talk about. She ran through a list of demons that all hinged on the same underlying principles: shame, anger, betrayal, abandonment, vice, and hollow. Wow. I didn't know anyone else had tumbled down the same dark pit as I had. I was not alone. I was not alone.

The end game in this counseling process was writing letters to people who represented large areas of pain in my life and reading them aloud to the counselor or group as a form of catharsis. The first letter I wrote was to my father, and right away, I felt something for the first time. A tiny flicker of warm light was trying to catch a steady glow deep in my chest. Then I read it aloud for my counselor to hear, and that propelled me into a third dimension. It was difficult to finish as my tears came out, and I had to take moments to catch my breath. But I got it all out, and I finally stood face to face with my own truth as the stranger who had confessed her truth to me hugged me and told me she was proud of me for being so brave.

The force inside me was unstoppable; I knew what I had to do. I carefully removed portions of the letter that could have been viewed as accusatory, and I was left with a long list of confessions and apologies for me to own. Then I called my papa and told him I needed to see him.

I was brittle and excited as I drove to his house. My father lived alone by then, a man of simple means, but there was nothing simple about the complexity of that man's intellect. He could run philosophical circles around most people but chose a meek life instead—an ode to his rural upbringing from a place where scarcity was the guiding principle of all life's choices.

He was always excited to see me those days when I stopped by. He was lonely, and his heart yearned for company. His eyes beamed when he opened the door, and a silly, schoolboy smile spread wide across his face. We stayed outside and had a cigarette together, paying homage to the first tradition we two ever cemented.

Inside, we sat at his kitchen table, but it was no ordinary table. My father did not throw things away, so there we were, twenty years after all the angst-filled kitchen-table conversations of my childhood, both of us having moved around more times than I could remember, and we came together, back to the source, sitting at the same kitchen table, from the house I grew up in, that he kept for all those years.

The table was made of dark oak, and the edges were worn and scuffed. On top sat a custom piece of glass, and between the glass and wood was a hand-knitted table spread, off-white, always perfectly centered. The chairs were a matching set of four originally purchased with the table in 1989. They creaked when I shifted my position, and my shirt stuck to the back each time I straightened my posture from the layer of congealed sweat and dirt left to soak over the years. On top of the table were old napkins, with swathes of light orange and tomato-soup red, neatly pressed flat and re-creased for future use by my peasant father. My God, I used to be so embarrassed of that shit.

In the background, a satellite radio played Croatian news at a conference whisper volume. A teakettle boiled over low heat on the stove, but nothing would be brewed that night. This was how the frugal immigrant added a little humidity to the air on dry winter nights. The house smelled musty, and the coffee table held a visible coat of dust on top. Such were the ways of a simple man.

"So how are you?" my father asked with slow words and a thick Croatian accent.

"Things have been tough dad. Things have been real tough. But I think I may have found some answers."

His smile disappeared, and his eyes focused. Every ounce of his being was at attention.

"Tell me. Vat is going on?"

"I told you last time I was here about the depression. I told you how I don't leave my house for days at a time, how it feels like something sucks the life out of me and all I can do is lie around and think about horrible things."

"Yes. You told me. Are you still feeling that way?"

"Off and on, I guess. Some days are better, but I can't quite seem to shake it this time."

"Have you gone to see a doctor?"

"I'm seeing a therapist, but I also started seeing a counselor my friend recommended."

"That's good. Is it helping?"

"Yes. Something happened. Actually, I realized something. Something about my life and the way I've been living. And that's why I'm here today. I need to tell you something."

"Okay. You can tell me anything," he reassured me.

I took a deep breath through my nose and exhaled audibly, then reached into my coat pocket and pulled out two folded pieces of paper.

"Please just listen, and let me read this all the way through."

"Okay."

> Dear Dad,
>
> I've taken time to reflect on our relationship, and I need to share what is in my soul. First, I know you do not have a dark heart. I have many emotions that have been pent up inside of me for a long time, and often those came out as anger toward you. In an attempt to explain why I feel the way I do and try to bring some kind of closure to this, I want to take some time to go through certain events in my life with you. So let me start by doing something I should have done long ago.
>
> I am deeply sorry for putting you in a place to have to stand up for what you thought was right at the expense of your relationship with me and mom.
>
> I apologize for stealing money and cigarettes from you. More importantly, I'm sorry for continuing to lie about it and putting you in an impossible position.
>
> I apologize for my use of drugs and alcohol. I'm sorry for bringing drugs into your house. I know the continual lies, stories, and cover-ups caused you a great amount of pain.
>
> I'm sorry for continually getting in trouble and counting on mom to bail me out. I knew I could manipulate her to save me, and I knew she would defend me from you.
>
> I'm sorry for continuing my selfish ways as an adult, for not taking responsibility for my actions, and for continuing to

347

*play the games I learned as a teenager in order to persist in
a lifestyle I knew was wrong.*

*I also need to tell you about the good memories I have of us.
I need you to know that I remember more than the anger.*

*When you taught me to ride a bike, the moment you let
go and I looked back and saw you smile, that is one of the
greatest memories I still hold on to dearly.*

*I loved the times we would get ice cream together after
visiting the doctor for my broken bones.*

*I remember how proud I was when you asked me to help
shoot the squirrels in the backyard.*

*I still smile when I think about the diploma around your
neck at my college graduation.*

My words began to round off at the edges, giving way to panicked
sips of air, as tears slowly trickled down my face. I was scared
and overwhelmed. I took a large, hurried gasp of air through my
mouth and kept going.

*One of the most moving times we shared was when you came
to Veronica's house after hearing I had cut off my fingers. I
felt so loved at a time when I needed it most.*

*I told you I understood your anger toward mom for not
letting you punish me in the manner you thought was best.
I know now why you did it, and unfortunately, I agree
with you. You wanted to teach me responsibility and how
to be accountable for my actions. You wanted to instill a
strong work ethic for the purpose of survival, not greed. You
wanted to show me that the world would bombard me with
vice, temptations, shortcuts, greed, lust, and all types of
other evil. You wanted to teach me how to be strong in order*

*to avoid the easy way and to take the difficult path instead.
All of this you wanted to teach me, so I could avoid being
exactly what I am today.*

*I have lied, cheated, and stolen my way into the world in
which I now live. I have never done things for the sake of
kindness or compassion. I have lived life for me and only me.
From the drugs to the money, the jobs, and the women—all
of it has been done for the sake of my ego. More importantly,
I have always lived my life knowing mom will bail me out
if I fail. I am now at a point where I know I need to change.
I think my constant return to depression is simply my soul
reminding me of all the unfinished business I have stuffed
down into my belly. All the apologies I need to make, all the
effort I need to focus on helping others, all the truth that has
yet to be spoken, all of it has been rotting in my gut, and I
have made myself sick because of it. It is time I admit what I
have done. I did what I did because it was easy. It was easier
to lie to you and have mom fight my battles than it was to
tell the truth and face your consequences. It has been easier
for me to use my charm and intelligence to get what I want
instead of rolling up my sleeves and working for it. I see that
now, and I see that you were trying to protect me from this.*

I could barely see the writing on the paper anymore, and my face
was sodden with twenty years of tears. The pitch of my voice was
narrow and constricted as my nasal cavities completely gave way
to mucus. I tried with everything I had to continue, and I didn't
know if my words were audible anymore. But it didn't matter. I
went on.

*The time has come for me to face my demons. This is where
I sit today, in a dark corner of shame and regret. I know the
changes I need to make. I know the man I want to be. And
I know through all our difficulties that you loved me and
wanted the best for me. If I have children, I will teach my
son all that you wanted to teach me. I have wasted enough*

349

time playing games. This will change. I will change.

This is the beginning for me, and I'm glad you are in my life to see it. I want you to know I love you very much, and I'm proud to be your son."

I was sobbing uncontrollably. I could taste the snot dripping out of my nose and down over my top lip. The paper was wet below me, and I sat curled over, staring down at the words, unable to look up.

And then I felt a hand on my shoulder. I stood up, and my father wrapped his arms around me. I held onto him desperately. For the first time in my life, my father was holding me with compassion and tenderness, like the moon holds the ocean on a calm, clear night. I squeezed, and I cried, and I thought I might just die right there.

"I'm so sorry, Dad. I'm sorry for everything."

"It's okay. I'm sorry, too."

There is no drug, no orgasm, no love, and no accomplishment that comes close to the bliss of speaking long-repressed truth.

When I walked out of my father's house later that night, I thought I was on a different planet. The sensations running through my being were so heightened, so elegant yet invigorating, that I was certain I had crossed a threshold into a fourth dimension. Everything seemed fascinating, and I felt wonderfully alive, like the first day in a new city. I could smell at a level of detail I never thought possible. Beyond the normal faculties, I felt as if I were connected by a new sense, something that had been lying dormant, to every piece of earth and sky I had ever walked by and never paid attention to, but had been waiting for me patiently all this time.

The cold winter air no longer stung my throat, and the stars were as bright as the sun's rippled reflection on an ocean horizon. For the first time in my life, I felt free, and I realized that was what I had been searching for all along. Instantaneously, I knew what I had to do. My mind didn't come up with a logical plan. No details were provided, and no steps were given. But deep inside, I felt something open, a compass of sorts, and I knew that moment was the first step in the long journey that lied ahead.

49348391R00220

Made in the USA
San Bernardino, CA
22 May 2017